Parents' Guide to
SPECIAL NEEDS SCHOOLING

Parents' Guide to
SPECIAL NEEDS SCHOOLING

Early Intervention Years

Ruth F. Cantor and Jeffrey A. Cantor

Auburn House
Westport, Connecticut • London

Library of Congress Cataloging-in-Publication Data

Cantor, Ruth F.
  Parents' guide to special needs schooling : early intervention
years / Ruth F. Cantor and Jeffrey A. Cantor.
      p.   cm.
  Includes bibliographical references and index.
  ISBN 0–86569–243–2 (alk. paper)
    1. Handicapped children—Education (Early childhood)—United
States.   2. Early childhood education—Parent participation—United
States.   3. Handicapped children—Services for—United States.
I. Cantor, Jeffrey A.   II. Title.
LC4019.3.C36   1995
371.91'0973—dc20   95–24262

British Library Cataloguing in Publication Data is available.

Library of Congress Catalog Card Number: 95–24262
ISBN: 0–86569–243–2

First published in 1995

Auburn House, 88 Post Road West, Westport, CT 06881
An imprint of Greenwood Publishing Group, Inc.

Printed in the United States of America

The paper used in this book complies with the
Permanent Paper Standard issued by the National
Information Standards Organization (Z39.48–1984).

10 9 8 7 6 5 4 3 2 1

Copyright Acknowledgment

The authors gratefully acknowledge the use of Lisa Irwin's "Family Album" essay,
"Look at the Good Side," which appeared in *Exceptional Parent* Magazine (March 1991, p.
100). Reprinted with the expressed consent and approval of *Exceptional Parent*, a monthly
magazine for parents and families of children with disabilities and special health care
needs. Subscription cost is $24 per year for 12 issues; call 1-800-247-8080. Offices at 120
State Street, Hackensack, NJ 07601.

The inspiration for a work such as this must come from a very special person. That person is our son Adam. To Adam we dedicate this book.

Contents

Appendixes

Figures and Tables

TABLES

Preface

As parents of children with special needs you will confront many obstacles in your journey to acquire the best possible education and care for them. Like all parents, you want the best for your children, whether they are hearing impaired, learning disabled, developmentally delayed, or autistic. Many parents, however, do not feel that they are equipped with the knowledge or educational background to challenge the "system"—even though they believe they know their child best. This book is designed to explain the processes involved in evaluation, diagnosis, and treatment in the educational setting as well as placement procedures, how progress is measured, and the steps parents can take to promote the best learning environment for their children. It provides baseline guidance on how to interact with the school system. Our aim is to help parents gain access to all the information they need to feel comfortable in making decisions that affect the life of their disabled child and the entire family.

Parents' Guide to
SPECIAL NEEDS SCHOOLING

Introduction

Even though we don't know you personally, it is more than likely that if we met you today for the first time, we could talk for hours about our mutual experiences—our triumphs and hardships—parenting a special needs child. Parents of special needs children face many challenges, and when given the opportunity, we should share and exchange information and establish support systems to help each other cope with the emotional and physical stress we undergo.

We have noticed that in most cases communication among parents of special needs children is very limited. But why? When was the last time someone spoke to you directly (either by telephone, at the local supermarket, or at a school function) to give you a hint or suggestion that might benefit you, your child, or your family—or, for that matter, provided a shoulder to lean on? And how much interaction do you have with parents of your child's classmates? Time is also a problem. We are sometimes set in our ways, with a routine that makes it difficult for us to be flexible. These problems are compounded by the lack of information on how to interface with those who provide services to special needs children. One goal of this book is to provide such information.

Providing the best education for all children is a difficult task. The process is constantly being challenged by changes in government regulations and laws, economic conditions, and social values. Most change, however, results from parents working together as a team to influence political and educational leaders. This activism on behalf of children is very encouraging. To be effective as "change agents," however, we need to acquire the information and skills that will enable us to be persuasive. We must convince the members of the educational community that we will pursue all avenues to obtain the services that will prepare our children to lead independent lives in society. This is why we have written this book.

In many situations it is up to parents to take the first step, such as asking a child's teacher about a problem encountered at home (e.g., "I have noticed that Johnny cannot concentrate long enough to complete a simple task, and wonder if this also occurs in school."). Have you expressed concern that your child is not receiving a necessary service, such as occupational therapy, or making substantial academic progress? Or have you sought help to identify funding sources for specialized equipment to be used at home? What if you do not feel comfortable talking with your child's teacher; or you do not want to question authority; or you are embarrassed by your child's condition; or you cannot take time off from work to attend meetings or can't find a babysitter? Many parents may want to communicate with their child's teacher and participate in the larger educational community, but often feel intimidated and reluctant. This may be due to the highly technical and specialized concepts relating to their special needs child. Parents confront fears of the unknown, and many are unable or unwilling to accept the reality that their child has a disability (National Board for Professional Teaching Standards, 1987). This book offers suggestions on how best to approach these concerns.

How do we become change agents, when, as parents, we are not communicating very well with each other or with our children's teachers? The results of a national survey confirm our suspicions (see Figure 1.1). A common parental response is that most of us do not want to be viewed as assuming an adversarial role, and many do not feel comfortable making suggestions to professionals in the field. This book aims to provide guidance, suggestions, and examples that will give you the information and self-confidence you need to be active partners in your child's education.

COMMUNICATION: THE KEY TO SELF-CONFIDENCE

We believe that an important first step in developing your self-confidence is to establish an open communications network. This begins with identifying your personal community—a circle of important people who play key roles in your child's schooling. The purpose of developing this communications network is to have a well-defined structure for the exchange of information. One element is access to daily information needed to make decisions that positively impact the child's learning environment (Schleifer & Klein, 1990). Additionally, learning how information is used to formulate the procedures and processes involved in planning and conducting a special education program is key in becoming an active member of the decision-making team. Decisions are based on

Figure 1.1
Parental Involvement Survey

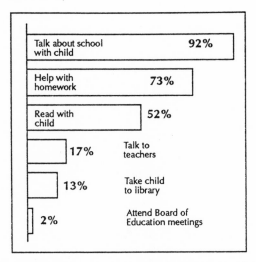

Source: PTA/Dodge National Parent Survey. As published in *Newsweek.* Fall/Winter, 1990.
Special Issue, Education: A Consumer's Handbook, How to Teach Our Kids, p. 61.
Reprinted with permission of Newsweek, Inc., 1995.

how well we synthesize and understand the information gained through communication channels.

A TEAM APPROACH

Special education programs for any disability always involve more than a classroom teacher. Services such as speech pathology and audiology, psychological services, occupational therapy, and school health services can be prescribed and thus become important components of the program. In order to establish a program that takes into consideration all of a child's needs, the communications network needs to include a vehicle for interaction between you and your school-based professionals, as well as outside providers such as doctors and therapists.

THE COMMUNICATIONS NETWORK MODEL

This book stresses what we term the Communications Network Model, which fosters family support through effective communications. In the Communications Network Model the parent is the focal point for coordinating these activities (see Figure 1.2). This is part of a growing trend. In the 1990s, society is turning its attention to the state of the family unit, recognizing that action must be taken to keep families together. Educa-

Figure 1.2
Communications Network Model

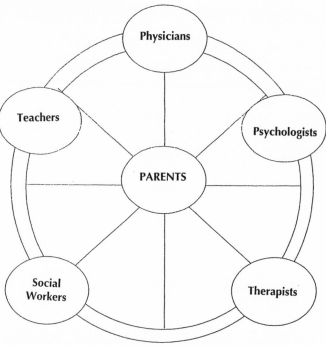

tors, government officials, and politicians have all climbed aboard the bandwagon. This is a perfect climate in which to establish a communications network with those who provide services and programs to help children be successful in school and in the community. Agosta et al. in Iowa (1990) state: "Children belong with families. As with all children, children with disabilities need to be members of both families and communities to develop to their fullest potential" (p. 5). Much emphasis is being placed on programs that are family-centered, culturally sensitive, community-based, and well coordinated. The nationally recognized family support movement is based on this premise. Three potential sources are public, private, and informal supports (see Figure 1.3). The leaders of this movement believe that parents are best suited to be "case managers" and that with the proper training, fiscal support, and information they will be empowered to be effective. The family, as a unit, will then work with the school and the community to educate a special needs child.

A STARTING POINT

Education is a lifelong process. Parental involvement in a child's education is often concentrated in the early grades, usually decreasing as

Figure 1.3
The Family and Three Sources of Potential Support

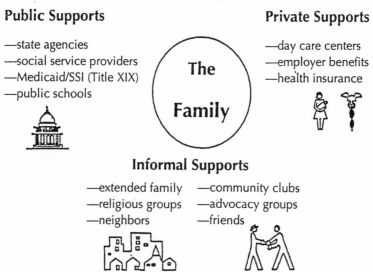

Public Supports

—state agencies
—social service providers
—Medicaid/SSI (Title XIX)
—public schools

The

Family

Private Supports

—day care centers
—employer benefits
—health insurance

Informal Supports

—extended family   —community clubs
—religious groups   —advocacy groups
—neighbors   —friends

Source: Iowa (1990). Reprinted with permission of Iowa Governor's Planning Council for Developmental Disabilities, 1995.

the child gets older. As parents, we can become discouraged—a form of burnout—usually because we are so emotionally and physically exhausted that our minds and bodies need to "chill" for awhile. Sometimes we feel that we are in the minority and that our position will not be taken seriously. The effects of less-than-desirable economic conditions (either ours personally, or budget problems within governments, social service agencies, or school districts), an unexpected medical crisis, or the inability to convince those in decision-making roles that our child needs a service or program can lead to a decrease in parental involvement. These are all barriers to parental involvement, but we must carry on with our commitment to educating our children with special needs. We need to adapt to change if necessary, but always keep plugging away. Through this book we hope to inspire our fellow parents to act and to give inspiration to each other. Educating a child is a full-time job, and we propose to make your job a little easier. We will continue to learn and to become better partners in the schooling of our children if we perceive that we are valued as equal team members and that our opinions and suggestions are heard and sometimes implemented.

To ensure appropriate identification of interventions and services for a child, parents must be able to access school-based professionals and other community people. We must be able to talk with appropriate authorities, express our opinions, and receive information to help us make decisions. Parents need to be an integral part of the decision-making process. Our model describes a partnership arrangement for the purposes of clear and open communication, exchanges of useful information, sharing of knowledge, group participation, and continuous and clear feedback. The members of the team include parents and teachers, school-based professionals, therapists, physicians, and the community. The following chapters highlight how these team members interact to remove obstacles in order to implement an appropriate education for the child.

DIAGNOSIS

You may assume that your child's education begins in preschool or kindergarten—not so! Education is a lifelong process.

Chapter 2 concentrates on the diagnosis of your child's special needs. Your child may be diagnosed with a disability or special need at various points in life: at birth, in the early grades in school, or after a trauma or accident. The implications of a problem may not be known until school age or beyond. Chapter 2 describes how to act as a detective, gathering information that will help to confirm your suspicions of a potential difficulty or problem that needs to be brought to the attention of medical or educational professionals. Learning how to observe your child in various situations and how to describe these manifestations will be important when you communicate with doctors, therapists, and teachers. We describe how to keep a chronological and narrative diary of your child's development. Several examples of how a problem may manifest itself are included, along with typical reactions of parents to these events.

Your pediatrician is one of many important members of your family's communications network in the first six years of a child's life. Your doctor's expertise is invaluable in identifying potential problems or specific needs and in directing you to appropriate resources. We offer suggestions to help you feel more comfortable in communicating with your doctor, and to help you create positive and productive relationships with other medical personnel.

Finally, we describe the types of support available to parents through medical centers, as well as in the community, while undergoing this long and emotionally draining process.

SECOND OPINIONS

A child's welfare is of primary concern to a parent. When confronted with a condition that will affect our child's health or ability to learn— whether for a week, a month, a year, or for life—we immediately question whether the diagnosis is accurate, and to what extent the condition will inhibit or delay the child's growth.

Many parents opt for a second opinion, and in some cases, three or four opinions. Chapter 3 provides information designed to increase your comfort level as you seek to confirm or correct a diagnosis. The first step in this process is to learn more about the various medical specialists and professionals who can help confirm a diagnosis.

Chapter 3 will help strengthen your research efforts in finding appropriate sources for second opinions. We show how to access information on clinics sponsored by national organizations (e.g., United Cerebral Palsy, Easter Seals) and provide an outline of how the medical and educational communities are structured to evaluate symptoms or make diagnoses.

There are numerous child development clinics around the country, usually affiliated with hospitals or universities that specialize in reviewing diagnoses. These clinics provide many other services to help parents cope with medical and educational diagnoses. Many will make suggestions and propose strategies to the family and your inner circle and provide a follow-along plan to improve the delivery of services to your child. The cost of a second opinion may be the deciding factor for many families. Several options are detailed to help you assess your ability to pay for these services. A discussion on how to best use your insurance coverage is included. Chapter 3 also discusses how you can effectively communicate your concerns and needs to the professionals on the child's evaluation team. You will gain self-confidence in working with these professionals so that the outcomes of this evaluation can be utilized most effectively by all members of the inner circle communications network.

COPING STRATEGIES

Chapter 4 emphasizes developing and strengthening positive relationships and attitudes so that your family can act cohesively to advocate the best schooling for your special needs child. To this end, it is important to recall the feelings and concerns you had when you first found that your child had a disability. The emotional stages and parental responses to this new situation (e.g., denial, fear, guilt, confusion, powerlessness, disappointment, and rejection) are discussed so that you can start or improve the healing process and develop or strengthen coping strategies. Any type of coping strategy is implemented step by step, one day at a time.

Personal accounts of how to cope emotionally on a daily basis will help you identify with your own situation, and a sense of not being alone will begin to unfold. From this point, a support network can assist you and your family in identifying a course of action to help you relieve and minimize the stress you experience with a special needs child. We offer specific suggestions on how to identify and access a support network within your community.

This is the start of developing a communications network. The next step is to learn all you can about your child's condition. A directory of community resources, national organizations, and designated regional informational centers is included to help you find out about the essential characteristics of your child's disability.

As parents we must not overlook the overall effect a diagnosis has on relationships within the family, as well as among extended family and friends. How a family can work together to deal with the traumatic event of diagnosis is discussed. You must be a positive role model for your child as well as for other members of your family. If your children see that you can cope, they will be more likely to follow your lead.

ACCURATE ASSESSMENT FOR PLACEMENT

Once you have completed the process detailed in Chapter 4, it is time to extend your inner circle to include the educational community in your local school district or region (as appropriate) if you haven't already done so. Now is the time to identify appropriate schooling opportunities for your child. An assessment of your child's educational abilities will be made before a school district can place your child in a program. Children may be eligible to participate in programs if they meet established criteria. It is important to be familiar with all of the components of the assessment process because the outcomes dictate actions that the school may take on behalf of the child. In addition, an assessment also determines the types of related services your child may need and be entitled to receive (e.g., occupational therapy, physical therapy, speech therapy). These early intervention services may be critical to your child's development.

Chapter 5 familiarizes you with the assessment process. We give suggestions on how to prepare your child for an accurate assessment and ensure that a positive test-taking environment is provided. We describe what takes place when professionals meet with you to discuss the results of the assessment and suggest how to use the results of the assessment to access the services you need. A questionnaire is included to help you rate your level of satisfaction during each step of the process.

Legal issues are also covered, including obtaining parental permission for testing and laws on confidentiality and access to information. Parents' and children's rights are discussed.

TESTS FOR LEARNING DISABILITIES

Chapter 6 describes the types of learning problems a disabled child may face in school and at home and gives examples of typical behaviors observed by teachers and parents that may signal a potential problem. The information gathered from observations may indicate a need for further testing. We discuss tests that are commonly used in the assessment process. Infant development scales, preschool and school-age intelligence tests, achievement tests, reading tests, math tests, speech/language/auditory tests, and tests used in the assessment of learning disabilities are described. We will alert you to those tests that are not appropriate for specific student populations. The limitations of their effectiveness are noted.

PROGRAM PLACEMENT

As a parent, you have significant leverage in determining the programs or service your child receives. Do not simply defer to professionals when decisions need to be made. You need to investigate the options available in your community. Chapter 7 describes various placement options and the philosophies behind them. Birth to three early intervention programs are highlighted. We describe factors to consider when choosing a program. The availability and quality of programs for very young children varies from state to state and town to town. In the past, most programs were organized and administered by nonprofit organizations such as Easter Seals, or by public sector institutions such as city or county health departments. With the passage of Part H of P.L. 99-457, the 1986 Amendments to the Education of the Handicapped Act, a federal mandate was established for the states to develop a plan to serve all children who, at the earliest age possible, were identified as in need of special education and early intervention. It also includes direct services to families to better cope and deal with the problems at hand. An Individualized Family Service Plan (IFSP) or "contract" is drawn up between you and the agency responsible for early intervention services. A list of services typically offered in this program is provided. Program flexibility and adaptability are never out of the question. Information in this chapter should encourage you, when necessary, to suggest a change in your child's schedule or program.

Chapter 7 also looks at how programs for children ages three to five differ from programs for younger children. The experience of transitioning into a new setting, including parents' feelings and the effects of these changes on the whole family, is discussed.

THE INDIVIDUALIZED EDUCATION PROGRAM PROCESS

Chapter 8 details the Individualized Education Program (IEP) process. The IEP, a legal contract between the parent and the educational professionals working with the child, is based on a mutually agreed-upon course of action. A sample IEP is included, as are timelines from assessment and testing to placement, with a detailed description of each phase. The IEP identifies a set of goals that your child will strive to achieve by a certain date, using specific approaches and strategies.

Developing an IEP agreeable to all parties is not a simple task. Topics covered include who takes part in IEP meetings, frequency of meetings, and how an IEP is written. How to set and evaluate goals is discussed in detail.

In some instances your school may not have the expertise or experience to provide your child with certain services. For example, highly trained staff in a given specialty may be available only through state agencies. Chapter 8 describes parents' rights to obtain services not available through the local educational agency. Even if the local educational agency does not have every resource you need, it is responsible for locating appropriate sources to fulfill the requirements of your child's program.

Chapter 8 gives information and suggestions on how to be a team player in developing your child's IEP. Educators want parents' perspective in the development of a student's IEP, and the law requires that parents have input. We discuss what weight parents' views should have on the development of the IEP process. Exercises are included to develop communication skills among parents, teachers, and administration. We show you how to be assertive in a positive, cooperative way. Suggestions on having a productive parent-teacher conference are given. And two questionnaires help you rate your level of satisfaction with IEP meetings and with your child's IEP.

DEALING WITH THE SCHOOL SYSTEM

There are times when parents have questions or concerns about their children's schooling. It is useful to know where to turn for help to resolve an issue. The seriousness and long lasting effects of the Individual Education Program Process in many instances determines the rate for success for a special education child. Situations may arise whereby the original IEP needs to be modified several times a year. Knowing how the school system is organized is important if communications are to be smooth and effective. Chapter 9 describes a typical school system's structure, including roles and responsibilities of each of the principal parties. We discuss how to advance up the chain of command to get issues resolved. When and how to approach board of education members is also described.

Chapter 9 also describes the funding mechanisms for a local educational agency (LEA) (your local school district) and how this affects program implementation. Parents seldom know much about budget lines and funding sources. However, parents have the right to know if the school district is properly disbursing the funds earmarked for special education students. We provide suggestions on how you can monitor the situation in your LEA.

As you become familiar with the administrators and they come to know you and your child, you may begin to see important issues you raise resolved more quickly. We discuss forming a coalition of parents of special needs children so that you will be ready to mobilize on time-sensitive issues.

DUE PROCESS

Parents can feel discouraged, desperate, and angry when things are not going well. You may have tapped all the resources available through normal channels and still feel that decision makers have not fairly understood your case. Chapter 10 covers when and how to initiate a due process complaint when all else fails. A list of protection and advocacy organizations is included.

We discuss how to state the complaint clearly and the procedures to follow to process it at the state level. Cases that have been brought to due process are described, including the authors' own account of a due process claim. The consequences for the child, the parents, and the administration following a due process complaint are discussed.

LOOKING TO THE FUTURE

Throughout this book we make suggestions to encourage you to get more involved in your child's special needs schooling. You also need to evaluate the effectiveness of your past actions (e.g., at the annual review, or when your child is ready to move into a new educational setting). To create the best educational climate for your child, both now and in the future, you need to educate the community on who your child is and what contributions he/she is making to the school and the community. Chapter 11 ties together the information presented in the book into a plan of action to help parents of children with special needs be their best advocates.

Your Child Is Diagnosed with a Special Need

As a parent you are your child's primary care-giver. You are most often responsible for alerting the medical and educational communities to problems your child experiences. If you suspect that something is wrong, act. Don't wait. Learning disabilities are defined as "neurological disorders affecting a child's motor, visual-spatial, perceptual, language, cognitive and/or abstract reasoning skills" (Jason & Van Der Meer, 1989, p. 253); they include *sensory integrative dysfunction* (an irregularity or disorder in brain function that makes it difficult to integrate sensory input effectively); *dyslexia* (inability to see or perceive letters and words as they really are); *aphasia* (loss of ability to comprehend spoken or written language or to express words in speech, writing, or gesture); and *attention deficit disorder* (characterized by deficits in being able to organize one's thoughts and actions in the environment). Early recognition is important if your child is to succeed to the maximum extent possible. You would not want a learning disability to run its course without appropriate treatment, as it can leave your child stranded in a maze not of his own making. With proper support you can help your child find his way around any obstacles in his path and proceed along a course of proper cognitive and physical development (Novick & Arnold, 1991).

To help you deal effectively with your child's problems, this chapter describes how developmental and cognitive problems are best identified and how to confirm your suspicions that something is not right. We discuss how to collect information to support your feelings, and how to locate resources to further clarify a problem. The roles of professionals who are most likely to make the official identification are also discussed (e.g., doctors, psychologists, and educators). And most important, we highlight how you can actively ensure that all issues are addressed and that an appropriate identification of a problem is made.

A CHRONOLOGICAL CONTINUUM

Problems During Pregnancy

Following a chronological continuum, let's first discuss problems identified during pregnancy. In most cases these are discovered by doctors through medical tests. However, mothers can also alert doctors to potential problems by discussing conditions that may affect the health of the fetus. They may inform their doctor about medical problems experienced during pregnancies by other family members. When genetic predispositions exist, it is best to arrange genetic counseling before a couple plans to have a baby. In many cases, however, counseling occurs during pregnancy. Appendix A lists support groups for genetic related diseases. You may want to contact the National Organization for Rare Disorders (NORD) (see Appendix B under "Rare Disorders") for a more comprehensive list, as well as an annual resource directory issue of *Exceptional Parent* magazine.

Problems at Birth

At birth, potential problems can be identified, based on a newborn's appearance (malformations) and behavior. Some medical tests are routinely conducted if the newborn's weight is below 2,500 grams (5 pounds, 8 ounces). Close monitoring by hospital staff as well as by parents may also identify a problem (e.g., reactions to sounds, light, or touch). How well a newborn adjusts to his or her new surroundings is closely monitored.

If problems are identified, further developmental testing and close observation by parents and a pediatrician are called for during the first year of life. Opinions differ on when you should become concerned about your child not meeting a milestone. (This is discussed later in the chapter.)

Problems as a Toddler

Not all problems are identified at birth or during the first few years of life. As your child grows, you will rely more and more on his or her behavior and actions to identify potential problems. It is easier to identify problems in toddlers (one to three years old) because they have a more sophisticated communications system at their disposal. For example, if your child's total vocabulary consists of only a few words at age three, and he/she would rather point than verbalize, this may indicate an expressive language deficiency. If your child does not use direct eye contact with individuals around him and is unwilling to develop an emotional attachment with his family, this may be a signal that something is not right (research has shown a link between this type of behavior and autism). You and your pediatrician will observe your child together. This is an integral step in the problem identification process.

Problems at Preschool

At the next stage, preschool through age six, educational professionals join with parents and doctors to identify problems or special needs. As your child gets older, the complexity of a potential problem may intensify (e.g., poor vision or lack of mobility); some problems become very obvious, but in some cases they remain hidden. As an example of the latter, a child may demonstrate aggressive behavior because he is easily frustrated due to lack of achievement, triggering low self-esteem. Uncovering the underlying causes of this behavior may require a concerted effort by the parents and medical and educational professionals. Identification of a problem may require a longer assessment (observation) period. A problem may affect how a child learns as well as his opinion of himself. This is a critical time for identifying problems. Parents and teachers need to work collaboratively to find an appropriate intervention to optimize the educational and social well-being of the child. Let's now talk in more detail about each stage on the continuum, and how problems are identified.

Warning Signs During Pregnancy

An increasing number of pregnancies are deemed high-risk. These pregnancies may be divided into several categories. The first is based on the health of the mother. An increasing number of pregnant women abuse alcohol or drugs. Babies born to these mothers have a higher risk of developmental brain dysfunction, also termed inefficient brain function (Novick & Arnold, 1991).

Adolescents and older mothers constitute a second high risk category. Adolescent mothers often lack information on proper prenatal nutrition and care, and run the risk of having low-weight, premature babies. There is a direct relationship between a woman's nutritional status and the brain growth of her unborn child. Cells cannot grow without a sufficient supply of nutrients (Novick & Arnold, 1991). A child may be born with permanent brain damage if its mother does not have good nutritional habits. Older women are more likely to have problems during pregnancy due to the fact that their eggs have been around for a longer period of time. And there are high-risk pregnancies due to environmental hazards (e.g., lead dust). Improper growth of the fetus and genetic anomalies may occur for various reasons.

If you are in one of these high-risk categories, there is a better-than-even chance that you may deliver early, increasing the likelihood that your newborn will need special care. It is imperative that you be prepared for *any* emergency that may arise. If you feel your obstetrician is not qualified to continue to handle your case, it is your job to find one who is. Find out whether your doctor is affiliated with a hospital that has a neonatal intensive care unit (NICU); or ask whether your doctor can have temporary privileges at the nearest regional hospital with an NICU.

Do not leave it up to your doctor. If you have concerns, ask for an honest opinion. Inquire whether your obstetrician feels competent in continuing with you as a patient. If the doctor does not, ask for a referral to a specialist who has more experience. More than likely, your doctor will send you to a university-affiliated hospital for testing, where you will probably see a perineonatologist. You may feel comfortable seeing both doctors.

Table 2.1 shows symptoms that may signal serious problems during pregnancy. With advances in medical technology, possible irregularities and lack of development in the fetus can be detected earlier, and a course of treatment can be prescribed by the doctor and followed by the patient to increase the probability of bearing a healthy child. Helpful interventions include monitoring the mother's nutritional intake, making the necessary hospital arrangements for intensive medical care if needed, and establishing a working relationship between doctor and patient (Messenger & Gliedman, 1980).

Table 2.2 lists terms you may encounter when meeting the specialists who will work with you for the next several months. At this point, you and your family are under a lot of stress. Highly trained professionals are available to give you the support you need to weigh all your options and make informed decisions on what course of action to take. Genetic counselors, geneticists, and social workers in regional medical centers are well equipped to counsel you. If your pregnancy is in jeopardy there are support organizations to call on to help you through this tough time. Table 2.3 lists some of them.

Warning Signs at Birth

Once your baby is born, routine medical protocols are followed by the attending physician. The most widely practiced protocol is the "Newborn Scoring System—Apgar Score." Your newborn will be observed within one minute of birth and after five minutes of life. The newborn's

Table 2.1
Situations During Pregnancy That May Warrant Further Investigation

Warning Signs	Noted by:	Action taken
Decreased fetal activity in womb	Mother	1) Questions Doctor 2) Sonogram & non-stress tests administered 3) Doctor monitors patient more closely with frequent visits and fetal monitor techniques
Little or no weight gain	Mother Doctor	1) Diet closely monitored 2) Periodic Non-Stress Tests and/or Sonograms to monitor fetus
High Blood Pressure	Doctor	
Previous miscarriage	Mother Doctor	1) Meeting with OB to discuss reasons for miscarriage 2) Possible Referral to Geneticist and Genetic Counseling 3) Genetic Testing 4) Diagnostic Testing—Amniocentesis or Chorionic Villus Sampling
Contractions well before scheduled due date	Mother	1) Consults with Doctor 2) Bed Rest 3) Medication prescribed to stop contractions—(Beta Adrenergic drugs) 4) Ultrasound
Bleeding or bloody discharge from the vagina	Mother	1) Consults with Doctor 2) Bed Rest

condition is assessed using the five criteria shown in Table 2.4. Medical professionals assign a number from 0 to 2 for each vital sign. A total Apgar score of 7 to 10 indicates that your newborn is in good condition.

The Apgar score allows the medical team to assess your newborn quickly. It is a routine activity that is used to determine if any immediate medical intervention is needed to assist your child in adapting to his new environment. Doctors will also observe your baby for jaundice, a condition that exhibits itself in approximately three-fourths of premature babies. It is a yellow discoloration of the skin and eyes, caused mainly by the immaturity of the brain stem, which metabolizes and excretes bilirubin (Simkin & Edwards, 1979). Treatment, usually phototherapy (bilirubin can be decomposed through the skin, because it is light-sensitive), is started to control the accumulation of bilirubin and to prevent large doses from entering the brain.

Table 2.2
Medical Terms Commonly Used During Pregnancy

Term	Definition
Amniocentesis	Test done where a needle is inserted into the amnio sac and fluid is removed for study.
Amniotic sac	The bag of waters which surrounds the fetus. The bag is composed of a membrane called the amnion.
Antepartum	Before labor and delivery—also called prenatal.
Congenital	Present at and existing from the time of birth—acquired during development in the uterus.
Gestation	Length of time a pregnancy is carried.
Neonatal	From birth to 28 days of life.
Oxytocin	A drug which causes the uterus to contract.
Premature	An infant weighing less than 5 1/2 pounds at birth or is less than 37 weeks.
Trimester	A period of three months; in pregnancy, there are 3 trimesters—first: 0–3 months; second: 4–6 months; third: 7 months to term.
Ultrasound (Sonogram)	A diagnostic test commonly used during pregnancy (also at other times) where a picture is made with sound waves of internal organs and structures within the body.

An Apgar score is only one diagnostic tool to help a physician identify a newborn who might be experiencing difficulties. Blood tests (e.g., PKU) are also performed routinely to make sure your newborn is healthy. As mentioned earlier, mothers may identify situations that need to be addressed by medical personnel. Examples include an infant not wanting to bond with the mother, difficulty in the sucking reflex, and excessive crying and unresponsiveness.

If appropriate, your newborn may be taken to a neonatal intensive care unit. In many hospitals, a team of nurses will be assigned to the care of your child. You will develop a close relationship with them. There may also be a nurse practitioner on staff who has extra training and is allowed to perform medical procedures including inserting intravenous lines and endotracheal tubes (allowing the infant to be hooked up to a respirator). These nurses have many responsibilities, the first of which is to provide primary care to your newborn. Second, they will inform you of the condition and progress of your baby. Third, they will educate you on everything from how to touch and hold your baby, to breast-feeding techniques (including how to express milk) so that when your baby is

Table 2.3
Examples of Resources to Contact to Help You Through Pregnancy

Neonatal illness/prematurity	Parent Care 9041 Colgate Street Indianapolis, IN 46268-1210
Bereavement support	A.M.E.N.D. (Aiding Mothers & Fathers Experiencing Neonatal Death) 4324 Berrywick Terrace St. Louis, MO 63128 Center for Loss in Multiple Birth PO Box 1064 Palmer, AK 99645 (907) 746-6123 Compassionate Friends PO Box 3696 Oak Brook, IL 60522 (708) 990-0010
Parent education	National Maternal and Child Health Clearinghouse 8201 Greensboro Drive, Suite 600 McLean, VA 22102 (703) 821-8955 ext 254, 265 March of Dimes 1275 Mamaroneck Avenue White Plains, NY 10605 (914) 428-7100
Local religious social service agencies	Catholic Charities United Jewish Appeal Federation

ready he/she can benefit from its nutrients, to changing a baby, to explaining the physical appearance of your newborn (e.g., angel's kiss—clusters of small pink patches on the midforehead; Mongolian spot—a dark pigmented area on the buttocks; fontanel—the soft spot on your baby's head). But perhaps most important, they will be part of your support network along with your doctor and family. They will share your emotional highs and lows and give you encouragement and support. These professionals are ready to answer your questions to the best of their ability. Many books are available that will help you become familiar with the daily activities of the neonatal intensive care nursery. Appendix C lists books that are useful for parents of preemies.

Table 2.4
Newborn Scoring System—Apgar Score

Vital Signs	Characteristics Demonstrated (circle one only)	Score Given
Heart rate	0 less than 100 over 100	0 1 2
Respiratory effort	absent slow irregular good crying	0 1 2
Muscle tone	flaccid some flexing of arms and legs active motion	0 1 2
Reflex irritability	no response cry vigorous cry	0 1 2
Color	blue and pale body pink—arms and legs blue completely pink	0 1 2

Warning Signs During The First Year of Life

As new parents you have been watching in amazement the miracles of life. You will be observing your child doing many things. Very basically, you will be looking at how your child responds to light (very passive—or very fussy); distinguishes your voice from others'; greets you with a smile; holds his head up; turns his head to follow sounds; coos or babbles. Absence of these events or milestones can indicate possible problems. Parents of preemies need to remember that their child's first two years of growth and development will be assessed based on the child's corrected age, that is, the age the premature baby would have been if born at forty weeks gestational age. In other words, your child will be given an extended period of time to catch up.

We know that human development follows a set path. However, the time it takes to go from one step to the next varies from child to child. The pace and adequacy of a child's developmental process varies based on the child's developing nervous system, experiences, and personality (Novick & Arnold, 1991). Many psychologists believe that neurological factors have the greatest influence, especially during childhood. The pattern of neurological development is basically similar. That is why we notice that almost all one-year-olds are able to demonstrate the same skills.

If you feel that the time between each developmental gain is not quite

Table 2.5
Baby's Activities at Various Ages

1 Month	3 Months	6 Months	9 Months	12 Months
Grasps your finger.	Reaches for objects and may grasp and hold them for a few seconds.	Transfers an object from hand to hand easily but doesn't know how to let go purposefully.	Grasps and handles objects skillfully.	Gives and takes a toy in play. Rolls a ball toward you.
When alert, watches your face and listens to your voice.	Responds to a greater variety of stimuli. Likes objects of different colors and textures.	Studies your face intently, touches it, pulls your hair.	Understands simple instructions such as "Bring Me."	Plays with one or two favorite stuffed animals, loving and sometimes pushing them.
Rolls part way from back to side.	Leans on elbows while lying on stomach and holds head up.	May sit alone, though she still can't get into a sitting position by herself.	Raises himself to a sitting position, has good head and body control.	Spends much of her time walking & standing. Prefers standing to sitting. Loves to climb.
Searches for a nipple, sucks and swallows.	Coordinates looking, grasping and sucking. (Tries to put everything in mouth.)	Shakes things to see if they make noise. Interested in sounds she can make and compares them.	Understands relationships between certain objects such as keys and lock.	Skilled at handling objects and testing what they can do (turning light switches on and off).

Source: Adapted from Mead Johnson & Company. 1990. *Your baby's first year: A guide to infant growth and development.* Evansville, IN.

right, and you feel confident that you have provided your child with a nourishing and stimulating environment, it is appropriate to make your feelings known to your doctor. Table 2.5 describes various activities your child may be engaged in during the first year of life. Table 2.6 is a checklist for speech, language, and hearing. Table 2.7 shows fine motor/adaptive milestones. These tables will help you begin to understand where your child is on the developmental continuum and to identify his or her strengths and weaknesses. Average responses or behavior demonstrated by an average child at an average age are listed. These data will activate your thoughts on how your child responds to certain stimuli. Consider whether you should act on your suspicions or uneasiness. Pick up the

Table 2.6
Speech, Language, and Hearing Checklist

Average Age	Question	Average Behavior
3–6 Months	What does he do when you talk to him? Does he react to your voice when he cannot see you?	He awakens or quiets to the sound of his mother's voice. Baby typically turns eyes and head in the direction of the source of the sound.
7–10 Months	When he can't see what is happening, what does he do if he hears father's footsteps? the dog barking? the telephone ringing? his own name?	When he cannot see what is happening, he turns his head and shoulders toward familiar sounds. These sounds do not have to be loud to cause him to respond.
11–15 Months	Does he respond differently to different sounds?	Jabbers in response to human voice, is apt to cry when there is thunder, may frown when he is scolded.

Source: Adapted from Montgomery County Public Schools. 1967. *Speech, Language, and Hearing Checklist.* Rockville, MD: Montgomery County Public Schools.

phone and call a professional. You have taken an important step in identifying a potential problem and finding an appropriate course of action if necessary.

During the first years of life your child will be seeing the pediatrician frequently. Visits are scheduled at two months, four months, six months, and so on. Find out how many visits you need to schedule and what will be occurring during these visits. During the routine examination, the doctor should explain the simple tests performed and the results. As part of the exam, the doctor should routinely and matter of factly ask questions on your daily routine, and ask if you have any other concerns that you would like to discuss. When examining your child's eyes, for example, the doctor may ask: "Does your child seem to use one eye more than the other? Does your child bring objects in front of his eyes? Does your child rub his eyes frequently?"

Your doctor will make typical inquiries into your child's eating and sleeping habits; activity level—whether he or she is passive or aggressive; eye/hand coordination; ability to imitate your actions; ability to discriminate between objects; and so on. This will help the doctor assess your child's growth. Learn to make your responses precise so that the medical professional gets a genuine picture of what your child is doing.

Over time your pediatrician will get to know you, your child, and your

Table 2.7
Fine Motor/Adaptive Checklist

Average Age	Questions	Average Behavior
3–6 Months	When there is a mobile in the stroller, crib or playpen, how will your child respond to it?	When there is a mobile with brightly colored items attached to it, he will try to reach for it and turn it.
7–11 Months	When sitting in the high chair, and small pieces of food are placed on his tray, what will your child do?	Child will use thumb-finger grasp to pick up small pieces of food.
12–19 Months	How does your child play with blocks?	When given a box of blocks a child can build a tower of 2 blocks.

Source: Adapted from Montgomery County Public Schools. 1967. *Fine Motor/Adaptive Checklist.*

family very well. Always ask your doctor for suggestions on the "how to's." Doctors should have handouts on parenting as well as notices for public events and seminars on child development. Ask for copies. They should be concerned with all aspects of what your child is doing and how he interacts with others. It is imperative that you take advantage of your doctor's experience and resources.

As you observe your child's growth, you and your doctor will compare it to the growth and development experienced by other children. Developmental milestones have been established that identify the average age at which children are able to complete certain tasks. Through past experience and research, the medical and educational community has come up with standards to which to compare your child's achievements, both physical (e.g., height and weight, head circumference) and developmental (e.g., grasping an object, smiling, turning over). Each child is an individual, and it is important to keep accurate records of when your child reaches developmental milestones.

Today, most pediatricians measure a child's growth by using the Denver Developmental Screening Test (Frankenburg and Dodds, 1969). It uses four basic categories to record developmental milestones from birth to age six:

1. Personal-social (skills that will help to develop independent living abilities);

2. Fine motor-adaptive (skills dealing with learning about objects and their use);

3. Language (skills in communicating information—begins with hand

gestures, body language, cries, and vocalizations, and then progresses to complete sentences and thoughts); and

4. Gross motor (skills enabling movements of the whole body).

A child's growth is usually very dramatic in the first year. Thus, if your child's growth lags, it is important to investigate. You and your doctor spend a lot of time with your child, both of you observing him closely. You can compare notes and observations. As a highly trained professional, your doctor is able to spot certain maladies or symptoms that may indicate a specific problem or developmental delay. With your help, the doctor can assess the situation and make recommendations and referrals. Together you can devise a plan to find out why your child has not acquired certain skills.

If the problem is associated with delivery (e.g., neuromuscular injuries such as brachial plexus) or chromosomal abnormalities (e.g., Down syndrome), then it is undoubtedly the physician who will alert the parent to the situation. In this case, your doctor should explain the potential problems as well as misconceptions about the condition, and refer you to either a support group or a professional organization for further information on the disease. Sources include the Down Syndrome Congress, National Organization for Rare Disorders (NORD), March of Dimes, Easter Seals, and other groups (see Appendix B). However, problems that are not readily detectable by a physician will often be discovered later by parents during the baby's early years.

On occasion you may not agree with your doctor's assessment or recommendations. If you feel that your doctor is shrugging off or refusing to acknowledge a serious problem, you always have the option to obtain a second opinion. Your gut reactions should not be ignored. Many parents we have spoken to regret not following their instinct that a problem needed attention, and are angry that they let their doctor convince them that there was no problem.

Warning Signs at Ages 1–3

The growth of your child is based on his ability to successfully gain control over his own body (using muscles progressively from head to toe), so that he may be able to test his environment and gain new skills. During the sensorimotor stage of development, the thinking processes are based on trial and error by exploration. If your child is having trouble manipulating objects because of his lack of motor control, or does not process the sensation of touch, he may not be able to benefit fully from his exploration of his environment (Novick & Arnold, 1991).

If your child's mobility and sensory motor experiences are limited, the emergence and use of language may be slowed. Language develops when a child is able to express his thoughts based on his experiences. A young child first learns about himself by exploring his environment (e.g., crawling to a mirror and looking at himself). Many songs and games for children this age contain words about different parts of the body. In order for a child to learn he first has to learn about himself. A child with limited motor ability may not be able to partake in all these experiences, and the ability to learn may be delayed. Teachers who have worked with them tell us that children who lack motor control are not totally aware of their body and have difficulty initiating and using it to complete tasks such as eating with a spoon (Keith, 1984).

You may notice that your child is having trouble swallowing food, and not realize that this is caused by low muscle tone, or by a condition called "tactile defensiveness." This may not only be a warning of a nutritional problem but may also signal a possible problem in speech development, since it might prevent your child from using the jaw, tongue, and lips to form words properly. Another scenario to watch for is the loss of a skill that your child has already attained. For instance, a young child might coo and babble, but then stop. A possible reason is a hearing deficiency. If he doesn't hear, he doesn't have any models to imitate, thus he is not rewarded and will cease the activity. It is important to observe not only when and how your child attains skills, but also if he loses ones he has already demonstrated or uses them infrequently.

When a child does not attain a milestone in a reasonable time frame, it may signal a potential problem, especially in the early years. If your child demonstrates no signs of an emerging new skill, shows no interest in exploration, is chronically unhappy or frustrated, has a very limited attention span, or is easily distractible—not willing to get close to you or other people—these are signs that he needs intervention services. It is important to observe carefully and be ready to investigate reasons for your child's behavior and actions. Your pediatrician should step in and help you identify problems, which then should be referred to the appropriate medical or educational agency to help make a diagnosis.

Warning Signs in the Prekindergarten Years

The federal law P.L. 99-457, Part H was passed by Congress to enable all children with disabilities in every state to receive special education at the preschool level as well as an opportunity to receive early intervention services. Each state designates a lead agency to coordinate referrals, assessments, programs, and placements, or to provide direct services to the family at home. A written Individualized Family Service Plan (IFSP) is required, wherein parents as partners in the planning process are given information, advice, and training in appropriate parenting skills. Eligibility for enrollment in this program varies from state to state. In fact, programs are available from birth in many localities. (See Chapters 5 and 7 for a more detailed explanation.)

In years past, children's learning difficulties were usually discovered in kindergarten or later by a teacher. Many children were left undiagnosed or called hyperactive. Or the teacher (or parent) might expect the child to outgrow the problem in time. In today's world of diagnostic tools and knowledge, specific brain function deficiencies can be identified (e.g., "process problem") through testing, both medically and educationally. Your child may not be successful in school if deficiencies in certain skills are not identified early. Visual motor and perceptual motor difficulties are noted quite often in children with neurological problems. These children usually have difficulty catching a ball, coloring inside a line, writing letters that are all the same height, and copying off the blackboard accurately. The attainment of these skills is a precursor to developing good thinking skills. If a child has difficulty exploring her world with hands-on experience, developing critical skills such as memory will be more difficult.

Table 2.8 lists some general skills your child should acquire before entering kindergarten. You need not worry if your child acquires these skills at a younger age. However, if any deficiencies in these areas persist for an extended period of time, this may signal potential learning difficulties when your child enters school. It is important that you observe your child more closely and be ready to discuss your observations with a professional.

Specific teaching methods can help your child deal effectively with a learning disability. Some problems still are not diagnosed early, but the chances of identifying a problem in preschool are better now than a generation ago.

DETECTING A POTENTIAL PROBLEM OR HANDICAP: STRATEGIES FOR PARENTS

As parents we are well-placed to identify problems and potential problems in our children's growth and development. We must express our concerns or suspicions to professionals, who can then take appropriate action. We first need to organize our thoughts to relay our suspicions effectively to others. How do we do this? First, write down signs that have alerted you to a potential problem. Recording the circumstances or events that led you to become concerned (e.g., responses or lack of them exhibited by your child) will help you acquire a true picture of what is happening in your child's life.

Many times a concern may come to the forefront when other children are using skills that your child is not. Very subtle differences may also

Table 2.8
Difficulties in Skill Areas During the Pre-Kindergarten Years That May Warrant
Further Investigation

Motor Movement	Auditory Skills	Visual Skills
Fine eye–hand control	Remembering various sounds	Visual Memory and Sequencing
Balance	Detecting differences and similarities in sounds	Visual Matching
Judgement in Space (Motor Planning)	Draws meaning from verbal direction	Eye Movements, eye–hand control

cause concern. You might be part of a parent-child play group where you observe other children and compare their play to your child's play. The following is a typical scenario.

Scenario: Your child is eighteen months old, and you are eager to form a play group. A group of four mothers with six children decide to meet one morning a week for two hours. You alternate hosting the play group.

Observation: On several different occasions, your child's peers are constantly battling over the same toy and eliciting their mother's attention to intervene on their behalf by hitting or screaming at each other. *Your child does not seem interested in the same toys, is very quiet, and plays with toys that are left in the toy box.*

Your actions: During the play group time you talk to your child and suggest that he/she play with a friend from the group. *Instead he/she refuses and runs into another room, or tells you that he/she wants to go home. When the play group is in your home, your child refuses to let the other children play with his/her toys.* You become frustrated and are considering abandoning the play group.

Your concerns: As a parent you know that a child goes through different developmental stages, but does your child's lack of socialization skills signal a problem that needs to be addressed?

Know How to Observe Effectively

Parents are usually very observant when it comes to their children's behavior. They know how their children respond to stimuli; their eating and sleeping habits; how they get along with other children; and their progression from simple to complex tasks (e.g., their ability to gain control over their bodies, progressing from holding the head up, to grasping an object, to standing, crawling, and walking). However, not every incident, whether joyous or disappointing, can be remembered.

What are the advantages and benefits for writing down your observations? It is an exercise that helps develop an accurate picture of what your child is doing, allowing you to interpret your child's actions. This can be helpful for you emotionally, because it allows you to deal with concrete facts that can be addressed. In addition, developing skill in observing and interpreting your child's responses will affect your relationship with your child (State of Maryland Department of Education, 1982). Through observation and documentation, you will have gathered vital information that will help you establish and maintain a warm, loving environment which can enhance your child's learning and meet his or her needs. It is important to write down facts in a logical order or to group them in appropriate categories so that you can relay this information to professionals diagnosing the potential problem.

Also, small elements of a larger picture should be documented. When certain behavior, complaints, and appearances are listed, a potential problem can be detected (e.g., omits and/or substitutes certain sounds; turns head when listening; says "Huh? What did you say?" Conclusion: my child may have a hearing problem. I will take my child for a hearing evaluation).

What to look for in an observation. Observing your child includes noticing how she incorporates all five senses in confronting a stimulus or situation, her communication response (whether it be through body language or by voicing complaints), and her physical appearance. Noting any changes in temperament is also valuable in the observation process. One strategy is to create a daily log (Figure 2.1) and highlight your child's typical activities. Write down her responses to these activities, being as specific and descriptive as possible. Adults often dislike doing difficult tasks or ones that make them feel uncomfortable. This is also true of children. Note how long it takes your child to finish a task. A pattern may emerge that will help identify a problem or a need that should be addressed.

It is useful to observe your child's strengths and weaknesses at play or in a social situation. This is especially true for younger children. Your child will demonstrate many strengths and weaknesses. At play you can determine:

1. his gross and fine motor skills (e.g., How does he pick up blocks, put together puzzles, turn pages in a book, play with a busy box or shape sorter?);

2. how he plays and gets along with others (e.g., What activities does he enjoy alone, and how often does he play alone? When he is with others, what types of activities does he engage in?);

Figure 2.1
Daily Log

Date: _____

Activity	Skills or Behaviors Displayed (Body Language—Temperament During Task)	Amount of Time Taken to Complete Task	Motivation or Type of Assistance Needed to Begin or Complete Task
Dressing: choosing clothes; putting socks on; buttoning shirt; tying shoes			
Eating: holding cup, fork or spoon; swallowing and chewing food			
Movement: crawling; walking; sitting			
Socialization: play alone; play with others			
Communication: verbal; nonverbal			

3. his emotional coping skills (e.g., How does he react to failure or changes in routine?);

4. his ability to use speech to communicate his wants and desires; and

5. his attention span (e.g., When is it the longest, shortest? What distracts him and what motivates him?).

Planning to Observe an Event Based on your Concerns: Factors to Consider

When you decide to observe your child formally, identify the specific behavior or task that you are gathering information on; the key players; and the time and place of the observation (Anderson, Chitwood, & Hayden, 1990). We will demonstrate how to initiate a formal observation of a child's behavior by using the scenario described above. This parent wants her child to learn how to get along with others and make friends easily. To reach this goal, we will create a situation that parallels a controlled scientific experiment, but on a very simple scale. In this planned observation we will control four variables:

Who: neighbor's child who is your child's age.

What: how your child interacts with his peers.

Where: in your backyard.

When: in the morning on a sunny, warm day.

Record what happens: Johnny sits on one side of the sandbox and plays. His friend Jake sits directly across from him. Johnny refuses to share toys, and when Jake takes a shovel out of his hands, Johnny does not resist and proceeds to pick another toy. When Jake tries to bury Johnny's feet in the sand, Johnny gets very upset; he looks at the house, but he doesn't call for me.

List your impressions of the event: Johnny likes to have lots of space for himself and does not like to be touched. He has trouble communicating verbally.

It is important to record your child's behavior or appearance before, during, and after the encounter or task being observed. Set up times to observe similar situations so that you can get a general impression of how your child reacts.

Family History

Family history is an important factor in identifying a potential problem. Hereditary factors may be the cause of certain actions. Talk to your family, including grandparents, aunts, and uncles to determine whether other relatives demonstrated the same types of behavior. A fun and very productive activity is to complete a family tree. You can learn about your ancestry as well as identifying problems that might have been exhibited by others in your family. Finally, writing down a complete account of your pregnancy may help developmental professionals find factors that have contributed to your child's problems.

POINTS TO REMEMBER

It is not easy for parents to admit that their child may have a significant delay in achieving age-appropriate developmental and cognitive skills. If we suspect that something is wrong, we may postpone acting because we do not know what the future will bring. Even though a very young child may not be able to do much (eat, sleep, and cry), the maturation process is already in full swing. The quality of growth is dependent on many factors, including the environment and the amount of stimulation and interaction with persons and objects around them. Thus a parent's role in the child's growth and development is crucial, especially in the early years. You may decide that it's too early to discuss your suspicions with your doctor or early childhood educator. But why wait? The first year passes by quickly, and you can never bring it back.

In this chapter we have given you the tools to start gaining and organizing information about your child, so that you will feel more comfortable in accepting the challenge of raising a child with a disability. It is important to realize that your actions can have a significant, positive impact on your child's progress. By identifying the characteristics of the developmental continuum in simple terms, you have gained a better understanding of what behavior is typical for an age group. Thus you have a point from which to begin to confirm your suspicions. Through close observation, you can gain a perspective of what your child's world is really like, find his or her strengths and weaknesses, and begin to gather information that will be vital when you communicate your concerns to professionals. And, finally, you do not have to feel that you are alone. Many families and professionals are out there to give you support and encourage you to accept the challenge of being a parent with a special needs child.

The Benefit of Second Opinions

When confronted with the possible existence of some condition affecting our child's health or ability to learn, our first concern is the extent to which this condition will inhibit or delay the child's long-term growth and development. We question whether an accurate diagnosis has been made. We may feel uncomfortable with the results of the testing and decide to have a more comprehensive assessment. When to call upon others to confirm a medical or educational problem or diagnosis depends on various factors. In fact, you may proceed with the process described herein more than once during your child's schooling. You may wait until your child has been in a school program for a period of time before calling upon others for diagnostic assistance, or you may seek a second opinion immediately, as soon as a problem appears.

REASONS WHY PARENTS CONFIRM A DIAGNOSIS

Your first priority should be to identify your child's specific educational needs. To do this you will assess his strengths and weaknesses. In essence, you will be looking for specific strategies to help your child succeed in school and in the community, seeking guidance and direction from experts in the field. However, it is important to remember that you do not have to accept the recommendations and conclusions made by the first professional that you consult, and certainly not just because he or she is well known. It is important that you feel comfortable communicating with the specialist, and that you and your child look forward to visiting with this person. You also seek this person out to give you helpful advice and support. Finding appropriate support for your child and the entire family is an important goal.

LACK OF CONFIDENCE IN PROFESSIONALS

Many parents seek a second opinion because they feel uncomfortable with the way a particular professional interacts with them and their family. Having spent some time in consultation with a given person, you may not feel that they are on target, or you may not like the person's ultimate conclusions and recommendations. As a parent you are a consumer of professional services, and you have the right to choose someone with whom you feel comfortable.

LOCATING THE SPECIALIST FOR YOU

The consultation process can be very time-consuming and stressful. This is an age of specialization in the medical and educational communities. Numerous medical specialists and educational professionals are available to assist you in confirming a diagnosis or perceived problem. Information on specialists' training and credentials can be found in the *American Medical Directory* (published by the American Medical Association) or the *The Official ABMS Directory of Board Certified Medical Specialists;* both are available in public libraries. It is important that you come prepared to meet with the professional. When you do go for second opinions, talk in a very descriptive fashion, outlining your child's abilities and weaknesses in detail. We suggest that you pick a recent event and describe your child's behavior during that time. Make sure the professional you are dealing with has met your child in person and is not just reading a list of facts from a piece of paper.

CATEGORIES OF PROFESSIONAL CONSULTANTS

Most children with disabilities will be referred to several specialists for testing and evaluation. They may visit a neurologist, a psychologist, a geneticist, an ophthalmologist (vision), an audiologist (hearing), or an orthopedist (bones and muscles). For example, if, after reading articles or books on the subject, parents suspect that their child exhibits characteristics of attention deficit disorder (e.g., inability to complete a task within a reasonable amount of time; disorganization; restlessness) they will probably call upon a psychologist who has had experience with this age group to test for achievement and aptitude, or they might consult a pediatric neurologist who will be searching for an organic cause for the problem. Parents may also consider seeking out two medical specialists that we have encountered over the years; the developmental pediatrician and the physiatrist. These specialists concentrate on children with developmental disabilities.

Your neighborhood pediatrician's practice typically deals with routine matters that occur during childhood. A small percentage of its total patient caseload may include children with disabilities. You may consider seeking a pediatrician who has more specific training in child development, and thus more familiarity with growth and development issues. But this does not mean that a pediatrician you like in your local area cannot meet your needs. You may want to consult both. A physiatrist works in the physical medicine arena. In a sense he or she is a doctor of physical therapy. It may be worth taking a look to see if a physiatrist is available near your home.

In addition, you may encounter other specialists, such as speech and occupational therapists. Occupational therapists work closely with children who have sensory and visual perception difficulties. A child who exhibits tactile defensiveness, where tactile sensations (touching smooth, rough, hot/cold objects) create negative emotional reactions such as distractibility, restlessness, and behavior problems, will probably be referred to an occupational therapist for evaluation and treatment (Sensory Integration International, 1986). Children who have difficulty with motor planning (the ability of the brain to conceive or organize and carry out a sequence of unfamiliar events), known as apraxia, may also be seen by an occupational therapist. An occupational therapist evaluates perceptual and neuromuscular factors that influence a child's ability to function, and concentrates on development of fine motor skills. Physical therapists evaluate a child's orthopedic structure and neuromuscular functions, concentrating on the child's gross motor skills. Examples of motor planning are learning how to tie shoes, ride a bike, cut with scissors, and skip. Some physical therapists may have extensive training in working with neurologically impaired children (Neurodevelopmental Treatment [NDT] certified).

A TEAM APPROACH TO CONFIRMING A DIAGNOSIS

A team approach often is used with young children (infant to age six), whereby many professionals specializing in various areas of child development will come together to observe and evaluate a child's abilities. There are various child development clinics around the country, usually affiliated with hospitals or universities, that specialize in confirming a developmental or physical diagnosis. These clinics provide many other services to help parents cope with the medical/educational diagnosis. Clinic staff will make suggestions and propose strategies to assist your family. They will provide a follow-along plan employing various interventions to improve the quality of delivery of services to your child.

One source for locating a multidisciplinary team is the *American Association of University Affiliated Programs (AAUAP) in Mental Retardation and Developmental Disabilities*. There are also federal health information centers and clearinghouses that can refer you to appropriate locations in your area that may help. The National Information Center for Children and Youth with Disabilities is a good resource, as is the Council for Exceptional Children. If you suspect your child is deaf, you can contact the National Institute on Deafness and Other Communication Disorders Information Clearinghouse for guidance in finding a local setting to help you and your child.

Other clinics are sponsored by nonprofit organizations such as Easter Seals or United Cerebral Palsy. The nonprofit Regional Center for Infants and Young Children in the Washington, D.C. metropolitan area specializes in the diagnosis, treatment, and prevention of emotional and development disorders in infants and young children using a multidisciplinary approach. Funding for these organizations comes from various sources, including client fees, contracts between the organization and state and local agencies, and third party payments (Medicaid). Your local hospital, pediatrician, or government agency (department of health or children and youth services) may be aware of such centers in your community.

FACE THE FACTS

In many cases an accurate diagnosis can take years. A pattern of behavior or symptoms may not appear consistently for a long time. Remember, each child with a disability may not match completely with all of the characteristics of a known syndrome. We suggest that you not become overly consumed with finding a label for your child. Also, with medical technology changing daily, definitions of certain disorders can change. In particular, be cautious about accepting unquestioningly the diagnoses given to your child. Designations like PDD (pervasive developmental disorder), ADHD (attention deficit hyperactivity disorder), and similar labels change rapidly (Rimland, 1989). However, diagnosis is helpful in some situations (e.g., certain medications can control behavior that may have an adverse effect on your child's behavior or learning ability).

LABELING: WHY IT IS APPROPRIATE TO SOME SITUATIONS AND NOT TO OTHERS

The intent of Section 504 of the Rehabilitation Act of 1973, a civil rights act that protects disabled individuals from educational or work-related discrimination, was to "demand that individual standards be employed when evaluating a child's progress or the appropriateness of his educational placement. By imposing this standard, Congress hoped to avoid labeling children, a practice which leads to broad, and often false, assumptions about the abilities of general classes of people with disabilities" (Cluman, 1987, p. 49). You do not want educators or medical personnel to make judgments before they have an opportunity to become personally acquainted with your child. It is important to use appropriate language to describe your child accurately in the best light. Thus, describing your child with stereotyped phrases is not recommended. And don't let labeling consume you. L. and J. Tommasone (1989) give the following advice to parents of autistic children:

> It may take awhile but someday you will wake up and realize that something has changed, your mind will be clearer and you will feel more optimistic. Without really knowing when, you will have accepted your child's autism and also another momentous fact—namely that your child is exactly the same person he was before you got a label for his condition. He hasn't lost a single one of the qualities that endeared him to you before his diagnosis; only your perceptions have been temporarily distorted. (p. 40)

When dealing with the world outside the family, it sometimes is practical or convenient to give your child a label. This is most often true when you interact with the medical and educational communities. The insurance and educational communities seem to feel more comfortable working with a child who can fit into certain stereotypical categories. There is no need for an extensive interpretation of your child's condition; rather, a label makes the processing and paperwork easier to handle. Decisions on services can be made more easily with a label in place. Your child fits into a neat definition. But is this fair to your child? We know that stereotyping can be very dangerous and can prevent children from being treated equally.

Some parents try to assimilate their child into society to an extreme. Some hide the fact that their child has a disability. I remember watching a segment on *Sixty Minutes* several years ago, about parents of children with Down syndrome who elected to have their children undergo plastic surgery to remove the "common facial features" exhibited by the syndrome. In their opinion too many negatives were attached to the Down syndrome child, and they decided to take extreme measures to prevent it from happening.

Some parents need to fit a label to their child so that they can cope better with the problems at hand—and that's O.K. They need to know in general terms what to expect. The parents' questions were answered, and they were able to deal with the situation. There is a sense of relief.

WHAT DO YOU REALLY WANT TO KNOW?

In our experience, no one will actually predict the achievement or learning rate of your child. What you really want to ascertain are what types of supports are available to help a child grow physically, emotionally, and educationally. By identifying these supports you can enrich your child's environment to enable him to learn.

To this end, it is important to learn more about how your child thinks, feels, and behaves. Areas that are important to identify early are the activities that motivate your child to learn and think; how your child perceives his environment; barriers that impede learning; and best learning style. Information is needed in these areas to initiate a program that will be compatible with your child's strengths and that will address your child's needs. But affixing a label to a specific condition is not necessary, especially if your child is under five years of age. Chapter 5 discusses in detail the guidelines school systems use for identifying children who may need extra help to succeed in school.

How to Find Out What You Really Want to Know From Professionals and Consultants

Parents rely on professionals to help us understand the underlying reasons for our child's problems. We seek explanations for why our children are not learning at the pace we expect. We anticipate that these experts will be able to identify the factors influencing our child's behavior and tell us what we can do to help our child succeed. By enlisting professional help, we are really seeking relief and comfort from those who can help us make some sense of what is happening to our family. We seek their advice because we feel they will be able to help us make changes that will make our daily lives more bearable and worthwhile. We may even want them to be able to make the problem disappear completely, even though we know in our hearts that that may be impossible. We are trying to make sense of what is happening to our child.

It would be foolish to think that professionals have all the answers, but their suggestions and recommendations may help parents create a more positive environment for the child and the family. In order for this to occur, parents need to describe their child objectively, without being highly emotional. We found it very beneficial to discuss with a consultant the reasons why we were seeking his help. Do not be afraid to fill the consultant in on previous consultations with other experts if you think he is a truly independent thinker. For the consultation to be valuable, we need to understand why we have come together. The consultant will tell you what he or the testing itself can and cannot do. Usually the consultant will tell you what he will be doing (e.g., what types of tests, procedures, and follow-up activities are planned). After listening to his approach, do you believe it will be beneficial to you and your child? Also, do you believe that this approach is reasonably sound, and that useful information can be extracted? Most important, you must decide whether or not your child will be able to get along with the consultant (if applicable).

We expect such a professional to be honest and sensitive to the fact that we are confronting a situation that may evoke painful and stressful emotions. It is important that the professional use appropriate diagnostic tools and be experienced in administering these tests. He needs to be adaptable and creative in the assessment process because no two children will react the same way. Most important, the professional must be willing to try to answer your questions and concerns, and not stifle your conversation. You may decide to talk to your child after the session to gather his impressions. Depending on his level of self-esteem and whether this was the first time he has been in such a situation, he may have enjoyed the session (thinking it was like school), or he might have felt a lot of pressure. Your child may complain that he was not able to follow the consultant's directions (e.g., spoke too fast, used words he could not understand), and so on. You may want to share this information with the consultant.

It is a good idea to schedule a follow-up meeting to discuss the report with the consultant. On occasion, it is not possible for both parties to get together for another face-to-face meeting and the report is mailed to the parents. If you have a choice, we suggest meeting in person. You and the consultant should read the report together, stopping at any point when you feel something needs to be explained in further detail. When going over the report, is the consultant describing the services performed in language you can understand? Also request a copy of the material (e.g., tests) used in the evaluation or consultation. This information will help you decide whether the recommendations are based on actual data the consultant collected when observing your child. In many situations, professionals use a set of criteria developed by experts in the field to determine your child's disability. Can the consultant describe the criteria used in making recommendations or a diagnosis and can he detail how your child meets these criteria or standards? It is important for you to ask the source of these standards (e.g., the American Psychiatric Association's definition of autism). It is important to find out how much time he has spent with your child. Carefully listen when he describes your child. Can he talk about your child without constantly referring to his notes, and has he included a narrative that makes sense to you? By focusing in on these tasks you can obtain the information that really is important—and throw out any information that seems useless.

SELECTING THE RIGHT PHYSICIAN OR EDUCATIONAL PROFESSIONAL TO HELP YOU FIND OUT WHAT YOU WANT TO KNOW

It is important that you select a doctor or educational professional whom you trust and who you can talk to when you have a concern. Recommendations are very important. Talk with other parents and describe the qualities you are looking for in a consultant. Determine his availability to talk to you on the phone. Is he a sole practitioner or member of a large group? Does he keep abreast of the latest developments in technology? Are his mannerisms and personality compatible with yours? These are all areas that you should rank in importance to you and your family. Tell the receptionist your intentions when seeing the professional, so that sufficient time can be blocked off for the meeting. Learn to be frank, and ask all the questions you need to ask. Tell him your concerns, and expect him to give you an answer or get back to you, or to make a referral to another doctor if necessary. Also, ask about whether he is willing to share information with your pediatrician, other specialists, and your case manager.

OTHER FACTORS TO CONSIDER WHEN THINKING ABOUT OBTAINING A SECOND OPINION

Financial

When they are contemplating seeking a second opinion, parents need to ask themselves some questions:

"Can we afford to? What new information will we receive that will help Johnny? Will they just repeat what they have said to us before? The cost incurred for a second opinion may be prohibitive for many families. Factors to consider include travel costs incurred to get to the clinic; length of time necessary to test and evaluate; and laboratory fees and associated medical costs. Parents are often frightened and anxious about these financial issues. To help them assess their ability to pay for these services, several options are available.

Funding sources. Your medical insurance is one funding source. Parents need to be very familiar with their individual insurance packages, including caps and deductibles. Many plans limit the family to a specified number of consultations per year for each specialty, such as speech, occupational, or physical therapy. To contain your family's health costs it is important that you tell your physician or case manager what type of insurance coverage you have. But it is your responsibility to find out whether the specialist is a participating provider in your health coverage system, and whether your plan will cover various testing procedures.

Tests performed on an inpatient basis are often covered, but outpatient services are another matter. Also, if the tests are related to a medical condition, the probability of coverage will increase, but an insurer might require that a particular site be used. It is best to speak directly to representatives of your insurance carrier, and not to your benefits officer. Obtain a copy of your certificate of insurance. This document is the actual contract between employer and health provider (Preferred Provider Organization [PPO], Health Maintenance Organization [HMO], or individual company).

There are state agencies you can tap to help you access funds for evaluations. In our son Adam's case we called on the Board of Education Services for the Blind to fund a psychological evaluation. Adam is eligible to receive annual funding from this organization for services that are appropriate to meet his school needs. These funds took a lot of pressure off the family and helped provide a needed service for Adam. State agencies for the deaf and hearing impaired, state departments of rehabilitation services, and the department of health should be accessed.

Many community service organizations may help provide funds. The Lions Club, Rotary, and Telephone Pioneers work closely with children with disabilities and their families.

Determine the Specific Components of the Assessment Process: Are They Different from Those Used Before?

It is important to know what course of action your consultant is planning to take. Find out what testing instruments will be used (e.g., aptitude, achievement) and the location for his observations (e.g., clinic, classroom, your home, or a combination of various settings).

Time

Question the consultant about how long it will take to observe, evaluate, and prepare a report that fulfills your expectations. You will want to know if the consultant will be able to complete all tasks in a reasonable amount of time. It is better to ask at the outset or before you visit the consultant, so that valuable time is not lost.

Credentials and Background

When selecting a consultant it is important to determine whether he has the necessary knowledge and skills to evaluate and diagnose your child. You may feel more comfortable with a consultant who has done a lot of research on the topic and has published his findings. Find out what professional organizations he belongs to. This information will be helpful in making a decision.

POINTS TO REMEMBER

Confirming a perceived medical or educational problem or diagnosis in most cases is an evolutionary process. Parents expend a lot of effort, time, expense, and emotional energy looking for answers and support. However, the most important factor in deciding whether or not to continue this process is how the outcome will affect the child and the family. Are the recommendations useful in everyday life, and will they make a difference in family relationships—between husband and wife, parent and child, parent and siblings, and among siblings? Is this information needed so that parents can agree on the best approaches to raising the child and teaching the child at school? As parents we may feel that we do not know what to do to help our child, and we need direction.

We also have to consider how this directly affects the child. How does your child react when he is taken from professional to professional for more testing? Is he uncomfortable meeting new people in white coats? We need to ask, will this effort help give us confidence in our role as parents, and at the same time give our child a better chance to succeed in school and in life?

4

Coping Strategies for Parents

When we planned this book it was a simple task to write the outline for this chapter. But now that we are embarking on the details, many deep-rooted feelings are beginning to emerge. Some of these feelings we have experienced in the past, but reflecting on the past ten years, new feelings have also emerged about our reactions when we realized that our son would always be significantly behind his peers.

It is not easy watching neighborhood children who are the same age as your child being able to run, speak, and participate in daily activities without constant intervention or assistance by a parent. You suffer when your child has been singled out by other children because of how he looks or acts. And it is even harder when you have older children that have been going through the growing pains of a "normal" childhood.

But let's stop for a minute and really think about what we have just said. What is normal? All children have problems. Every family has to deal with some unexpected event, whether it be a death, divorce, or loss of a job. But these crises usually pass over time, or you are able to put them behind you.

Once you know you have a family member with a disability, you try very hard to accept the situation, and try to look at your child's strengths. This is especially true when your child gives you positive feedback (to lift your spirits) when you least expect it (throwing you a kiss or a hug). But then again, you still ask yourself, "What would it have been like if my child was able to walk by himself, or feed himself, or dress himself?" As you go through your daily activities and routines, you do not constantly think about your child as one who has a disability (e.g., a child with only a motor disability vs. a cognitive disability). Rather, you think of your child as a child first, one who has needs, one who looks to you and others in the family for love and respect, one who yearns to be a valued member of the family. The point we are trying to make is that, sure, at times we would have liked to have denied that our son has disabilities, especially in the early years, when signs of a disability were not blatantly evident. But does his inability to walk limit the contributions he can make as a member of our family? We love our son and want to give him the most we have to offer.

We accept our son as an individual and as a valued member of the family, but we always think about how his disabilities have changed and will forever continue to change our lives. For we think about who will take care of him when we are not able to. Will he have a job? Will he be accepted in the community? Will he have friends? Will he be safe and happy? All these questions run through your mind when you first learn that your child has a disability. And you have every right to think about these issues.

FIRST COMES DENIAL

One of the first emotions psychologists and educators have said parents go through when a crisis occurs is *denial*. It is a coping mechanism that is simple to employ. Once the existence of a problem is confirmed, you and the family have reached a point where your life will be different from what you expected it to be like. Perceptions on family life are going to change drastically in a very short time. It is human nature to avoid change, especially if this change is viewed negatively. Thus it is easier to deny that change will occur.

In our case, we could not deny that there was a potential for problems because even before birth, we knew our son Adam was going to be small. His actual size, detected by ultrasound, was below the fifth percentile of all fetuses his age (therefore a diagnosis of "interuterine growth retardation," and thus the label at birth "small for gestational age"). Numerous nonstress tests were performed to determine the well-being of the fetus. The fetus's heart rate during contractions is recorded on a monitoring strip, similar to an EKG machine. Having these tests twice a week always produced a *fear* of the unknown, and not knowing what the outcome would be was very scary. This is a common feeling expressed by many parents. In our case we raised the following questions: Does small mean that he will not be able to function like any child his age? Will he be able to catch up if he is born prematurely? Will he need constant medical attention?

After twenty-four hours of pitocin-induced labor, Adam was born by vaginal delivery, weighing 3 pounds, 12 ounces. He was in no apparent medical distress, but careful observation was mandated. Looking back, I never asked the doctor his opinion on a C-section delivery, and I might have if I were better prepared. During labor you are intensely preoccupied with the activities of the moment, and your ability to make decisions is based on your tolerance of pain and the trust you place in your doctor and your spouse. The risk of potential problems in the birthing process increases (e.g., an inadequate supply of oxygen to the baby's brain may occur, resulting in serious birth defects) with an extended period of labor. That is why it is so important to discuss in detail before delivery what measures your doctor will take in emergency situations, as well as your concerns about the birthing process. We suggest taking a course for expectant parents offered at your local hospital.

THEN REALIZATION SETS IN

After Adam's birth, a wait-and-see approach was taken by the medical team, which can be very stressful. Testing may not result in a definite diagnosis. Usually a series of tests is done to rule out conditions or syndromes. Doctors do not have all the answers. And this can be very painful for parents. In most instances, doctors do not want to give parents false hopes, nor do they want to be too negative. You have many hours to think about the course of events, and you are likely to put the *blame* on yourself. You go over and over the past. Did you take an aspirin when you shouldn't have? Did you exercise too much? Did you fail to get enough sleep? Even if the doctor tells you that it was beyond your control, you still question what you might have done wrong and may have a deep sense of guilt.

The way the professional presents information gathered from the evaluation process may affect how you react to the news and what course of action you will take to follow up on the diagnosis. Sometimes physicians or psychologists say things that embarrass parents, such as "You're just a nervous parent." Without being aware of it, professionals may use nonverbal messages (e.g., facial expressions) when conversing with parents that give the impression that parents might be doing something wrong in raising their child. It is important for the professional to respect parents and be empathetic to their needs. If parents are unable to find professionals who value their opinions, they may wait longer before they seek help for themselves and their child. This is not fair to the child or to the parents. As program directors of the Connecticut College Program for Children with Special Needs, Sheridan and Radlinski have seen this occur often and are quite troubled by it (McGovern, 1991). Teacher training programs as well as medical schools must make a concerted effort to train professionals on proper communication skills so that all members of the team will be able to share information and develop appropriate strategies.

NOW ESTABLISH A FRAMEWORK FOR UNDERSTANDING

When signs of average growth are not seen, a doctor will probably use the term "developmental delay." This can be very *confusing*. The term is nondescriptive and does not answer many questions parents may have, such as, "What will my baby be like one year from now, or five years from now?" Parents may feel very *helpless* and *powerless* and not know where to turn for help. You think: "What effect will this labeling have on my child when he/she enters school? How will it affect the emotional and physical well-being of other members of the family?"

After watching our child closely, we were *disappointed* that Adam did not reach milestones at the normal age of development. We were even more upset and disappointed by his inability to gain weight. This was a deep concern in the early months, because we were afraid that it might affect his health. His growth was minuscule, and he fell off the pediatrician's growth chart. To this day, his growth is very, very slow. Every time Adam visits the doctor, we anticipate a weight gain or a height change, trying to be optimistic, even though his prior history shows that his growth is very slow. We try to prepare ourselves ahead of time, but sometimes emotions cannot be suppressed. And that is usually a good thing.

TAKE AN ENVIRONMENTAL PERSPECTIVE

As a parent of a special needs child, on occasion you will also feel that you have been *rejected* by the community around you. On weekends and holidays we have thought about attending special community events such as parades, concerts, and festivals, all the local events that make our town feel like home. However, sometimes it may be difficult to reach the event with a wheelchair (e.g., attending a softball game in the neighborhood park, or even going to the playground); the number of people may be overwhelming, especially in a confined area; or the hustle and bustle of the event itself (e.g., the loud noises of firecrackers during a Fourth of July Celebration) may cause us to leave early or decide not to go at all. Or we may decide to leave Adam at home with a sibling or family friend.

As you shop in the grocery store, others may stare at you and your child. Strangers may even approach and ask questions. This happens to me quite often. The typical question I get is, "How old is he?" Sometimes I tell the truth, and people react in disbelief (usually noted through non-verbal signals); on many occasions I say he is much younger so that I can go on my way. If I give his correct age, I usually explain why he is small for his age. I have a need to explain, but this is really not necessary. I have tried to control myself and not go into an explanation, but at

were able to muster as parents of a special needs child. Having a child with a disability may create strains in your marriage. Recognize that you and your spouse may have disagreements on how to raise your child or what medical advice to seek. A support group may provide the environment you need to release your feelings. You gain perspectives from other couples that may help you cope with your anxieties. We want to emphasize that you will probably have to seek out the support group. Don't wait for them to contact you.

Locating Support Groups

Parent to Parent is a grassroots national effort whereby parents volunteer to talk to other parents with a child with a disability or special health care need, usually on a one-to-one basis, to help direct them to the available resources or answer personal questions on various topics. Some parent to parent groups are subgroups of larger organizations, while others are organized independently by groups of parents to help others who may not know where to turn. Parent to Parent can be sponsored by a national organization such as the Association for Retarded Citizens, an advocacy organization, or a hospital. There are chapters of Parent to Parent in all fifty states.

Figure 4.1 lists organizations that provide support to families. The National Fathers' Network publishes a quarterly newsletter written by and for fathers who have special needs children. In addition, every issue of *Exceptional Parent* contains an article written by fathers called "Fathers' Voices." Here fathers can share with others their reactions to raising children with special needs.

National organizations have been formed for specific disabilities and conditions. Over the last thirty years, the number of these organizations has increased as new syndromes and conditions have been identified. Parents of children with Beckwith-Wiedemann syndrome and Wolf-Hirschhorn syndrome, for example, have established support networks to collaborate and communicate with other families with similar needs and problems. Many of these organizations have newsletters and telephone hotlines. Every year *Exceptional Parent* magazine publishes a resource directory issue. The National Organization for Rare Disorders (NORD) can also be helpful in locating these groups, as well as the Alliance of Genetic Support Groups, or the National Information Center for Children and Youth with Disabilities (NICHCY), and Parent Training and Information Centers sponsored by the federal government throughout the country.

If you are looking for written materials, especially on first learning that your child has a handicap, refer to the "Disability Fact Sheet" published by (NICHCY). Or you might be interested in the "ARC's Family

Figure 4.1
Resources for Support

Alliance of Genetic Support Groups	35 Wisconsin Circle Suite 440 Chevy Chase, Maryland (800-336-4364 or 301-652-553)
Association for Retarded Citizens (The ARC)	500 E. Border Street Suite 300 Arlington, TX 76010 (800-433-5255 or 817-261-6003)
Loma Linda University	School of Medicine Department of Pediatrics Loma Linda, CA 92354
Maine Parent Federation	P.O. Box 2067 Augusta, ME 04338-2067 (207) 582-2504
March of Dimes	1275 Mamaroneck Avenue White Plains, NY 10605 (914) 428-7100
Parent Care	The University of Utah Medical Center, Room 2A210 50 North Medical Drive Salt Lake City, UT 84112 (801) 581-5323
The American Academy of Pediatrics	141 Northwest Point Blvd P.O. Box 927 Elk Grove Village, IL 60009 (708) 228-5005
The American Association of University Affiliated Programs for the Developmentally Disabled	8630 Fenton Street Silver Spring, MD 20910 (301) 588-8252
The Center for Parenting Studies	Wheelock College 200 The Riverway Boston, MA 02215
The Council for Exceptional Children	1920 Association Drive Reston, VA (900) 845-6CEC
The National Fathers' Network	James May, Project Director The Merrywood School 16120 N.E. Eighth Street Bellevue, WA 98008 (206) 747-4004

Figure 4.1 (continued)

The National Information Center for Children & Youth with Disabilities (NICHCY)	P.O. Box 1492 Washington, DC 20013 (800) 695-0285
The National Organization of Rare Disorders (NORD)	P.O. Box 8923 New Fairfield, Connecticut (800-999-6673 or 203-746-6528)
National Rehabilitation Information Center	8455 Colesville Road, Suite 935 Silver Spring, MD 20910-3319 (800) 346-2742
The Sibling Information Network	62 Washington Street Middletown, CT 06457-2844 (203) 344-7500
The U.S. Department of Education Office of Special Education and Rehabilitative Services	Clearinghouse on Disability Information Washington, DC 20013 (202) 205-8241
United Way of America	701 North Fairfax Street Alexandria, VA 22314-2045 (703) 836-7100

Book" published by the Association for Retarded Citizens (ARC). You may want to read personal accounts written by parents for parents, such as *After the Tears: Parents Talk about Raising a Child with a Disability*, by R. Simon (1987).

Your telephone directory's yellow pages are a great source of information. Use them. Also, the United Way in your area, as well as your local hospital or school district, may have listings of these groups. In Connecticut the United Way sponsors an Infoline, a telephone referral service that will put you in contact with various social service agencies. The United Way supports information and referral services in communities nationwide. The names of these services may be different (e.g., Helpline, Information and Referral, or First Call for Help), but the purposes are the same: to "provide information about community services that help people in need; explain how to get help from these services; talk with people who need help, to refer them to the most appropriate agencies or services they need; and act as advocates for people who need help, when they are unable to represent themselves" (United Way of America, 1992, p. 1). Parent Care is another clearinghouse that has a directory of parenting groups.

In response to budget reductions at many nonprofit agencies, community partnerships have emerged to provide services in a holistic manner. As part of their efforts, many of these partnerships have published resource directories. Check with your local library or Chamber of Commerce to see if there is such a partnership in your town. Your local newspaper usually has a calendar of events, noting the location and time various support groups meet. Catholic Family Services or your local Jewish Federation has knowledge of the local support groups as well as city and state agencies.

If you are interested in establishing a support group, literature is available to help you through the process. For example, the Center for Parenting Studies at Wheelock College has published *Organizing Support Programs for Parents of Premature Infants.* The Maine Parent Federation has a workbook entitled *Parent Support Networks: A Workbook for Creating Successful Community Support Groups.* Also refer to *Parent's Guide: Accessing Parent Groups* by Ripley (1993), which is available from NICHCY. The Sibling Information Network is a federally funded organization that will provide assistance with establishing a sibling group in your area. They offer information on the process and refer you to local organizations and groups that have sibling programs or support groups. They also publish a quarterly newsletter for siblings and parents.

Table 4.1 lists types of support groups that you may find in your hometown.

DO A LITERATURE REVIEW ON YOUR CHILD'S DIAGNOSIS

Your first step is to talk to your doctor and obtain any written material that he or she has on the subject. Make sure the doctor explains the terms so that you can understand them. Your next step is to go to your local library. The reference librarian can direct you to a database that lists all the books in the system. The library at your local hospital can help. NORD can provide you with a fact sheet on a specific disorder. Every month *Exceptional Parent* has two sections, "Parent Search" and "Parent Respond," for parents in need of information, advice, or support, and parents who may have answers or suggestions to these questions or concerns. For example, in the February 1994 "Parent Search" column parents asked for help on a wide range of issues from increasing parental involvement at PTO activities, to identifying other families who have children with Rasmussen's syndrome, to the advantages and disadvantages of riding a school bus.

In 1976 the Maryland State Planning Council on Developmental Disabilities published *A Reader's Guide for Parents of Children with Mental, Physical, or Emotional Disabilities;* an updated version appeared in 1983. This comprehensive bibliography contains listings of where to write for information on disabilities in general, specific disabilities, and the early years—how to teach, train, and play at home. It includes the cost of each publication and a short annotation describing the contents of the re-

Table 4.1
Support Groups That You May Find in Your Hometown

Support Group	Sponsored By	Types of Activities Offered
Parent to Parent	Parent to Parent Network of CT—Family Center, Newington Children's Hospital	Provide one to one emotional and informational support by matching a trained and experienced parent with parents who are newly referred to the program
Children with Attention Deficit Disorders (C.H.A.D.D.)	National not-for-profit parent led group	Parent group whose children have attention deficit disorder
Parent to Parent and Support groups	Jewish Social Service Agency of Metropolitan Washington	Support group for parents of severely handicapped children
Family Network on Disabilities of Broward County Florida	Funded by Part H of the IDEA Act	Monthly support group meetings and one to one support.
United Cerebral Palsy of Montgomery County	(Not-for-Profit Agency)	Peer support for families with a child with a disability. Professionals from the local health and recreation agencies are involved for reference and referral
Parents of children with emotional & behavioral difficulties	Sponsored by State Agency—CT Department of Mental Health	Parent support group—meets once a month
Parents Organization Supporting Special Education (Danbury, CT)	Group formed with the help of the school district.	Parent support group organized when parents wanted to communicate with each other; have a good working relationship with school district; and become valued members of the community.

source. Another section includes specific topics of interest, ranging from attitudes, behavior modification, genetics and genetic counseling, rights of children, to sexuality and sex education. Also included are a bibliography for the younger reader—books for children about children with handicaps—and a list of journals, directories, and indexes.

There are numerous associations whose mission is to educate and lobby for the benefit of children with disabilities. The reader's guide mentioned above will help you find an association that best meets the needs of your child. For example, the National Association for Parents of the Visually Impaired will help you locate resource materials on making your child's environment safe and stimulating. They will also put you on a mailing list to receive their newsletter and information on current research in visual impairments and educating children with this disability. The Council for Exceptional Children is the national headquarters for the Educational Resources Information Center Clearinghouse on Handicapped and Gifted Children (ERIC). You can access information on programs, parent education and counseling, and evaluation methods, to name a few.

Regional hospitals and universities collaborate to provide the community with services that are needed by parents and children. Various independent clinics have been established. Their special departments work with hospitals and schools, both public and private. The American Association of University Affiliated Programs for the Developmentally Disabled is one source to identify programs in different parts of the country. In addition, Loma Linda University, School of Medicine, Department of Pediatrics has a series of pamphlets called "Introduction to Your Child" which provides basic information on handicapping conditions. The American Academy of Pediatrics (the professional organization representing pediatricians) may also have information that can prove useful.

The federal government awards contracts to organizations that provide information services to the public. Once such organization is the National Rehabilitation Information Center. The National Center for Education in Maternal and Child Health publishes a catalog that lists resources for various chronic and genetic disorders.

The Internet

The Internet gives parents the ability to obtain information directly from their home computer. One database that may be helpful is the Cornucopia of Disability Information (CODI). There are over 800 bulletin boards that offer information on disabilities. Table 4.2 can help you get started locating information on a specific topic or finding workshops or organizational meetings that you may want to attend. It is an ideal way to meet and communicate with parents from all over the country and throughout the world.

GAIN SELF-CONFIDENCE IN APPROACHING PROFESSIONALS WITH YOUR IDEAS AND OPINIONS

As a parent of a special needs child, you will often need to interact with medical and educational professionals. In some cases you will re-

Table 4.2
Information Accessible on the Internet

Title	Address	Description
Cornucopia of Disability Information (CODI)	*val-dor.cc.buffalo.edu*	
The National Institute of Health	*gopher.nih.gov*	to access research libraries
The Library of Congress	*marvel.log.gov* or *locis.loc.gov*	
Index of Bulletin Boards	*handicap.shel.isc-br.com* PATH: */pub/bbslists/**	
Autism and Developmental Disability List	*bit.listserv.autism*	Bulletin Board
Deafness	*bit.listserv.deaf-1*	Bulletin Board
Down Syndrome	*bit.listserv.down-syn*	Bulletin Board
Learning experiences for the disabled	*alt.education.disabled*	Bulletin Board
Students with handicaps or special needs	*k12.ed.special*	Bulletin Board

quest that evaluations be done and outcomes and recommendations be explained. These meetings are always anxiety-inducing because the outcomes are unknown. Such meetings may be unproductive if you were unhappy with previous visits with other professionals. Learning how to communicate effectively will make these encounters less stressful. How you perceive your communication skills has a strong effect on how you build effective relationships. This perception can be based on how professionals have reacted to you in the past. For example, perhaps you let the doctor do all the talking; he or she used medical jargon and terminology, and at the end of the meeting you felt that your questions were not answered and you were more confused than when you entered the office. You would have felt better if the doctor responded directly to your questions.

The next time, try to ask specific questions about your child's condition, and relate specific incidents you have recorded that bother you about your child's development. With this approach, the doctor will be more likely to take a deeper interest in your case. If the doctor senses that you know what you are talking about, he or she may answer your questions in more detail. As a result, you may get more information that will be useful, or serve to answer some of your concerns and thus lessen your anxiety. If you are calm, logical, and direct in your questioning, your relationship can be fruitful. Try to communicate your questions, concerns, ideas, and opinions in a strategically appropriate way to get responses that make sense to you and that are reasonable. If you feel uncomfortable with the doctor's responses, you will have the confidence to ask more probing questions, or ask why, or ask for a second opinion.

After you have taken your child for testing on several occasions, you will begin to ask yourself, "Was the time my child and I spent with this professional worthwhile?" If your self-confidence is high, you will ask yourself, "Did I gain any information that will be helpful?" By gaining a sense that you control the situation, you will increase your self-confidence. If you feel that the meeting was beneficial you will gain confidence in your ability to work with professionals and will be willing to interact with them more often when the occasion arises. With important information at your fingertips you will become more confident in making decisions that will affect your child's future.

What about professionals? How can they improve their communication skills with families? How can we work together to improve the professional-parent relationship? The Parent and Professional Alliance (PAPA) was formed in South Carolina "to promote understanding and cooperation among physicians, parents of developmentally disabled children and those with chronic health needs, along with agencies and health care professionals who serve them" (*Exceptional Parent*, August 1994, p. 26). PAPA sponsors presentations at medical training programs. They distribute handouts to medical personnel on parent support and resource groups in the community as well as information on disabilities and current legislation. Parent panels and videos of family life are included. The purpose of these presentations is to sensitize the medical community to the daily joys and difficulties of raising a child with a disability. They also give parents the opportunity to understand the physician's point of view. This parent-professional collaboration can be started in your hometown. The video *Parent and Professional Alliance: How to Get Started* can be obtained by writing The Citadel, Department of Psychology, 171 Moultrie Street, Charleston, SC 29409.

COMMUNICATE OPENLY AND FREELY WITH YOUR FAMILY

Some families have an endless, free-flowing communication system. But most of us have to work very hard to let our feelings and views be known to our loved ones. We want to be in control and not cry. And with our busy schedules, it sometimes seems that there isn't enough time in the day to have a one-on-one conversation or a family sharing time.

Men often have a harder time talking about their feelings because they do not want to get wives or children upset, or add to the conflict or tension that already exists in the household. Or they may have a harder time accepting that their child has a disability, because they always wanted a child who would follow in their footsteps or wanted to be able to coach them at football or soccer. They may not want to share their disappointment or anger. Recent research suggests that fathers are more likely to set the tone for the family's acceptance of the child. Don't leave men alone to struggle to make sense of what is happening in their lives. We need to reach out to them. We have to talk—start the conversation on a positive note by relating something funny that happened. Express your feelings. Share your happy and sad times. Lean on your spouse a little—support one another. S/he might say something that will make you feel better, and vice versa. Don't wait for a crisis before you both react (e.g., a sudden hospitalization of your child). We know that's hard to do, but we have to try.

By spending time together, you increase the likelihood that you will share your feelings. Get him involved in taking care of your child. Bring him to meetings with you. Act as a couple. Plan activities with the entire family. And don't isolate yourselves from the community. Get out there with your child as soon as you can. Participate in block parties and school functions. Go shopping in the malls together. You are a family and you need to function like any other family.

Go out alone with your spouse. Have a chance to be together without the distractions of crying and demanding children. Emphasize physical closeness. Take time for a walk around the block or a drive to the local store. The car is a good place to talk because you are close to each other and can't escape each other's conversation.

You might prefer to use writing as a way to release your innermost feelings. If you keep a diary you may want to share it with your spouse. Talk openly about your feelings and do not make judgments. Listening is very important. The ultimate goal is for your family to be able to reach a consensus when important decisions need to be made.

Your other children are indeed going through pain and suffering when they see a sibling who is unable to do things that they can do. They may ask why this has happened to their sibling and not to them. They may have the same feelings you do, but do not know how to deal with them. They definitely are jealous of the time you spend with your child with a disability. They may try to attract your attention by misbehaving, or do poorly in school, or nag you constantly and physically surround you.

Set aside time every day to spend alone with your other children. Let them help you with simple tasks. They can read to their sibling, or brush and comb his or her hair. They may want to make items for their disabled sibling. This makes them feel good. Our daughter Julie's fifth grade science project was to make a simple machine. She decided to make a toy for her brother. She was very excited and proud of her invention. It was displayed in the school fair and then given to her brother's class.

Julie has written about her feelings for Adam:

> I don't really remember much about when Adam was first born, or about those first few years. I was only two when he was born. All I really remember was Adam being born, and being put in an incubator. I don't remember what I thought. For all I know, I could of thought he was a baby chick.
>
> What I do remember, is feeling so defensive of him. When people would talk about handicapped kids, I would go all off, and tell them what they were really like. Just people with a disability, and they shouldn't talk about them. They're human beings, just like everyone else. I would really get defensive when they would talk about him. There was always someone who would always make fun of him. My motto was, if they make fun of someone with a disability, they must really be insecure about themselves. My friends realized why I was so defensive, and they became defensive too. I was glad to have someone on my side.
>
> There were times when I felt jealous of him, and times when I really got angry, but I could never stay angry at him. I think that having him as a brother, made me a little more patient, sensitive and caring. And he made me so that I could never stay angry at someone. He gave me a gift, a gift that can never be matched, himself.

And you may notice that your children will talk about their sibling all the time in school to their teachers and friends. They are excellent storytellers. It is a way for them to communicate their feelings. Julie would do this constantly. Sometimes I thought it was *all the time* and quite embarrassing, but now that I think about it, I realize that it was her way to release her feelings and gain compassion from others around her. This probably will happen in your family as well. Don't be surprised by it.

You may have children who are very quiet and do not display their emotions so openly. That is true of our other son, David. He may have talked about his brother to his friends, but somehow it never came up in our conversations. He expressed his feelings by asking questions about Adam's schooling or medical condition. Both David and Julie have been excellent role models for Adam. They have been caring, loving, and nurturing siblings.

It is imperative to let your children know that they can always come and talk to you about their feelings or concerns. Never shut them out. Usually they come to you at the least favorable time—the witching hour of 5 P.M. Be firm and say, "I want to talk too, but now is not the time. Let's talk at bedtime or after supper."

You may want to start a family album—a series of photographs or videos of good times you've shared together. Your album may include trips you have taken to Disney World or to a local playground. Maybe you want to collect writings your children have done over the years. For example, *Exceptional Parent* has a series called "Family Album," where siblings talk about their brothers and sisters with disabilities. From your children you gain strength. I found one essay by a sibling very touching. In the March 1991 issue Lisa Irwin wrote an essay entitled "Look at the Good Side", about her brother Davey. We would like to share it with you.

> My brother Davey is 11 years old. He has cerebral palsy and also uses a wheelchair. Davey has a lot of seizures. I think he is very cute. Why do people always think it's so sad being handicapped? Davey won't have to go into the war. And Davey won't have to boss me around as a big brother.
>
> Davey hears weird sounds, like a hairdryer, electric knife, and blender, and laughs at them. Sometimes he even laughs at nothing.
>
> When my brother dies, he will go to heaven and be able to walk and talk. I love my brother. He is too cute to be true.

RESOURCES AVAILABLE FOR FAMILIES

Many books are available to help your child cope with the stresses of family life when one sibling has a disability. When siblings read stories that contain scenes they can relate to, they realize that they are not alone. They also may be inspired to strengthen bonds with their sibling. Appendix D is a bibliography of helpful books for siblings. Appendix E lists resources on coping strategies for parents.

A book the whole family may want to read is *It Isn't Fair: Siblings of Children with Disabilities*, by Klein and Schleifer. It is a compilation of articles by parents, siblings, and professionals published in *Exceptional Parent* magazine since 1971.

POINTS TO REMEMBER

Parents of children with special needs who build human relationships for support will be better able to develop a repertoire of effective coping strategies. Figure 4.2 is designed to help you identify your support network.

Figure 4.2
Support System People—Resources Worksheet

Below is a description of some of the functions which human relationships can provide for us. Please read the descriptions, then in the spaces below enter the names of the people in your life who provide you with that function and your relationships with them. Think of friends, family, neighbors, work associates, etc. While some individuals in your life can provide you with more than one specialized function, try to think of individuals who provide you with a single special resource.

1. *Intimacy:* People who provide you with closeness, warmth and acceptance. You can express your feelings freely and without self-consciousness. People whom you trust and are readily accessible to you.

——————— ——————— ———————

2. *Sharing:* People who share your concerns because "they are in the same boat" or in similar situations. People who are striving for similar objectives. People with whom you share experiences, information and ideas. People with whom you exchange favors.

——————— ——————— ———————

3. *Self Worth:* People who respect your competence in your role as a teacher and parent. People who understand the difficulty or value of your work or performance in that role. People whom you respect that can recognize your skills.

——————— ——————— ———————

4. *Assistance:* People who provide tangible services or make resources available. People who don't just lend a hand, but whose assistance is not limited by time or extent of help. People you can depend upon in a crisis.

——————— ——————— ———————

5. *Guidance:* People who provide you with advice and methods to solve problems. People who mobilize us to take steps toward solving problems, achieving goals and otherwise taking action.

——————— ——————— ———————

6. *Challenge:* People who make you think. People who make you explain. People who question your reasoning. People who challenge you to grow.

——————— ——————— ———————

Source: Adapted from Montgomery County Public Schools (n.d.).

5

The Importance of Accurate Assessment for Placement: Birth–Five Programs

Having verified a child's disability or learning problem, we as parents often recognize that we do not have all the training or parenting skills necessary to effectively assist our child. Thus, we turn to others for help and guidance. More than likely we will seek out and rely on the local school district for assistance and direction.

IDENTIFYING SCHOOL OR AGENCY PERSONNEL RESPONSIBLE FOR COORDINATING THE ASSESSMENT PROCESS

The first person parents usually contact in the school district is either a neighborhood school principal or a district administrator responsible for special education programs in the town. The principal will refer parents to an organization or person who screens and evaluates children entering the school system. In our town, a nonprofit organization called Child Find screens and evaluates preschool youngsters for the school district. This organization conducts an assessment of the child's strengths and weaknesses and determines if the child will need extra help to succeed in school.

Children can be referred to Child Find by parents who have concerns about their child's development, or by a doctor or social service agency providing services to the child and his/her family. The Individuals with Disabilities Education Act (IDEA) establishes the state grant program to serve infants and toddlers. It is considered a discretionary program. If your state participates, the state agency designated by the governor as lead agency is responsible for coordinating services for children under two and one-half years of age (e.g., the Florida Department of Health and Human Resource Services). Unless the agency has its own trained staff, it probably will call on the school district to do the assessment.

More preschool programs have been made available by the passage of P.L. 99-457, Part H. State agencies have the option to run their own programs, to fund the local school districts, or to contract with private providers to operate programs and services.

Most programs for children three years of age and older are available through your local educational agency (LEA), which is usually your local school system. The special education administrator in many school districts is also responsible for pupil services (ancillary services provided to children). A look at a school system's organization chart shows that psychologists, social workers, guidance counselors, and physical, speech, and occupational therapists all report to the special education administrator. This individual is authorized to make decisions on scheduling, class structure, class size, curriculum, and so on. In most cases, however, there is an intermediary between teacher and administrator, often a special education supervisor who does all the legwork in the field. This person usually makes sure that all procedures are explained properly and accurately to parents, discusses concerns, coordinates the testing sessions and follow-up meetings, and helps establish a plan for the parents, the teacher, and other specialists to put into effect to work with your child. He or she is an important team player, one with whom you need to establish a good working relationship.

Before your child participates in a program, his or her educational abilities need to be assessed. The outcomes of the assessment are critical, as they dictate the actions that the school will take. For example, assessments in the child's early years may lead to tracking or labeling. Parents may or may not want this to occur. In addition, an assessment also determines the related services your child may be entitled to receive (e.g., occupational or physical therapy, speech). These early intervention services are critical in the growth of your child.

WHAT ARE EARLY INTERVENTION SERVICES?

Early intervention by professionals (early childhood educators, speech therapists, occupational and physical therapists, social workers) allows them to work together with parents to promote optimal development of young children. Services include:

1. providing information on child rearing practices for parents.
2. one-on-one services (e.g., a vision specialist making regularly scheduled home visits [possibly once a week] to suggest ideas on playing with your child. She may suggest toys that are most appropriate for your child and lend them to your family. She may

also suggest specific activities to strengthen visual stimulus, and will answer parental questions).

3. parent and child co-participating in a program where other parents and children with disabilities get together to play and learn.

A PRIMER ON ASSESSMENT

One of the most stressful parts of parenting your special needs child involves undergoing extensive assessment at various times as the child grows and progresses. The first time you are involved in an assessment, you will probably get a general idea about the following:

1. the amount of intervention and support that may be necessary to enable your child to learn;
2. the ease with which your child can adapt to new situations and gain important socialization skills;
3. the physical limitations that may impede his/her access to opportunities in the community; and
4. the general outlook for his/her future success in school, at home, and in the community.

An educational assessment can include the following: formal testing using standardized tests; informal testing through observation by both parents and professionals; and information gathered by questioning parents and collecting a medical history.

Your family may be entitled to services by simply filling out a form listing general biographical data. In some cases you may have to fill out a long financial statement, or have your child undergo an intensive testing process. An extensive assessment is overwhelming at first, but parents need to take one step at a time. We also need to remember that assessments are done periodically and can change dramatically over time. It is important to be patient. Your expectations for a quick assessment will most likely be diminished as you go through the process. We can also control some of the environmental factors during an assessment. Parents can always disagree with an assessment and question the procedure, the testing skills of the administrator of the test, or the subjective or objective conclusions arrived at from the scores, and if necessary can request that the assessment be repeated with more documentation.

ASSESSMENT IN PERSPECTIVE—WHERE WILL IT LEAD?

To devise a plan of action to help children succeed in school and in the community, we need to uncover their strengths and weaknesses. The only way to do this is to evaluate how they can accomplish tasks and gain skills and to identify the level of support they might need to achieve success in school. Thus the assessment process is needed. The Division of Special Education, Maryland Department of Education (1981), defines an assessment as an

> extensive procedure given to all children who have been identified through screening as potentially in need of special education programs. It shall consist of reading, math, spelling, written and oral language, and perceptual motor functioning as appropriate. Cognitive, emotional, and physical factors shall also be assessed as appropriate. Each assessment report shall also include a description of the child's behaviors which establishes the existence of a handicapping condition; a statement which describes, in terms of special education services needed, the child's performance as it deviates from developmental milestones and/or general educational objectives; a statement of criteria used to establish the deviation of the child's behaviors; and the signature of the assessor. (p. 21)

School districts, medical providers, and local, state, and federal agencies all rely on assessments, to various degrees, to determine the eligibility of your child to receive services or to participate in programs as well as to make decisions about specific placement settings. An assessment also determines the kinds and amount of related services your child needs to benefit from an educational program (e.g., occupational therapy, transportation, speech) (Montgomery Community Public Schools, n.d.).

If your child has more than one handicapping condition or disability, he will be entitled to receive intervention services from several individuals or agencies based on the results of the assessment findings. The definition of a disability, according to a school district's perspective, is "a physical or mental condition that substantially limits learning to the extent that the child requires special or extra educational services" (Montgomery Community Public Schools, p. 5). The adjectives and definitions describing the conditions affecting the limits of learning differ from district to district, and may be vague or very specific. Definitions are listed in the special education manual of all school districts. However, school districts as public agencies are mandated to follow local, state, and federal guidelines. How programs are set up is likely to vary from one school district to another, based on size, the number of children in special education, the amount of monetary support from local, state, and federal sources, and the parental pressures put on the school system. Table 5.1 lists eligible handicapping conditions.

For example, if your child is visually impaired and has an orthopedic impairment, the agency responsible for vision services, as well as a provider for physical therapy, will be called upon to do an assessment. After explaining the results of the assessment, the lead agency, represented by a case manager, with assistance from representatives of other agencies providing support, will devise a plan using their observations, results from standardized tests, parental input, and their knowledge of child development. This plan—either an IFSP (Individualized Family Service Plan) for young children (birth to age three) or an IEP (Individualized Education Program) for children three to twenty-one years old—identifies goals for the child and includes specific means for achieving those goals through a coordinated team effort. The purpose of early intensive intervention is to work with families to ready children for school. Figure 5.1 shows the steps in a typical assessment.

A PARENTS' PREROGATIVE

We must alert you to the need early on in your child's formal learning experience to communicate strongly the types of services you feel your child needs based on *your* observations. It is important for you to convey your thoughts to the key people who make decisions based on the criteria gathered on the assessment instruments. As parents, we want to do whatever it takes to prepare our children for school and help them succeed. Thus, we need to monitor the assessment process carefully to ensure that the system has made accurate evaluations of our children's strengths and weaknesses. A plan must be practical, fulfill the needs of children and parents, and access the best curriculum and strategies. Remember, if necessary, a program can be established to center specifically on your child's needs. *Individual* is the key word. You probably will encounter many roadblocks along the way (e.g., professionals who reject your proposals, taking the attitude that they know more than you; freezes on hiring), but it is important to keep the faith in what you believe is the right program for your child. To get through these frustrating times, seek support from other parents or organizations. If your child is in need of a given intervention, a program must be established to provide it. You don't have to agree to a program or service if this is not appropriate for your child. Parents have rights called "procedural safeguards" that will let you be an equal partner in the planning and implementation of a program for your child.

INITIATING AN ASSESSMENT

Referrals for assessments have been described in previous chapters, but to recapitulate, you and your pediatrician are the most likely initi-

Table 5.1
Classifications and Abbreviated Definitions of Handicapping Conditions (Fairfax County, Virginia, Public Schools)

Condition	Definition
Autism (AUT)	AUT—A severe disorder of communication and behavior characterized by deficits in language ability and sustained impairment of interpersonal relationships with others.
Emotional Disability (ED)	ED—A condition exhibiting one or more of the following characteristics over a long period of time and to a marked degree, which adversely affects educational performance: inability to learn which cannot be explained by intellectual, sensory, or health factors; inability to build or maintain satisfactory interpersonal relationships with peers and teachers; inappropriate types of behavior or feelings under normal circumstances; general pervasive mood of unhappiness or depression; tendency to develop physical symptoms or fears associated with personal or school problems.
Hearing Impairment (HI)	HI—Hearing loss (after all necessary medical treatment, surgery, and/or use of hearing aids) which significantly restricts benefit from participation in the general classroom program and necessitates a modified instructional program.
Mental Retardation Mild Retardation (MMR) Moderate Retardation (MOD)	MMR—A reduced rate of intellectual development and a level of academic achievement below that of peers. Deficits in adaptive behavior are concurrently demonstrated. MOD—A difficulty in acquiring necessary skills as determined by a substantially reduced rate of intellectual development. Deficits in adaptive behavior are concurrently demonstrated.

Condition	Definition
Multihandicaps (MH)	MH—Concomitant impairments (such as mental retardation-blind, mental retardation-orthopedic impairment, etc.), the combination of which causes such severe educational problems that they cannot be accommodated in special education programs solely for one of the impairments.
Orthopedic Impairment (OI), Other Health Impairment (OH)	OI, OH—Physical conditions and/or special health problems which result in the need for special provisions for educational purposes. Included are organic, orthopedic (skeletal, muscular, and neuro-muscular), and neurological conditions affecting motor activities.
Preschool (PS)	PS—A significant delay in one or more of the following areas of development: cognitive ability, motor skills, social/adaptive behavior, perceptual skills, communication skills. Any of the handicapping conditions listed in this section may be used.
Severe Disability (SD)	SD—Severe and profound disabilities that severely impair cognitive and/or adaptive skills and life functioning. There may also be associated severe behavior problems and physical and/or sensory disabilities. Included are those students with severe and profound mental retardation and those who exhibit two or more severe disabilities.

Table 5.1 (continued)

Condition	Definition
Specific Learning Disability (LD)	LD—A disorder in the area of an identified processing skill(s) accompanied by an objectively observable discrepancy between ability and skill development in one of the following areas: oral expression, listening comprehension, written expression, basic reading skills, reading comprehension, mathematics calculation, and/or mathematics reasoning. The discrepancy must be "severe" as evidenced by measured achievement significantly below expected performance based upon measured intelligence.
Speech/Language Impairment (SH)	SH—A communication disorder, such as stuttering, impaired articulation, language impairment, or voice impairment, which adversely affects educational performance.
Visual Impairment (VI)	VI—Vision, which after best correction, limits ability to profit from a general or modified educational setting. Impairments include visual acuity of 20/70 or less in the better eye with best correction or a severely restricted field of vision.

Source: Adapted from Department of Student Services and Special Education, Fairfax County Public Schools. (1991, March). *Special Education Handbook: Information About Services for Students with Special Education Needs.* Fairfax, VA: Author, p. 11.

Figure 5.1
Steps in an Assessment

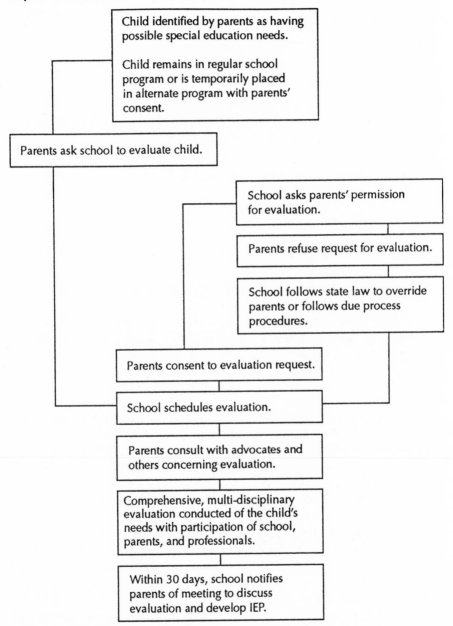

Child identified by parents as having possible special education needs.

Child remains in regular school program or is temporarily placed in alternate program with parents' consent.

Parents ask school to evaluate child.

School asks parents' permission for evaluation.

Parents refuse request for evaluation.

School follows state law to override parents or follows due process procedures.

Parents consent to evaluation request.

School schedules evaluation.

Parents consult with advocates and others concerning evaluation.

Comprehensive, multi-disciplinary evaluation conducted of the child's needs with participation of school, parents, and professionals.

Within 30 days, school notifies parents of meeting to discuss evaluation and develop IEP.

Source: Adapted from Children's Defense Fund (1989). Reprinted with permission of Children's Defense Fund, 1995.

ators of referrals. In recent years there has been an increase in the efforts of hospitals, educational organizations, and social service agencies to reach the community to provide needed services. Some of these programs are under federal entitlement programs, such as P.L. 99-457, Part H, commonly known as birth to three programs. These programs are discussed in detail later in the chapter. The next step is to describe how to obtain an appropriate assessment from this referral.

Steps Leading to an Appropriate Assessment

The following chain of events will most likely occur for both medical and educational assessments. A preliminary screening is usually the first step in the assessment process. It may be done by your pediatrician or Child Find, or at Kindergarten Roundup.

In the following case study, the pediatrician was the case manager. (In an educational setting, the case manager might be a social worker in a state agency or an educational specialist in a school system.) A parent can coordinate the assessments with assistance from a social worker or case manager (from a variety of sources such as nurse specialists from local hospitals, parent advocacy groups, the state department of children and youth services, or the state department of mental retardation).

When our pediatrician examined our son Adam at seven weeks of age, she noticed a lack of coordinated eye tracking, a skill a child of seven weeks should possess. Because Adam was born a month early, this was a warning of a possible problem. Our doctor suggested further testing to determine the cause of the lack of appropriate eye movement. We agreed and were referred to a pediatric opthalmologist (an eye doctor trained to work with children) for follow-up. Adam's records were requested by the specialist.

To accurately diagnose a potential problem, a specialist needs records of previous medical history and treatment. These records cannot be released to the specialist without your consent. In addition, the parent or guardian must authorize treatment by the specialist. To expedite matters, you may consider requesting your own copy of medical records and then passing them on to the specialist. In this way, you exercise more control over the flow of information. You are able to read the report before the specialist sees it. It may contain information that you would not otherwise be aware of. You may find that your pediatrician or other medical or educational professionals have made observations that you disagree with. You may discover opinions held by your doctor that have not been made known to you. More often than not, you will experience an emotional reaction when you see the information in print. Somehow when written on paper, it becomes more real, something you can not avoid, because it is permanent, not just part of a conversation that has ended.

In our case, the referral was made promptly, and within weeks a doctor with experience in diagnosing infant eye disorders was able to share his expertise and knowledge with the referring pediatrician and our family. It helps if your pediatrician has had previous contact with the specialist he has referred you to. In our case, our pediatrician was in telephone contact with the ophthalmologist, and they had previously worked together. This is an ideal situation. You may want to talk on the telephone with the specialist before you make an appointment to find out whether he or she is right for you and your child. Ask about the specialist's background and whether he or she has seen other children with similar problems. Consult other medical professionals for references. You may ask your pediatrician for the names of two specialists, and gather information on each. As a parent you have the right to decide which specialist can best meet your needs.

What to Expect When Visiting with a Specialist

Before the specialist examines your child, he or she will ask about how your infant behaves, whether he is alert, how he reacts to stimulation, and his general demeanor. After an intensive physical eye examination (we were amazed at the abundance of attention-grabbing toylike diagnostic tools used by the ophthalmologist) the specialist suggested that it was appropriate for Adam to have a brainstem visual evoked response test (using electrodes to monitor brain waves in response to light) and to see a neurologist, since the results of the exam indicated a possible neurological problem. This is not uncommon. You may be referred to various specialists. You should take a step back every time, analyze the situation, and decide with the help of your primary doctor (pediatrician) or case manager whether this step is necessary.

You also need to assess the quality and quantity of evaluative services your child receives. As you wait to see the specialist, does the environment make you feel comfortable? Look around the waiting room. Is there a play area with stimulating toys, or maybe a fish tank or other attention-getting objects suitable for the specialist's patients? Is reading material available on appropriate topics? How about the other support staff in the office? Are they friendly and willing to answer all your questions? This may influence how you evaluate the advice you receive and whether you accept the specialist's recommendations. Also talk things over with your spouse (even if he/she was not able to go with you). Think carefully about what the doctor/professional said. Does it make sense to you? Ask what the next referral will accomplish. Basically, it comes down to trust, instinct, and whether the information you have gained by going to the specialist answers most of your questions and parallels your thoughts.

Your decision should not be based on emotional reactions. Sally Smith (1978) describes "flight" as a feeling typically experienced by parents in reaction to an assessment or diagnosis. You might think, "These doctors jump to conclusions. We're going to see another specialist. They're only out to make money with more tests and more examinations. They probably get a kickback from the other doctors they recommend" (p. 67). Emotional reactions like this are perfectly natural. Sometimes fitting all the pieces together to form an accurate diagnosis may take many years. Doctors and educational professionals are learning all the time. Your child may exhibit some signs of a particular syndrome, but may be free of others. A label may make it easier for a school district to define services for a child. In some cases a child may be mislabelled. However, school districts are becoming more family-centered and child-focused and will classify children under five as "developmentally delayed" without attaching a specific syndrome or condition to them. We suggest you read "Heather's Story: The Long Road for a Family in Search of a Diagnosis." This article, published in *Exceptional Parent* in March 1991, is an account of a family's struggle to find an accurate diagnosis for their child. Their experiences may parallel some of your own.

Continuing Our Search

We felt that the ophthalmologist's recommendation was useful. We proceeded to see a pediatric neurologist, who suggested a CAT Scan (x-ray of the brain) to determine possible physical damage. We recognize that doctors need to have information before they can come up with an accurate assessment of a condition. But it is important for the specialist to talk to you about the alternative diagnostic tools available, the risks involved in performing tests, the likelihood of making a diagnosis at this time, and whether the facility's staff is qualified to perform the tests and read the results. At the end of the session, it is important to let the specialist know that you want feedback. We suggest having a copy of the physician's report sent directly to you at home. You must request this every time. Ask for a time frame for feedback. Some results may come back immediately; others may take a week. But ask for a follow-up visit to discuss results, a telephone call, a letter, or a combination of the above. And make sure the specialist gets back to the referring doctor. In most instances the report will be addressed to the referring doctor. Be aware that at this point many professionals, from radiologists to neurologists, may be involved in this process; you will need to be patient for results.

Where Do We Go from Here?

At the next pediatrician's visit we were able to discuss the reports from both specialists. They suggested that we closely monitor Adam's progress and note when he reached milestones, for example, reaching for objects and manipulating them, sitting up, and crawling. Adam's inability to grasp toys and inability to follow objects from side to side were due to his motor involvement and visual problems. These behaviors indicated that early intervention services would be most appropriate to foster his educational progress. In February 1985, when he was eight months of age, we contacted the local school district and requested an early childhood placement.

At the time we requested help there was no federal mandate requiring all school systems to provide services to infants, but federal subsidies were available if school districts wished to offer programs. Most programs for infants then available were funded by local departments of health, not-for-profit agencies such as United Cerebral Palsy or Easter Seals, or private educational providers. The state of Maryland, however, felt that early intervention services were important and encouraged local school districts to establish such programs. In 1975 Part B of the Education of the Handicapped Act (P.L. 94-142, or EHA) required that all states provide "a free and appropriate public education" to all eligible school-age children regardless of their disability. In 1978 changes were made in the law to include three- to five-year-olds. The 1986 amendments to EHA, commonly referred to as P.L. 99-457, included a part called "Infants and Toddlers with Disabilities." This part gave states monies if they adopted laws to allow these children access to appropriate services. Children from birth through age two were entitled to receive services.

Each state was allowed to set its own eligibility requirements as well as an administrative structure responsible for coordinating services. Those eligible usually included children with developmental delays and, in some states, children who due to their physical or mental condition were at risk of exhibiting developmental delays in the future (Beckman & Boyes, 1993). This legislation was based on research that suggests that providing early intervention services can lessen the severity of a disability. Thus laws have changed over the years when parents and educators have come together to inform legislators of the vital need for early intervention services.

The Road to Identifying an Appropriate Program

In many cases, medical reports establish a foundation for educational assessments in order to determine the services most appropriate for a child. This was what happened in our case. When we had our initial admission, review, and dismissal (ARD) meeting with our local school district, the medical documentation presented to the committee, a parent questionnaire describing our concerns about Adam's slow development, and medical health form (standard health record including immunizations) were the only material needed to admit Adam to an early intervention program. The fact that Adam was born prematurely with visual and motor development problems made him eligible for the program in Maryland. (Note: Check your library for a copy of your state's law regarding special education.) Adam's placement was made before Part H of P.L. 99-457 became law. By the time this law was passed Adam was already placed in the system, thus any eligibility requirements established after 1986 would not cause Adam to be removed from the program.

Documentation of Delay and Determination of Eligibility in Birth to Three Programs

In Connecticut, the birth to three programs stipulate that the parents, a service coordination center (SCC), or another agency (school district or public or private provider) can screen students for possible referral into the system. An "intake" (information for referral) is done by the SCC (located in strategic regional areas of the state), or by contractual agreement by the school district or public/private providers. Screening is defined as follows: "Information is gathered in preparation for eligibility evaluation if deemed appropriate" (State of Connecticut, 1990, p. 5). Then an eligibility evaluation is done: "Perform multidisciplinary evaluation in accordance with established standards to determine eligibility for early intervention services, areas of need, and services to meet that need" (State of Connecticut, 1990, p. 5).

The following are the established Connecticut standards:

A combination of quantitative and qualitative procedures will be used to document delay and determine eligibility. In situations which preclude using quantitative procedures only qualitative procedures will be used (i.e., clinical judgment of a team of qualified professionals will be used to systematically document developmental delays and/or significantly atypical development). In the first phase of the plan, a child will be eligible for early intervention services if s/he met criteria in either (A) or (B). A child will be monitored by the system if s/he meets the criteria in (C) below.

(A) *Developmental Delay:* A child must show a developmental delay in the following developmental areas—cognitive, physical, speech and language, psychosocial and self-help skills.

Delay is determined by:

2 or more standard deviations below the norm
25% delay in one area
20% delay in two or more areas
Clinical Judgement

(B) *Categories of Established Risk Conditions:* A child must have a diagnosis of a physical or mental condition that has a high probability of resulting in developmental delay.

1. Genetic Disorders
2. Chromosomal Abnormalities
3. Significant Exposure to Teratogen
4. Major Congenital Malformations
5. Sensory Impairments
6. Neurological and Neuromuscular Disorders
7. Other physical conditions, atypical developmental patterns, and psychosocial conditions congruent with established risk of developmental delay.

A list of specific established conditions for the categories listed above will be determined at a later date.

(C) *Multiple Risk Factors:* A child with three or more environmental/biological risk factors or all children with a documented delay which does not meet the criteria in (A) above. (State of Connecticut, 1990, p. 5)

Parents' Role in Assessments

Assessment is a key element in your child's schooling. Therefore, you need to know many facts about the assessment process, including information on testing. Chapter 6 discusses testing in more detail. Foremost on parents' minds are the following questions and concerns.

1. Will we be able to meet with the test administrator to go over the general procedures used during testing?
2. Who will decide which standardized tests are given? Is it school district policy, or is the decision made by the administrator of the test or the school psychologist?
3. Who will administer the test? (Will the reading specialist, school psychologist, or teacher give the test?) Is it an informal test, a standardized test, or a combination? Who will share the results of the test with us? Who else may look at the results?
4. Are adaptations made to testing so that our child can demonstrate his strengths (e.g., testing in stages for young children)?
5. Can we bring previous evaluations to the table? Will they be considered in the assessment process?
6. Can we see a copy of the test? (Can we see a blank version and our child's answers?)

BECOMING AN ACTIVE PARTNER ON THE ASSESSMENT TEAM

Know the Law

P.L. 94-142, Subpart E was amended in 1990 by P.L. 101-476 and was retitled the Individuals with Disabilities Education Act (IDEA). In the interim IDEA has been amended by P.L. 102-119. Ask your local reference librarian for the latest copy of the IDEA's regulations: Code of Federal Regulations, Title 34; Education; Part 300–399.

The procedures the school agency must follow to be in compliance with the federal law are detailed below. Knowing them will help you to ensure that the assessment follows the letter of the law. Most important, as parent or legal guardian you must be given notice that your child is being screened. Eventually you will be asked to give your permission for the assessment to proceed. Before you authorize the agency to do the assessment, the following information must be given to you:

1. The reason for the assessment.
2. How information will be distributed.
3. To whom reports will be distributed.
4. Who will have access to the information.
5. How long each record will be maintained.
6. The right to challenge record contents.

If you decline an assessment, the school system, if it feels very strongly that there is extreme need for testing, has the right to initiate "due process." In other words, the school system becomes the child's advocate if they believe that the child has not been given the opportunity to be granted services that are due him based on the law. The local school district will ask the state education agency due process board (usually three qualified impartial educational professionals) to examine the record. The board can authorize an assessment at state expense if there are compelling reasons to do so. This is discussed further in Chapter 10. Note that many school districts will not proceed because of the financial cost incurred in this process, except in cases where there may be a history of child abuse or parental neglect as documented by records submitted by other state agencies.

Highlights of IDEA include the following:

1. An evaluation is undertaken to determine whether a child has a disability and to discover the nature and extent of special education and related services that are needed.

2. The evaluation process must be done by a multidisciplinary team.
3. The testing and evaluation materials and procedures must be selected and administered so they are not racially or culturally discriminatory, and shall include all areas that may be related to a child's suspected disability.
4. The tests must be administered in the child's native language or other mode of communication, unless it is clearly not feasible to do so. Tests must be administered by trained personnel.
5. No single test or procedure can be used as the sole criterion for determining an appropriate educational program for the child.

The assessment process will usually look into five areas: educational, medical, social history, psychological, and other. You may refuse to give permission for this testing. Also, if you dispute the results of the testing, you can ask for an independent evaluation at public expense. You always have the right to review records.

Family Educational Rights and Privacy Act of 1974 (P.L. 93-380)— Buckley Amendment. The Buckley Amendment is the legislation adopted by Congress to preserve family rights over disclosure of educational records that are maintained by institutions receiving federal education funds (including your local school district). The school district is required to disclose the types of education records collected and maintained and the location of these records. In addition, the state's policy regarding release and destruction of these materials must be made available to you upon request. Only personnel with a legitimate educational interest in the records may have access. A list of those persons must be kept by the school district (NICHCY, 1993). In order for persons other than direct school personnel to review files or receive any information about your child, you must sign a waiver giving the school authority to release the information. When releasing information, you must specifically name the individual or organization who is to receive it. You may also specify the types of materials you wish the party to receive.

As parents you may inspect and review your child's school records upon written request. (See Figure 5.2 for a sample letter.) One copy of your child's records is available to you at no cost. You also must be given the opportunity to review records before any official meeting is held during any phase of the IEP process. You may find reports by psychologists and consultants in your child's records. You may request correction of any information that is inaccurate or misleading. You may also want to exclude information in your child's permanent record. If the author is unwilling to edit the report, you may challenge the appropriateness of the information at a formal hearing, and request removal.

If you are uncomfortable with proceeding with an assessment for your

Figure 5.2
Sample Letter Requesting Review of Records

Today's Date (include month, day, year)

Your full Return Address

Name of Principal
Full Address

Dear (name of Principal):

I am writing to schedule a time to come to school and review all of my child's records, both cumulative and confidential. My child's name is...his/her grade is...,and his/her teacher is.... I will also need copies of all or some of these records.

Please let me know where and when I can come in to see them. (I need these records by...). You can reach me during the day at (your daytime phone number).

I look forward to hearing from you soon. Thank you for your consideration.

Sincerely yours,

Your full name

Source: Ferguson and Ripley (1991).

child, consider our suggestions. They may help you decide on your course of action. We believe that as you learn more about the process, and participate and communicate with the multidisciplinary team, your comfort level will increase and you will move forward to stimulate your child's growth and development. And certainly ask what you can do to prepare your child for testing if you decide to proceed.

Figure 5.3 is a sample authorization for assessment. You may also be asked to sign an additional consent form for a psychological evaluation.

Acquaint Yourself with the Test and the Testing Procedure

The first step is to understand the testing procedure. It is certainly okay to ask the testing administrator to describe the ways in which your child will be asked to respond to questions. You might ask: "Will my child respond orally to questions, or must he write down his answers? Will she work with manipulatives (i.e., shapes, blocks) and demonstrate a task (identify two similar shapes)?" Tell about your child's behavior, attention span, and likes and dislikes so that the administrator can grab her attention and make the session run smoothly. An important aspect of the evaluation will be how well your child followed directions.

Figure 5.3
Authorization for Assessment

Office for Special and Alternative Education MONTGOMERY COUNTY PUBLIC SCHOOLS Rockville, Maryland 20850-1744	AUTHORIZATION FOR ASSESSMENT *CONFIDENTIAL*

ART I: INFORMATION

Student Name _____
       Last   *First*   *MI*

Student ID # _____

Parent/Guardian _____

Work Phone (_____)_____

Address _____

Home Phone (_____)_____

School(s): Current _____

Date of Birth ____/____/____

       Home _____

Age ____ Grade (yr./mo.) ____/____

Classroom/Homeroom Teacher _____

Primary Language _____

Form Completed By_____
           Name   *Title/Position*

____/____/____
   Date

PART II: TYPE OF ASSESSMENT: Check (✔) each category with Yes or No

Yes	No		Yes	No	
☐	☐	Educational	☐	☐	Vision
☐	☐	Speech/Language	☐	☐	Auditory
☐	☐	Occupational Therapy/Physical Therapy	☐	☐	Vocational
☐	☐	Psychological (Consent obtained by psychologist)	☐	☐	Other (specify) _____

In completing the form the above named person certifies that he/she has explained to the parent(s)/guardian(s) and student (if 18 or older) that Check (✔) all that apply

1. ☐ the individual assessment has been requested for the following reason _____

2. The obtained information will be used to:
  ☐ help determine whether there is a handicapping condition
  ☐ help determine educational placement
  ☐ develop instructional/program recommendations

3. Reports will be distributed to the:
  ☐ student (if 18 or older)   ☐ parents   ☐ central office
  ☐ school confidential file   ☐ field office   ☐ other (specify) _____

4. ☐ record of the results will be maintained in a confidential folder and access to the report(s) will be granted to MCPS staff on a need-to-know basis, and record will be maintained documenting the name and reason for each reviewer. Parent(s)/guardian(s) and eligible students may request/authorize release to another agency/professional

5. ☐ the record will be destroyed 5 years after graduation

6. ☐ assessment results will be shared with parent(s)/guardian(s) prior to taking any action and parent(s)/guardian(s) and eligible students have the right to challenge the accuracy of the report contents and to have information which is proven inaccurate expunged from the record

7. ☐ due process rights were distributed and discussed

8. ☐ the assessor has an ethical obligation to serve the best interests of the student

9. ☐ other _____

The above statements have been carefully explained to me and my signature below indicates my consent to the recommended assessment.

_____
Signature, Parent/Guardian or Student (if 18 or older)

____/____/____
  Date

MCPS Form 336-31

NOTE: This is a multipart form No carbon paper is required. Remove 4 copies and complete.
DISTRIBUTION: COPY 1/Confidential folder; COPY 2/Parent; COPY 3/Assessor(s); COPY 4/Pupil Services (if psychological assessment)

Rev. 7/93

Find Out What Standardized Tests Will Be Used

Standardized tests are developed to measure an individual's skills, knowledge, or abilities based on a specific population's norm. They are validated for use with that specific population. There are two different types, norm-referenced and criterion-referenced. "Norm-referenced tests compare a student's performance to that of a select group of students called a norm group. In a criterion-referenced test a student's performance is measured against specific standards." (What Every Parent Should Know . . . , 1992, p. 1). Testing for special needs children raises a lot of questions and concerns from both educators and parents. How much weight should we put on these tests for an accurate assessment? "The Americans With Disabilities Act (ADA) requires that every examination accurately reflect an individual's aptitude and ability, not his or her disability." (What Every Parent Should Know . . . , 1992, p. 3).

Typical tests used. In recent years educators and researchers have directed their efforts toward developing testing tools that can accurately reflect the abilities of children with disabilities. See Chapter 6 for more information. "EARLY—LAP: The Early Learning Accomplishment Profile for Developmentally Young Children: Birth to thirty-six months" (Glover, Preminger, & Sanford, 1978) is one such tool.

Reduce the Anxiety Level for Both You and Your Child

Visit the place the test will be held a day or so ahead of time. Show your child around. Let him meet the testing administrator ahead of time, and introduce him/her as a teacher. You may tell a very young child that he is going to play games. Pay lots of attention to him. Let him talk about his family and favorite stories or activities. If at all possible, request that testing be done in your neighborhood school, where his brother or sister goes; this can make your job easier, because younger siblings always want to go to school like their sisters or brothers. If he is an only child, or the oldest, look to neighborhood children as role models. Children are afraid of strangers. We want to make sure they feel comfortable with the environment and surroundings. This will help your child relax and do well.

Your Role During the Testing Session

Depending on your child's feelings on separation, you may or may not want to stay in the room while testing takes place. The testing administrator may request that you leave. Find out ahead of time so you can prepare your child for either possibility. If you stay, let the teacher lead the session. The person in charge has a lot of training and experience working with youngsters and can handle most situations. Prompting your child is not a good idea. If you have any questions, it is appropriate to ask them before the session begins, or hold them to the end of the session.

Your Role After the Testing Session Ends

Praise your child for doing a good job. Reward him with a special treat. Let him express his feelings about this new experience. Was it fun? Was it frustrating? This will give you a clue to how he might do in a structured learning environment and what you may need to do to help him get ready to enter school.

Meeting to Get Results

A meeting will be scheduled to go over the test results. Ask that a written copy of results be mailed to you at least a few days before the meeting. Be familiar with common terms used in testing (e.g., scatter, psychomotor). Read the report carefully and note any statements you disagree with. You can evaluate a report by considering the following factors:

1. Accuracy: Do they report fairly what your child can and cannot do (to the best of your knowledge)?
2. Do you understand all the terms?
3. Do the recommendations seem reasonable to you? Do the test findings mesh with the recommendations?

Take advantage of this meeting and go over in depth the process that was undertaken. The multidisciplinary team should also ask or discuss the following information at this meeting:

1. Previous school history.
2. What are your primary concerns both academically and behaviorally?
3. Medical information and history, including nutrition background, any medications taken, vision and hearing.
4. Family information—language spoken at home; other members of the family.
5. Your child's behavior when alone. Describe his personality, his attentiveness/distractibility, mood, level of self-esteem.
6. Your child's behavior when in a group. How does he play with his peers? Does he have any friends? Is he a leader or a follower?

7. Your child's strengths. What does he enjoy doing? What can he do well?

8. How do you motivate your child to participate in academics, group and individual activities, family functions? What works and what doesn't work?

9. Discuss reports and test results from all involved on the team. The testing team will describe the skills your child was able to master on the standardized test, as well as any gaps in certain areas, such as a lack of physical coordination in manipulating objects, inability to complete sentences, etc. They will describe in narrative form how your child reacted when presented with certain situations. They will describe what he can do, whether it is age-appropriate, and the success rate of completing a task. For example, they will tell you if he needed to be prompted, or began the task but gave up in the middle, etc. They will describe his behavior in terms of his temperament, willingness to cooperate, and willingness to complete a task.

10. Staff recommendations. The multidisciplinary team will make a recommendation as to whether they feel your child is eligible for special education services.

Digest What They Have Said

At this point a lot of information has been given to you. The results of the assessment (evaluation) will determine what special education services your child is eligible for. The bottom line is determining whether a child will *benefit* from participating in a special education program. What does "benefit" mean? How can we predict whether a child will make progress if she is included in a program? After collecting information on a child's learning style (including how she best receives and processes information; what she already knows; and what skills are lacking to achieve further skills), a program can be developed specifically for the child that will enhance her learning ability.

Parents' Actions to Foster Desired Outcomes

Bring as much documentation as you can to support your claim that your child can benefit from a special education program. This includes your child's records (e.g., reports from consultants you have used previously). Be prepared to describe your child, what types of activities she engages in, and what she needs help in. Also describe what kinds of skills you would like your child to acquire. Choose skills that are realistic and have a good chance of being mastered. Basically, you are presenting the team with a course of action for your child. It will be harder for the team to criticize your proposal if you give them factual information based on observable behavior. The team has seen your child only briefly. Thus, they may put a lot of weight on information that you provide them. Make sure the team has a true picture of what your child is like. The team will use the testing results to confirm what you have said.

Present your ideas very enthusiastically and optimistically. Accentuate your willingness to participate actively in your child's education, whether through communicating frequently with teachers or engaging in class activities.

If you wish, you can bring someone with you for moral support, perhaps an expert in the field or a parent advocate. You may also bring legal counsel if you so desire. And you may bring along a tape recorder. Continue to ask questions until you clearly understand the procedures and recommendations.

Before you enter the meeting you should have some idea about what the team will recommend. Make a list of the reasons why you feel your child would benefit from participating in a program. Articulate these reasons to the group. If you feel uncomfortable, you can always put them in writing. But always make your opinions known.

What If You Disagree with the Test Results?

The following options are open to you if you disagree with test results. Parents may:

1. request an independent evaluation at public expense;
2. proceed with independent evaluation at private expense;
3. request an informal hearing; or
4. initiate due process.

How Much Importance Should a Parent Place on an Assessment?

Parents need to be aware that the assessment findings may be used to place children automatically in specific programs set up by different agencies, including school systems. Although this may be advantageous in some instances, in others it may not. If your child's assessment determines that he needs many services, this does not necessarily mean that he must attend a school that serves only children with multiple disabilities. You may put extreme importance on the closeness of the facility to your home or the importance of inclusion. Some programs are established to serve the specific needs of one special population, and a target audience is sought to fill that program (e.g., to keep a program going to keep the funding mechanism active).

POINTS TO REMEMBER

We suggest that parents take a very close look at the assessment process and monitor and scrutinize every step. We have included a questionnaire that you can use to rate your level of satisfaction during each step of the process (see Figure 5.4). After completing the questionnaire, analyze your answers and decide which procedures you would like changed or modified to better meet your needs and the needs of your child in the assessment process. Make an appointment with the administrator in charge of the evaluation process and discuss your suggestions. If you are indeed committed to making changes, you might want to get together with other parents, compare notes, come up with a list of suggested changes, and present it to those in decision-making roles.

Figure 5.4
Evaluation Questionnaire

Evaluation	Strongly Agree	Agree		Disagree	Strongly Disagree
I feel I was properly notified about my child's evaluation.	5	4	3	2	1
I believe I was accurately informed about my child's testing before my child was evaluated.	5	4	3	2	1
I believe the tests given to my child were appropriate.	5	4	3	2	1
I knew who in the school to call if I had any questions before my child was evaluated.	5	4	3	2	1
I believe the evaluator/s who tested my child had good rapport with my child.	5	4	3	2	1
I believe that my child's "evaluators" complemented each other so I obtained a complete picture of my child's abilities and needs.	5	4	3	2	1
I believe the evaluation results were clearly explained to me.	5	4	3	2	1
I believe the written evaluation reports were understandable.	5	4	3	2	1
I feel the written evaluation reports contained statements about my child's strengths as well as weaknesses.	5	4	3	2	1

Figure 5.4 (continued)

Evaluation	Strongly Agree	Agree		Disagree	Strongly Disagree
I believe the written evaluation reports accurately describe my child and will be helpful for future reference.	5	4	3	2	1
I feel the evaluation described my child's strengths as well as his/her weaknesses.	5	4	3	2	1
I believe that my child's evaluation was complete.	5	4	3	2	1
I believe the evaluation recommendations were understandable and made sense in light of the evaluation.	5	4	3	2	1
The school told me that I could ask for an independent evaluation if I disagreed with the school's evaluation.	5	4	3	2	1
I feel that the evaluation process helped/will help to insure my child obtains an appropriate education.	5	4	3	2	1
I believe my child is evaluated often enough to obtain necessary information.	5	4	3	2	1

Source: Special Education Parent Advisory Council. 1991. *Parental Survey.* Danbury, CT: Danbury Public Schools.

6

How Tests Help You to Understand Learning Disabilities

It is estimated that between 12 and 14 percent of all school-age children are affected by some sort of learning disability. Therefore, you are not alone in trying to understand your child's learning difficulties. By understanding the kinds of assessments (including testing) school professionals are doing, and what the findings can and cannot tell you, you will be in a better position to interface with these people to identify the best kinds of support for your child. What kinds of problems might you or the teachers note about your child?

CATEGORIZING LEARNING PROBLEMS

Listening Problems

A child with listening problems may not be able to follow simple directions or may become distracted in class when instruction is presented orally. For instance, she might score low on spelling tests because she cannot hear the words the teacher is asking the children to spell. As a parent you may be concerned that your child still has difficulty counting to five even though she has watched *Sesame Street* every afternoon for the past two years. A teacher may notice that during recess your child may not want to participate in circle games because she cannot keep up with the rest of the group. These behaviors may signal the need for testing. Various tests are available to diagnose listening problems. When you speak with your child's teacher, he or she may use the terms "auditory perception" or "receptive language." Auditory perception is the ability to obtain meaning from what is heard. Receptive language is the process of receiving and understanding written or spoken language.

Later in the chapter we discuss some of the tests available to help assess children's listening skills.

Speaking Problems

When some children first learn to talk, they are not able to reproduce all the sounds correctly because their vocal muscles are immature. These children have not had enough vocal practice to master all the consonant blends. As your child progresses in school his speech should improve. But what if your child's speech continues to be slurred or you cannot understand what she is trying to say when she is in second or third grade? For instance, the child may say "wif" instead of "with." Or what if she cannot speak in complete sentences? Again, there are tests to help isolate the specific learning problem.

Mathematics Reasoning Problems

Many parents tell us that on occasion they have sat down with their child to explain the mechanics of how to tell time, or how to convert inches to feet, only to find that the child cannot comprehend the reasoning behind the concepts. Some parents have used objects found in the home as teaching aids, or even worked with the child on the computer using high-tech, high-interest programs, often to no avail.

If your child has similar problems, her teacher may propose during a parent-teacher conference that she be tested on her ability to use "thinking skills," including mathematical reasoning to solve problems.

Many children have computational problems, often manifested by not remembering the multiplication tables, or relying heavily on counting on their fingers to solve problems.

Written Expression Problems

Some school-age children have difficulty writing complete sentences; others may be unable to organize facts in a logical order. The problem often results from getting too involved in the details of the writing assignment; the child is likely to get sidetracked and be unable to complete the task on time.

Reading Problems

Of all the learning difficulties a child may display, reading problems are the most common. A child may have difficulty in word recognition and analysis (word attack skills) and listening comprehension. When your child reads orally or silently he may use his finger to guide him

Table 6.1
Examples of Reading Difficulties

Confuses "B" and "D" reads "Bog" for "Dog" and often confuses B,D,P, and Q.
Confuses the order of letters in words. For example, reads was for saw.
Does not look carefully at the details in a word, guesses from the first letter. For example, reads farm for front.
Loses his place on a page when reading.
Cannot remember words from one day to the next, even though he mastered them previously, and will know them on a future day.
Does not have a systematic way to figure out unknown word.
Has no awareness of words expressed by written symbols.
Omits or adds words to a sentence to make meaning of symbols he is trying to encode.
Reads very slowly and tires quickly.
Reads word-by-word struggling accordingly.

Source: Adapted from Smith (1978).

across the page. You may notice that your child is having little success decoding words phonetically or extracting the main idea of a paragraph. Table 6.1 gives examples of problems that he may face.

INITIAL VERIFICATION OF LEARNING DISABILITIES

How can test results help the learning disabled child? Empirical data suggest that preschool children with learning disabilities are most likely to have problems in either language or visual perceptual-motor functioning. For a child to develop adequate speaking and listening skills, as well as to perform at or above grade level in basic reading, writing, and arithmetic skills, he must be able to perform rudimentary skills such as copying objects correctly (numbers, letters), cutting with scissors following a line, and matching simple geometric forms, to name a few. These are all examples of the rudimentary skills grouped under the category visual perceptual-motor functioning. If your child is having difficulty completing some or all of these tasks, you may request further testing by the resource teacher or reading specialist in your school or by a school psychologist to pinpoint the specific problem. Tests are one part of the assessment process that can help in identifying an appropriate learning program for your child.

MEETING WITH THE SCHOOL PSYCHOLOGIST

When teachers or parents believe that a child exhibits a delay or lack of attainment of skills, the child may be referred to the school psychologist for a complete assessment. A conference will be held to discuss your concerns in detail. The psychologist will compile a detailed written history describing general information on your child's development. In addition he or she will ask you to describe how the family functions as a social unit. One purpose of holding this meeting is to determine the positive and negative factors in your child's environment that may influence learning potential. This includes your attitudes toward your child's behavior and personality, often manifested by conflict in the household (e.g., arguments between mother and father and other siblings), and/or your level of interest in participating in a program for your child. The psychologist will also ask you to describe your child's behavior and will be interested in knowing how your child interacts with people and his immediate environment.

The role of the psychologist is to develop a strategy (what tests should be given) that will be used to determine discrepancies between your child's abilities and his current performance in the classroom (Lamm & Fisch, 1984). The first step in the process is to determine your child's ability to learn from experience, and solve problems. An intelligence test is used for this purpose. Table 6.2 lists commonly used intelligence tests.

WHEN SHOULD PARENTS REQUEST TESTING?

While you may not see the need to gain the insights of psychologists, you certainly will be discussing your concerns with your child's teacher if he is of school age. The teacher may ask you to come in and discuss how your child is functioning at home. Here is a golden opportunity to identify situations where you and his teacher can develop strategies to strengthen your child's self-help skills.

When your child reaches the primary grades your attention begins to focus on his academic success. Your anxiety level will be heightened, and you will want to know if he is able to understand the concepts being presented to him. Will he be able to match pictures to words on a worksheet? Is he able to sit still and listen attentively to the teacher? Is he able to socialize with his peers? Teachers should be asking the same questions. By observation, and by collection of written work, your child's teacher gets a picture of what your child can do and what he is struggling with. For example, your child may not like to get up in front of the class and share an experience or sing along with his classmates.

However, if this is combined with other behavior, such as always interrupting the teacher in the middle of a lesson, it can be a sign of a

Table 6.2
Tests Commonly Used in the Assessment Process

Title	Age Level	General Description
Infant Development Scales		
Battelle Developmental Inventory	Birth to 8 years	Criterion referenced and norm referenced personal-social, motor (gross and fine), communication (receptive and expressive), adaptive (self-help) & cognitive.
The Bayley Scale of Infant Development	2 months–30 months	Assesses early mental and psychomotor development. Standardized test yields mental level & psychomotor index. (norm referenced) (no adaptations for disabilities)
Brigance Diagnostic Inventory of Early Development	Birth–6 years	Criterion referenced test designed to assess performance levels in 6 areas. Psychomotor; self-help; speech & language; general comprehension; pre-academic skills (adapted for disabilities).
Denver Developmental Screening Test	2 weeks to 6 years	Screening Instrument for detection of children with serious developmental delays. Personal social; fine motor-adaptive; language; gross motor. Spanish version is available from publisher.

Table 6.2 (continued)

Santa Clara Inventory of Developmental Tasks	Preschool–7 years	Test assesses a subject's readiness for performing academic tasks either by observation or testing at specific times. Areas tested: motor coordination, visual motor performance, visual perception, visual memory, auditory perception, auditory memory, language development, and conceptual development.
Early Learning Accomplishment Profile for Developmentally Young Children (E-LAP)	Birth–36 months (E-LAP); Birth–6 years (LAP)	Simple criterion-referenced test for handicapped youngsters. Enables the teacher to identify developmentally appropriate learning objectives for each individual child; measure progress through changes in rate of development; and provide specific information relevant to pupil learning.
Early Intervention Developmental Profile (EIDP)	Birth–36 months; 35–60 months Modified for children with visual, hearing and neuro-motor disabilities	Criterion-referenced. Areas tested: perceptual fine motor, cognition, language, social/emotional, self-care, gross motor.

Preschool and School-Age Intelligence Tests

McCarthy Scales of Children's Abilities (NICHCY)	2 1/2 to 8 1/2 years Children within this age group who are thought to be learning disabled may be given this test instead of the Stanford Binet.	A. Cognitive Index—(3 subtests) 1. verbal 2. perceptual/performance (nonverbal thinking & problem solving). Can be used with bilingual or bicultural preschool children or children who have specific language or visual problems. 3. quantitative (number knowledge & reasoning) B. Memory Index C. Motor Index Limitations: Should not be used with children who are severely retarded.
The Stanford-Binet Intelligence Scale	2 years to adult Preferred test of intelligence for children ages 2–6.	Measures global or general intelligence. Binet tests six general areas: general comprehension, memory and concentration, arithmetic reasoning, visual-motor ability, vocabulary-verbal fluency, and judgement and reasoning. Limitations: 1. Does not provide subtest scores about particular strengths & weaknesses. 2. May not provide a fair assessment of bilingual or bicultural children. 3. Depending upon the child's age, the test requires vision, eye-hand coordination, hearing, and speech.
Wechsler Preschool and Primary Scale of Intelligence (WPPSI)	4–6 1/2 years	Used often with learning disabled children. 5 verbal and 5 performance subtests. Provides information about the particular areas in which the child is having difficulty.
Wechsler Intelligence Scale-Revised (WISC-R)	5–15 years	Measures overall ability and at the same time provides information about specific disabilities. Test most likely to be used to assess cognitive functioning of school-age children.

Table 6.2 (continued)

		Achievement Tests (Readiness Tests)
Basic School Skills Inventory	4 to 7 years	Standardized instrument measuring readiness skills critical for first grade: self-help, handwriting, oral communication, reading readiness, number readiness, and classroom behavior.
Basic Concept Inventory	Preschool to 10 years	Criterion-referenced checklist of basic concepts frequently used in verbal directions and explanations and considered necessary for primary grade achievement. Used as a basis for remedial instruction.
Metropolitan Readiness Tests	K–1	Measures word meaning, sentence meaning, information, matching, copying and numbers. Supplementary test requires that the child draws a man. Used to measure readiness for first grade instruction.
Peabody Achievement Tests	K–12	Screening test in math, reading, spelling, and general information.

Reading Tests

Diagnostic Reading Scales (SPACHE)	Grades 1–8; Slow Readers Grades 9–12	Designed to assess oral and silent reading skills and auditory comprehension. Pinpoints deficiencies that interfere with reading ability and indicate instructional, independent, and potential level of reading.
Durrell Analysis of Reading Difficulty	Grades 1–6 Appropriate for non-reader through the intermediate grades	Identifies specific reading difficulties. Subtests: oral and silent reading, listening comprehension, word recognition, word analysis, letters, visual memory of words, spelling, and handwriting.
Gates-McKillop Diagnostic Tests	Grades 2–6	Details specific deficiencies in reading performance. Tests oral reading, word perception, phrase perception, blending word parts, giving letter sounds, auditory blending, spelling, oral vocabulary, syllabication, and auditory discrimination.
Slosson Oral Reading Test (SORT)	Elementary Age	Assesses ability of a subject to pronounce words at different levels of ability. Used to identify children with reading handicaps.

Table 6.2 (continued)

		Math Tests
Key Math Diagnostic Arithmetic Test	Preschool to Grade 6 Individually administered	Designed to provide a diagnostic assessment of mathematic skills. The 14 subtests are organized into three major areas: content, operations, and applications. Each subtest contains items arranged in order of increasing difficulty. Provides a grade equivalent based on the total test performance in each area, with a description of each item's content and indicates whether the student has or has not mastered it.
Stanford Diagnostic Arithmetic Test	Grades 1–12 Individually administered	Identifies and diagnoses specific weaknesses in arithmetic. Focuses on an understanding of properties of the number system and on computation.

Speech/Language/Auditory Tests		
Peabody Picture Vocabulary Test	Ages 2–18 Individually administered	Test for verbal intelligence Assesses familiarity with vocabulary words without requiring child to speak.
BZOCH-LEAGUE Receptive/Expressive Emergent Language Scale REEL	Birth to 36 months Norm-referenced Individually administered	Screening test Uses informant-interview of parent to determine child's level of expressive and receptive language.
TOLD	4–8 years	Tests word discrimination, word articulation, picture vocabulary, oral vocabulary, grammatic understanding, sentence imitation, and grammatic completion.
Slingerland Screening Tests for Identifying Children with Specific Language Disabilities	Grades 1–8 Group	Educational Diagnostic Test Assesses information processing skills (visual and auditory).

Table 6.2 (continued)

Tests Used for Assessment of Learning Disabilities* (Tests in other categories may be used in conjunction with the tests cited below)		
Pupil Rating Scale: Screening on Learning Disabilities	Grades 3–4 Individually Administered by classroom teacher	Screening device for children suspected of having learning problems.
TPA—Illinois Test of Pyscholinguistic Abilities	2 years, 4 months–10 years, 3 months	Diagnoses specific learning disabilities. It evaluates abilities in the visual-motor and auditory-vocal channels of communication.
Meeting Street School Screening Test	5–7 1/2 years	Developmental Test—gross motor skills, fine motor, visual perception and language.
Slingerland	See above	See above
Detroit Test of Learning Aptitude (Auditory Visual Memory)		Measures auditory and visual memory and concentration.
Bender-Gestalt (Visual-Motor)	Norms given for ages 5–11 Psychologists may use for a personality assessment.	Child given 9 geometric figures one at a time and asked to copy them. Used to assess visual perceptual skills and eye-hand coordination. Used to predict school achievement, intelligence, brain injury, and mental retardation.
Berry—Developmental Test of Visual Motor Integration (VMI)		Tests the degree to which visual perception and motor behavior are integrated. Consists of 24 geometric forms, arranged in order of increasing difficulty, which the student is asked to copy.

Sources: Association for Retarded Citizens, Montgomery County. N.d. *Project TEAM: Training in Educational Advocacy and Monitoring Manual.* Rockville, MD: Author; Beckman and Boyes, (1993); Melton (1984); National Information Center for Handicapped Children and Youth (NICHCY) (1985, October).

more serious problem. You may notice behavior and actions at home that seem abnormal or uncharacteristic of a child your son's age. We suggest that you select a week and closely observe your child; record your observations using Figure 2.1.

If a teacher has a concern, a conference may be held. A teacher who suspects a problem may bring up the subject with colleagues (probably not disclosing your child's name), either formally or informally, before meeting with you. Usually the teacher will prepare a list of problem areas. The group may make suggestions on different approaches to take when teaching a concept to your child (e.g., peer teaching). The teacher may try this new approach, but perhaps it doesn't seem to help. He or she may then decide that the appropriate course of action is to refer your child for further testing.

At this point you have a meeting with the teacher, the principal, and the resource specialist. It is a good idea to bring your written observations to the meeting. The group should identify and develop a list of problems your child may be experiencing in school, both academically and socially. If a teacher notices problems in the classroom, the child will probably have the same problems at home. But what if you do not see any problems at home? How do you know that testing is necessary? It is always possible that your child and his teacher can't get along. This can have a negative effect on your child's progress in school. Here is where the school psychologist can be helpful. When interviewing your child he or she may discover this conflict and suggest a different class placement. There may be a sudden crisis in your family life such as divorce, illness, or the death of a loved one that may have an effect on your child's schooling. On many occasions schools will request a complete physical examination to rule out any medical causes for your child's behavior. It is important that these possibilities be ruled out before your child is tested.

If after pursuing the above steps no satisfactory reason for your child's behavior is found, a behavioral/developmental test may be appropriate. If the child is in preschool, the Santa Clara Inventory of Developmental Tasks may be administered. It indicates readiness to perform academic tasks. Test areas include motor coordination, auditory memory, and visual memory, among others. In other words, the test is divided into very specific categories, so that a precise area of difficulty can be identified.

For many parents, the first inkling of a problem may crop up during a scheduled parent-teacher conference in the fall. The teacher may express concern about your child's performance in school, alerting you to the possibility of a learning disability, and would like to consult with the school psychologist. Some or all of the behaviors listed in Table 6.3 may be identified by your child's teacher. With your permission, a series of tests will be given to your child. An intelligence test (measures

Table 6.3
Behavior That May Indicate a Need for Testing

Poor attention span.
No sustained focus.
Work takes too much time to finish.
Personal organizational problems.
Study skills lacking.
Low frustration tolerance—gives up easily.
Daydreams—appears to be lazy.

Source: Adapted from Smith (1978).

cognitive level—thinking ability) such as the Wechsler Preschool and Primary Scale of Intelligence–Revised will be given, along with an ahchievement test (measures the level of development in academic areas) such as the Peabody Individual Achievement Test. It is widely accepted that a child with possible learning disabilities should be given an intelligence test which measures overall ability and at the same time provides information about specific disabilities. Children must also be given an individual academic achievement test to measure whether their achievement is lower than expected based on their IQ score (National Information Center for Handicapped Children and Youth, 1985). The results allow the psychologist to identify or verify a child's barriers to achievement. Or your child may exhibit some of the behaviors listed in Table 6.4. Language instruments such as the Test of Language Development (TOLD) and the Peabody Picture Vocabulary Test–Revised (receptive language) are given to identify specific barriers.

When should you become concerned about your child's cognitive development? It is probably never too early. From birth, we can observe developmental milestones. In fact, it is the pediatrician who initially monitors cognitive development. Our pediatrician was the first to become concerned about our son Adam's cognitive development because he was not meeting the milestones set forth on the Denver Developmental Screening Test.

UNDERSTANDING ASSESSMENT AND TESTING

A test can be designated as a screening instrument (an initial measurement used to determine whether potential developmental problems exist and to determine the need for further testing); an instrument for diagnosis (the process of identifying the nature of a condition or prob-

Table 6.4
Behavior That May Indicate a Need for Testing Language Skills

Cannot say something in an organized, cogent manner.
Tends to muddle—starts in the middle of an idea.
Cannot organize words properly into a question.
Has trouble following long sequences of directions.
Doesn't enjoy being read to, but does like to look at pictures in a book.
Becomes distracted in class when directions are presented orally—likes to watch others to learn.
Trouble with abstract words—defines words by their concrete attributes or functions.
Very literal—misses inferences, subtleties, nuances, innuendos.
Can't tell a story in sequence or summarize.
Forgets names of things already learned—has to summarize them.

Source: Adapted from: Smith (1978).

lem. The child's development and performance are compared to those of children of the same age who are developing normally); an educational assessment tool (the process of obtaining and gathering different kinds of information to provide a suitable educational or therapeutic program); or a monitoring assessment tool.

Tests, when properly used, can help identify and diagnose disabilities in children. Not only is testing important in identifying disabilities, but it is always used as one measure to monitor and evaluate your child's special education programming.

The first series of tests of this nature is usually given in the primary grades, kindergarten through second grade. These are called readiness tests and are often given at Kindergarten Roundup. You may have noticed that your child is unable to walk a straight line, or has trouble tying his shoes, or that his drawings are totally abstract even though he tells you they are of persons. These behaviors may indicate that your child will have difficulty in the primary grades. Readiness tests will identify specific areas of underachievement. For instance, the Basic School Skills Inventory is a standardized instrument that measures readiness skills that are needed for the first grade (self-help, handwriting, oral communication, reading readiness, number readiness, and classroom behavior; see Table 6.2). If test results show that he lacks the appropriate self-help skills, the kindergarten teacher can develop a program accordingly. Information from the test helps the teacher prepare daily lessons.

Centers will be designed that emphasize self-help skills. A child who scores below the norm on these tests may be placed in a developmental kindergarten class. In this class the student-to-teacher ratio may be lower than in a regular class. An extra instructional aide or tutor may be assigned to the class. The curriculum may be slightly different, and the time spent on each objective may be longer. The teacher may focus on providing activities that promote visual and auditory discrimination skills if that is what is needed by the students.

A Further Understanding of Developmental Assessment and Test Instruments

In recent years educators and researchers have directed their efforts to developing testing tools that accurately reflect the abilities of children on a developmental continuum. "EARLY—LAP, The Early Learning Accomplishment Profile for Developmentally Young Children: Birth to thirty-six months," (Glover, Preminger, & Sanford, 1978), is one such tool. This test is divided into gross motor, fine motor, cognitive, language, self-help, and social-emotional categories. Each section is divided into headings: item to be tested, procedure, credit (what needs to be observed in order to pass this item), "Pre" column (date of initial testing), "Post" column (after the child has been in a program—test same item again, noting date tested), and comments section.

The test booklet describes the format for the tester to follow in determining where to begin testing on the continuum and where to end. The initiation of the assessment should reflect a series of skills the child is exhibiting. The starting point or basal for the EARLY—LAP is the positive demonstration of eight consecutive skill items. Positive demonstration of an item based on a specific criterion is indicated by placing + in the item box. Skills that appear to be emerging may be indicated by +/−. There is a section where a bar graph can be filled in so that the assessor can visualize the results of the test.

Alternatively, a psychologist may decide to administer the Pupil Rating Scale or the Meeting Street School Screening Test (MSSST) (see Table 6.2).

Important information has been collected. How does a parent make sense of the results of all these testing instruments? A report will be written, usually called "Report of Findings," describing your child's scores. For example:

> Johnny's IQ tested at above average intelligence as recorded by the _____.
> He has an average or above average IQ. He appears to have the readiness skills to learn how to read. However, he seems to have difficulty with visual motor integration.

With the scores, the reports will usually describe the observations made in the classroom (e.g., Johnny is unable to organize his papers, and his desk is always messy). Suggestions may be included (e.g., Johnny needs to sit close to the blackboard). The teacher or school nurse may initially request that your child be seen by a medical doctor to rule out a medical cause, such as a neurological problem (e.g., a tumor), or to investigate attention deficit disorder as a possible diagnosis.

How are tests developed, and are they reliable? For a test to be valid and reliable, the contents and procedures by which it is administered must be replicated consistently. This is the definition of a standardized test. Norm-referenced means that the score your child receives is compared to those of other children in the same chronological age group. The norm group, however, usually does not include children with disabilities. Thus your child may not be able to answer some questions because of his or her disability (e.g., a visual impairment). If your child cannot get credit for answering some items on the test for this reason, the results reported (e.g., cognitive level) may be inaccurate. Parents need to be aware of these situations in advance. For example, the Bayley Scales of Infant Development and the Battelle Developmental Inventory are norm-referenced tests. However, the Battelle allows the testing administrator to modify acceptable responses from children with disabilities. We need to check to make sure that the testing administrator is trained to use the test correctly, especially if a modification is used. In addition, when we review the results with professionals, we need to discuss this modification.

Other tests known as criterion-referenced tests are designed to evaluate a child's performance against a specific performance criterion or standard. The Early Intervention Developmental Profile (EIDP) is used by many professionals. I remember vividly that when Adam was in an early intervention program, he was given two tests. The Battelle was given to all children as part of a countywide research project. Two months later Adam was tested using the EIDP. There was a large discrepancy between the results of the two tests. Adam scored much higher on the EIDP across the board. We were very upset with the testing results and immediately thought, "How can this be? Which test is right?" We were concerned, and questioned Adam's teacher. When you sit down with the team to go over test results, especially when you are interacting with the system for the first time, the experience can be devastating. It was for us. Make sure you understand what is being tested and how. Most important, do not make all your decisions on test results alone.

Categories of testing instruments. A wide variety of testing instruments are available to the school system or private practitioner. Tests are categorized first by age level, then by purpose (e.g., screening, diagnostic, assessment, educational programming, monitoring). They are further classified according to domain (e.g., gross motor, speech/language, or more than one area, such as the EIDP, which measures six areas). Table 6.2 lists commonly used educational tests and highlights the major categories: (1) infant development scales; (2) preschool and school-age intelligence; (3) achievement tests (including readiness tests); (4) reading tests; (5) math tests; (6) speech/language/auditory perception tests; and (7) tests used for the assessment of learning disabilities.

POINTS TO REMEMBER

Testing is an important part of the assessment process, but test results should not be the only criterion used in placing your child in a program. Tests do have limitations, as noted in Table 6.2. Some children (e.g., those with disabilities or with multicultural backgrounds) may be at a disadvantage when undergoing testing. They may be unfairly evaluated due to a test's cultural bias, or a requirement that the child have adequate visual-motor skills (e.g., good eye-hand coordination), hearing, or speech to perform on the test. A child's score on a standardized test such as the Stanford Binet Intelligence Test may not present a true measure of his cognitive abilities. Many tests can be used in the assessment process, and parents need to insist that those used be selected on an individual basis to meet the needs of their child. The information gathered during the testing process and the interpretations of the test scores will become important factors in the development of an individualized education program. Learn about the testing procedures in your local school district, and take a close look at how school officials view your child after the testing procedure is completed. These perceptions may have serious consequences with respect to your child's schooling. Parents need to be adequately informed and involved in this process.

Parental Choice of Program Placement: Birth–Five Programs

Congratulations! You have cleared a major hurdle in the process of obtaining some of the services your child needs and is entitled to receive. Now it's time to put on your detective hat and begin to investigate the variety of existing programs that may or may not be appropriate for your child. Remember, you do not have to place your child in a program that does not meet his needs just because the school system operates the program. Many parents have elected to enroll their children in neighborhood preschool programs with direct support and consultation services from professionals employed by the local school system, various state agencies, or other providers (e.g., Easter Seals, nonprofit rehabilitation agencies). Many of these professionals provide on-site consultation. It is important to remember that federal statutes mandate that *all* of your child's needs be met.

THE IMPACT OF P.L. 99-457 ON PROGRAMS

Reform in early intervention services has come about with the implementation of P.L. 99-457, Part H. Changes that have occurred include the following:

1. Families are no longer at the tail end of the program delivery system. The family not only becomes an active participant in the decision-making process—either agreeing to or refusing to endorse specific services—but also becomes eligible to receive direct services (both parents and siblings).

2. Services to families cannot be fragmented but must be integrated into a single plan.

3. Ability to pay is no longer an issue for eligibility.

4. Children with intensive medical needs are given the medical support to allow them to participate in programs.

Family-Centered Programming

The delivery of programs and services to children who are identified as needing early intervention special education services can be home-based, center-based, or a combination of both. The delivery of early intervention services is changing to focus on a family-centered approach. In the past, intervention with young children with disabilities centered on providing educational, therapeutic, and medical services designed to remedy a specific condition and to enhance a child's development. Practitioners, therapists, and clinicians worked directly with children on activities designed to meet the child's specific needs. Parents and families were usually involved in providing home-based activities to reinforce the goals of the therapy or schooling. Early intervention services have expanded to include a comprehensive list of family services (e.g., family training, counseling, and home visits); health services; medical services (only for diagnostic and evaluation purposes); nursing and nutrition; respite care; transportation; and/or social work. In the family-centered approach, families are allowed to choose their role at each stage, and professionals are there not to direct, but to support the family and provide services. Sometimes the family assumes the leadership role, but not always (Dawkins et al., 1994). Thus, decisions on programming are based on you and your family's changing needs.

Individualized Family Service Plans

The adoption of the Individualized Family Service Plan (IFSP) provides a mechanism for infants and toddlers with disabilities and their families to receive a well-planned and coordinated program for early intervention services. How does a family receive what it needs? A multidisciplinary and family needs assessment will identify its unique needs. Services appropriate to meet those needs will be identified. The IFSP will include the frequency, intensity, and method of delivery of services. It also identifies a case manager who will be responsible for implementing the plan and coordinating with other agencies to make sure it is in place (Arcfacts, 1986). Case management is an active, ongoing process that involves

- assisting parents of eligible children to gain access to the early intervention services and other services identified in the Individualized Family Service Plan;

- coordinating the provision of early intervention services and other services (such as medical services for other than diagnostic and evaluating purposes) that the child needs or is receiving;

- facilitating the timely delivery of available services;

- continuously monitoring the appropriate services and situations necessary to benefit the development of each child being served for the duration of the child's eligibility.

The duties of the case manager are

- to coordinate all inter-agency services; and

- to serve as the single point of contact in helping parents to obtain the services and assistance they need. (State of Maryland Department of Education, Maryland Infants and Toddlers Program Interagency Coordinating Council, 1989)

Eligibility

Eligibility criteria for receiving early intervention services were enumerated in Chapter 5. These services must meet state standards and be provided by qualified personnel at no cost, except where federal or state law provides for a system of payments by families, including sliding fees (*Arcfacts*, 1986). With the change in the economic climate and the emergence and growth of the concept of privatization, some parents may be asked to underwrite (e.g., access their health insurance benefits) many of the costs associated with birth to three programs. These programs are administered through the states. Governors and state legislatures hold the reins for many of these programs. Some services are fee free, such as evaluations and assessments, services coordination, and development of the IFSP. Also note that inability to pay will not result in denial of services (Georgia ARC, June 1994). States receive funding based on U.S. Census data.

Health Services

Children are entitled to receive health services as part of their early intervention services. The following excerpt defines and gives examples of health services:

Services necessary to enable a child to benefit from the other early intervention services under this part during the time that the child is receiving the other early intervention services ... [include] (1) Such services as clean intermittent catheterization, tracheotomy care, tube feeding, the changing of dressings or osteotomy collection bags, and other health services; and (2) Consultation by physicians with other service providers concerning the special health care needs of eligible children that will need to be addressed in the course of providing other early intervention services. (Schleifer & Klein, 1989)

Other Relevant Information Parents Need to Know

Time lines. After a multidisciplinary assessment is concluded, the law states that the IFSP has to be written in a reasonable amount of time. The IFSP must be evaluated annually, and the family must be able to review the plan every six months.

Contents of an IFSP. Included in the IFSP must be a statement of the child's present level of development, a statement of the family's strengths and needs as they relate to assisting the child, the anticipated major outcomes to be achieved, and how progress is to be achieved. (Chapter 8 describes the contents of an IFSP more fully.)

The following procedural safeguards are mandated by the law:

1. The timely resolution of administrative complaints by parents and the right to appeal to a state or federal court.
2. Confidentiality of personal, identifiable information.
3. The opportunity to examine records.
4. Procedures to protect the child if parents or guardians are not known, unavailable, or the child is a ward of the state.
5. The provision of services pending resolution of the complaint. (*Arcfacts*, 1986)

Impact of These Changes on Families

After reading these few paragraphs, you now realize how far-reaching this piece of legislation really is. It will enable you to become more involved in your child's early development. However, it probably will put more pressure on your family. In order to make an intelligent choice, you will need ample information. You must be able to tap into appropriate resources, and feel comfortable working with professionals. This raises many questions. For example, you might ask, "Isn't my child too young?" Or "Should we start right away?" Or "Is too much intervention harmful?"

Dorros and Dorsey (1988) suggest that you do not have to rush into a decision. They feel that early intervention programming will be more successful for a child and his/her family when they are ready to participate in a program. They argue that there hasn't been any "authoritative evidence that intervention programs which begin at three weeks provide a noticeably greater benefit than those beginning at six months" (p. 73). Thus it is more important that you as parents feel comfortable in making this decision. According to Dorros and Dorsey:

> There are no explicit standards for judging the effectiveness of early intervention programs. There are no specific guidelines which a parent can use in choosing the appropriate program for his/her child. To the extent that the goals of all such programs are general and wide, they are all to some extent effective. Given all of this information, what do we recommend to all parents, once they find out that their child has a disabling condition? We tell them:
>
> 1. First and foremost trust yourself and take your time.
> 2. During those first days, medical needs should be first priority.
> 3. Talk to people you trust.
> 4. Seek out professionals for specific information.
> 5. Remember what may be right for one parent and child may not be right for you and your child.
> 6. Contact parent support groups.
> 7. Remember there is help available. Take your time to do what is best not only for your child, but for your entire family. (pp. 76–77)

More responsibility is placed upon you as parents—and rightly so. The following pages will shed light on what is out there and how you can be effective in planning the most appropriate program for your child.

Home-Based Programs

The definition of a home-based program is one in which one or more designated professionals travel to a child's home to provide one-on-one service. Your child may be eligible to receive more than one clinical service. The emphasis in this type of program is on early stimulation and therapy. As discussed in Chapter 2, infants develop very strong bonds with their mothers and care providers. Thus delivery of services makes sense on an individual basis. A very young child (birth to age two) is most comfortable in his or her familiar surroundings and most likely will benefit most from this environment. Also, much emphasis is placed on parent education. Time is spent on teaching specific skills to foster your child's growth and development; sharing information and directing you to resources that may help your child and the family; and answering your questions and concerns in depth, in a way that is tailored to your needs. You will discover that professionals in certain disciplines, most notably vision and speech and hearing, believe that children in need of these services will excel faster when provided with one-on-one service in the home setting.

Home-based services may be the delivery strategy of choice for medical reasons. However, this mode has been steadily declining in the past decade, especially for children over the age of five. Before 1976, almost all children with intensive medical needs were excluded from attending school-based programs because of their "medically fragile" condition. This term included many children with varying needs. Typically, children prone to have seizures were likely to receive services at home or in a hospital setting rather than in a center-based program in the local community. Schools were not willing to take on the responsibility of providing medical treatment for these children. Others may have had g-tubes (for feeding) or needed medication administered to them frequently.

However, as noted above, P.L. 99-457 removed the barriers that prevented children from attending center-based programs. It is important that communication between all members of the team (family, school and medical personnel) be open and flowing. Extensive preparation and coordination of equipment, medical paraphernalia, and so on must occur before your child enters the program. The classroom teacher and other designated individuals need to be trained to take care of your child's specific needs. Communication and training are critical. The staff must know your child's history, how to handle emergencies, and what protocols to initiate. As more and more children with medical needs have entered the school system, school personnel have gained experience and expertise in caring for them.

Center-Based Programs

Another alternative is the center-based program. As the name implies, space is provided by either the school district or program sponsor to house a program where a number of clients (parents and children) come together. Small groups are formed, and members interact in a planned environment. For instance, an infant/toddler class addresses each child's needs through classroom activities and topics. "Decisions about appropriate topics are based on the general needs of the classroom along with themes that children can be exposed to outside of school for carry-over" (Keith, 1985, p. 1).

FACTORS IN DETERMINING PROGRAM SELECTION

Once you have decided to secure early intervention services, it is important to write down the characteristics of the kind of program you are looking for. You need to think about the advantages and disadvantages of having an exclusively home-based program versus one that is delivered only by a center-based model. Will you feel comfortable in a class with other children and parents? On the other hand, will having a professional come to your home to work with you and your child suit you? Will you need to arrange day care for your other children and rearrange work and family schedules? We suggest that you make a checklist of the characteristics you are looking for. Figure 7.1 is an example.

Sources to Help You Identify Programs

Once you have written an outline, you can look around in your community to find programs that you can observe and gather information about. At your IFSP meeting you should ask for information about the programs that are available in your region. Your case manager should be familiar with or able to find out about available programs. Representatives of the agencies that will provide services indicated on your IFSP can be contacted, and a list given to you. You can also contact the Parent Training and Information Center in your state to locate such programs. Parent to Parent is another source you may use (see Chapter 3). Certainly the nature of your child's disability will influence your decision on which program will be most beneficial. For example, the Alexander Graham Bell Association for the Deaf suggests that you may want to consider a preschool that has both normal-hearing and hearing-impaired children in a program that places a heavy emphasis on listening and language development skills.

Thus, it is a good idea to contact a professional association closely linked to your child's disability; it can assist you in establishing which criteria to consider when deciding on an appropriate placement. Many organizations will send you information on what parents can do to help their children at home and school.

While you are thinking about a center-based program, you may also want to think about the pros and cons of a home-based program. State agencies will contact you to set up an appointment with specialists who may come to your home. You should interview these prospective providers. Realize that as the level of federal and state dollars available decreases, specialists will probably cover a larger territory. You may not have a choice of who will come to your home, and the times scheduled for visits may or may not be convenient. Most likely the same weekly appointment will be kept by the specialist. This will help you and your

Figure 7.1
Center-Based Program Observations

Name of Program: _____   Date Visited: _____

Categories	Yes	No	Comments

General
 	
1. Time length
   Does it meet your child's needs?
2. Schedule—will it be "workable"?
   (e.g. day care arrangements)
3. Medical support at site if needed.			

Location 1. Travel time reasonable 2. Can access public transportation			
Environment 1. Clean & Bright 2. Accessibility 3. Noise Level 4. Exhibits children's work 5. Information posted for parents 6. Class size			

Classroom attributes & deficiencies
 	
1. Space planning
   a. adequate space
   b. changing tables
   c. bathroom
   d. work areas
   e. sinks
 	
2. Observation room
 	
3. Supplies and materials
   a. equipment for: gross motor;
      visual stimulation; fine motor
      activities			

Teaching Philosophies 1. Interdisciplinary approach 2. Parent participation important part of program			

Figure 7.1 (continued)

Staff
 	
1. Qualifications
2. Personality
  (will child & family feel
  comfortable in establishing a
  relationship?)
3. Ratio teacher/student
4. Creativity
5. Willing to share info with others			

Supports available 1. Social worker 2. Parent educator 3. Nurse 4. Psychologist 5. Opportunity to talk to other parents			
Opportunities for inclusion 1. Housed in a neighborhood school 2. Peers as helpers in class 3. Child participates in many activities with peers			

family keep on a schedule. Specialists usually carry with them the equipment (such as balls, toys, mirrors, books, tapes, and tape recorders) they will use in each session. However, large, bulky equipment will not be accessible (e.g., sandboxes, pronestanders, wedges). Expect that there may be changes as different professionals are assigned to your case. This happens quite often. We cannot stress often enough that good record keeping is important, since you may be working with several professionals in one year.

Some states provide family support grants for programs such as early intervention services. You may want to get information about these programs. You may decide you want to use a private provider. Are you limited to the resources found by your case manager? Many professionals have established private practices. We have noticed that practices have sprung up in which professionals from three different disciplines have joined forces to provide services based on a multidisciplinary approach. These groups may come to your home at one sitting, or they may ask that you visit their office. For example, an occupational therapist, physical therapist, and speech therapist may have incorporated and started a small business whereby they work together to develop and implement a plan or program for your child. The choices are growing all the time. You may have to spend a lot of time on the telephone, but the program that is set up to meet your child's needs may be very creative and tailored to fit your family's needs.

How Age Three–Five Programs Differ from Programs Geared for Younger Children

Time length. You might assume that as your child gets older, the length of time he or she can access the services of a program will increase. This is not necessarily the case in all states. For example, in Georgia, a child receiving services through the birth to three program may attend a program five days a week, six hours a day; but when he reaches three, the program can be cut back dramatically. The reason is that once a child reaches three, a different organization is responsible for administering the program, and the program components can change as well. Early intervention (birth to age three) and preschool (three to five) programs are a part of the Individuals with Disabilities Education Act (IDEA), but the ways in which they operate are different (Georgia ARC, 1994). There may be a significant change or very little change in the amount and kinds of services provided to you and your child when your child turns three. Now you need to become familiar with not only the federal early intervention laws, but also with federal and state education laws regarding special education. Your local library as well as your school district will have a copy of applicable state special education laws and guidelines.

Location of services. You should expect that as your child reaches the age of three, services will probably be provided primarily in a center-based program. Preschool programs for children with disabilities may continue to be offered through a public or private agency. More children will probably be in a three to five program than in an early intervention program serving younger children, because as they get older more children will be identified as needing services. This may be an advantage because now you may have more programs to choose from.

Program emphasis. When your child moves on to a three to five program, the emphasis centers on meeting his educational needs through special education and related services (as deemed appropriate) rather than on his psycho-developmental needs (services directly provided to the family to help enhance the child's development). Your child may attend such programs without you. Most important, your child is entitled to a free, appropriate public education with an individualized education program that takes place in the least restrictive environment (LRE). In addition, as parents, you are entitled to implement due process procedures if you disagree with any portion of the program, including placement. The state or local educational agency (depending on who is responsible for the program) can determine that educational programming for your child can be satisfied in a program that runs for two hours a day rather than five hours a day. Much depends on what is already in place in your local school district.

REASONS WHY SCHOOLS OFFER THE PROGRAMS THEY DO

Chapter 8 treats this topic in greater detail, but we would like to give you an overview of the factors that influence the policy set by your local school district with regard to early intervention and special education preschool programs. This will give you a sense of what position your local school district will take when you suggest a program for your child.

IDEA and Programming

The most important factor is the procedures and guidelines mandated by federal and state laws. All children with special needs must be served. However, your school district may contract with a private agency to run the program. This is perfectly allowable under the law. Reasons for doing this may vary from district to district. Sometimes children come from several neighboring towns to a program run by a nonprofit agency. Your local school district pays tuition (the cost of having your child attend this preschool) to the nonprofit agency. Why do school districts opt for this approach? Usually for financial reasons. It may cost less to pay tuition than to hire staff and buy high-tech classroom equipment (e.g., augmentative communication devices, walkers, motorized wheelchairs). Many towns do not have enough classroom space for the entire school population. Thus limited space may be a consideration. In our school district, the preschool program ran only three hours per day. The administration felt that Adam needed to be in a full-day program. The only full-day program available was at a preschool for multihandicapped children run by a nonprofit community agency. Fortunately, the school was only five minutes from our house. Many families may find that a program is as much as an hour away. This may influence your decision to continue with a home-based program, or have your child stay in the program he is already in.

Parent participation. A major thrust of the law is that parents of children with disabilities participate in the planning and decision making for their child's special education. School districts want your input and suggestions regarding your child's education, but we have noticed that they will not volunteer every bit of information on programming (e.g., escort you around to all the special education programs in the district). In the past, special education programs have been low profile, but as of late they have been changing as more parents participate in programming. To continue this visibility, it is up to parents to gain information, set up their communications network, and visit programs. Information packets about special education are available from your local school district; ask for them. However, these materials may be very broad. Call up with specific questions, and, as mentioned previously, visit programs and observe.

Confidentiality. This is a major protection under the law. However, this sometimes may not make it easy to speak with other parents about their feelings or experiences regarding different programs. We suggest that you get involved in your school's PTO as well as districtwide committees sponsored by advocacy organizations such as the Association for Retarded Citizens (ARC) or Parent to Parent so that you can make acquaintances and keep on top of what's going on in the school district.

In Chapter 5 we suggested that you need to know your child's strengths and weaknesses, situations in which your child will excel, and what types of supports your child needs to do well. This knowledge increases your effectiveness as a member of the team and gives you the background you need to make an intelligent decision on programming. Ask for your child's records. There may be some items that you disagree with. As a parent you have the right to review records and to request that information be added or deleted. On occasion, the evaluative team may recommend a specific program based on testing; however, you may disagree. Do not be afraid to speak out. Talk openly and honestly to the other members of the team. They may see your point of view. If not, you can take further steps in due process (see Chapter 10).

Parental involvement leads to positive change. In many instances programs in school districts have been established by parents who have demanded programs that meet their child's needs in the least restrictive environment in their neighborhoods. More than likely, if you are satisfied with your child's progress and program you will never bother to read the law or question how it affects your child's program. Parents do know that their children are entitled to services, and put a lot of faith and trust in educators. Yet they are often unaware of how much input and influence they can have in the process. We suggest that you take advantage of the provisions of the law that give parents the opportunity to influence their children's programs.

The IEP Determines Programming

The IEP document is crucial in determining programming. If services are not written into the IEP, the local school agency is not responsible for providing them. Thus, if you want your child to receive services, you have to speak up and be heard.

Transitions from One Program to Another

There is no one set procedure for making the transition from the birth to three program to preschool programs. Each state has its own procedures. According to federal guidelines, however, three approaches may be taken during the school year your child turns three (for instance, a child whose third birthday is in February 1995 could be enrolled in an early intervention program in September 1994):

1. Your child stays in the early intervention program and is entitled to receive early intervention funding until June 1995, if the transition plan stipulates this procedure; or

2. Your child can enroll in the three to five program in September 1994; or

3. In February 1995, your child can enroll in the three to five program.

Each state has guidelines as to which option they will follow. In Georgia, a child immediately changes programs on his third birthday.

Monitoring Your Child's Program

According to federal guidelines, a program review must be initiated ninety days before a child's third birthday. Obviously you need to weigh your options long before this date approaches. This is another critical time in evaluating the needs of your child and how best to fulfill those needs. Monitoring your child's program should occur not only at transition times, but throughout the year. You should have an open dialogue with your case manager at least once a month. Also, after every session, if possible speak with the teacher or specialist for a few minutes to get her opinions on how your child is doing in school. Request a conference frequently to go over areas of concern as well as the progress your child is making. One of the components of the center-based program is to have parents get together for a part of the session to talk about issues confronting their child and their family. This is a good time to compare notes and impressions on how the program is going.

Also, do your own assessment using the guidelines provided in Chapter 5. Review the notes you collected during the assessment and eligibility meetings. Read over your IFSP. Have the objectives been met? How has your child fared? Has he made progress? Has he learned new skills? Refer to Chapter 8 to help you to proceed through this task.

There are natural transition periods in your child's schooling. The transition from early intervention to preschool is one of those times. But what if you feel that a change in programming is necessary at another time (e.g., a change from a medically-based model to a neighborhood model). If your child is in an early intervention program, you can withdraw your consent. A change in a three to five program is different and more complex. The first step is to talk to the professional most directly involved with your child, namely, your child's teacher. Questions arise: "How do I bring this issue up with the teacher?" Prepare some information to take with you. Here are some suggestions:

1. Observe your child during class time and note what he is doing. (Follow guidelines in Chapter 2.)

2. Observe your child at home doing certain tasks. Is he doing them differently at home than in school or vice versa?

3. Write your observations down in a log or book.

4. Talk to others who have observed your child. Do they see the same behavior? Is there a pattern or special time when it occurs?

5. If you desire, you can call your pediatrician or other trusted professionals to ask for their opinion.

When you do approach the teacher, we suggest that you request a meeting. Don't talk about these issues in front of the whole class. The teacher might be embarrassed and on the defensive. It is better to be polite and follow some simple rules. This is especially true if this is the first time you have a concern or disagreement.

1. Start off the meeting with positive comments.

2. Voice your concerns but do not talk down to the teacher.

3. Bring along your notes and documentation so that you have a basis for your conversation.

4. Allow the teacher to speak.

5. Request the records so you can go over them. (As part of the teacher's responsibilities, documentation should be on file on how your child is doing, including informal observations by the teacher, specialist, or supervisor, and formal reports or evaluations.)

6. Discuss how the curriculum might be changed to be more appropriate. You may request an IFSP or IEP meeting to change or modify some objectives if you feel it is necessary.

7. At the end of the meeting, decide on what you and the teacher will do to resolve the matter. Another meeting may be needed with others involved.

Chapter 9 discusses in detail the steps you can take to make extensive changes in your child's program if you are not satisfied with the results of this meeting or meetings.

POINTS TO REMEMBER

A parent's preference regarding program placement is always taken into consideration when a program is being developed. You can strongly influence the team's decision if you have relevant and accurate information to back up your opinions. The information shared with the team should answer the following questions:

1. How can my child learn best?
2. What does my child need to be successful?

If you choose a home-based program, be flexible in scheduling visits with providers. If a center-based program is your preference, visit several possible placement sites and select the program design that best fits your child's needs (e.g., local preschool, preschool that only serves children with disabilities; therapy-intensive medical model sponsored by a rehabilitation center or hospital such as Easter Seals or United Cerebral Palsy). In your deliberations, think about what types of classroom activities will foster your child's learning and whether your child will be able to develop a constructive relationship with his teachers. An important question to ask yourself is, Does my child have appropriate role models, and will he be able to interact with his peers? There are many program options open to parents. We suggest that you set aside a considerable amount of time to investigate all possibilities because this is an important step in initiating your child's formal education.

The Individualized Education Program: A Multifaceted Process

The previous chapters discussed the process of matching your child's needs to appropriate special education services in order for your child to be successful in school. The formal definition of special education in the United States Code is "a specially designed instruction, at no cost to the parent, to meet the unique needs of a handicapped child." Developing an Individualized Education Program for your child is a multifaceted process. The first step is to convene an IEP meeting of parents and school personnel to develop and write a specific educational plan (IEP) tailored to your child's needs.

PURPOSES OF AN INDIVIDUALIZED EDUCATION PROGRAM

There are several purposes for holding these meetings and writing a plan. The major purpose is for parents to be part of the decision-making team; another is to give parents the right to critique both the content of the plan and the services and types of delivery (placement) used to execute it.

The IEP document itself serves many functions. It is a monitoring and evaluation instrument that can be used to measure your child's progress in clearly stated objective terms. The IEP is, in fact, a written contract defining areas of concentration that the educational professionals will be working on with your child.

Specifically, the IEP process:

- mandates the establishment of a communication network between you as a parent and all significant team players involved in the education of your child.

- establishes a vehicle where parents and other team members can resolve their differences of opinion regarding the plan of action developed for the disabled child. It recognizes your child's needs, the services to be provided to meet those needs, and the anticipated outcomes.

- establishes in writing the resources that are necessary for your child to receive, such as needed special education and related services.

- is used as a management tool to guarantee that the special education program is designed specifically for your child to meet his/her individual learning needs.

- is used as a compliance and monitoring document to make sure that your child is getting the services you and the school have agreed are needed.

- measures your child's progress. (NICHCY, 1981)

If, after holding an IEP meeting, no agreement is reached, parents have access to a set of procedures that they may initiate if they are not satisfied with the response and actions of the agencies responsible for meeting their child's needs.

WHEN DOES THE IEP MEETING TAKE PLACE

The initial IEP meeting is held after the multidisciplinary team has had the opportunity to conduct an assessment of your child's abilities and needs. In some locales the results of that assessment may be discussed with you prior to the IEP meeting in an "eligibility meeting," but this is not always the case. The local educational agency calls an IEP meeting to discuss evaluation and placement. By law, this meeting must be scheduled no later than thirty days from the date of testing. Writing the actual IEP document officially begins at this point, for this is when the team begins to determine what intervention services and strategies are needed to help your child in school.

WHO SHOULD BE PRESENT

The law (IDEA) stipulates who is to participate in meetings (Section 300.344). Participants include (1) a designated official of the public agency qualified and authorized to provide or supervise special education; (2) your child's teacher; (3) a parent or both parents; (4) individuals requested to attend, either by the parents or the public agency; (5) the child, where appropriate; and in the case of the initial IEP (6) a member of the evaluation team, or one who is familiar with the evaluation procedures used with the child and with the results of that evaluation.

It is noted that the teacher should be one who has an educational background and experience in the area of your child's needs and suspected disability.

Terms of Notification

It is very clearly stated that the meeting must be scheduled at a mutually convenient time for all parties. Written notice of the purpose, time, and place of the meeting, including those who will be present, must be sent to parents. If you are unable to attend, the public agency must make every attempt to use other methods to get your input, preferably through verbal communication (e.g., an individual telephone call or conference call). In some cases parents are not willing to attend. The school district may decide to hold the meeting without the parents in attendance; if the meeting does proceed this way, the school district must keep accurate documentation of its attempts to have parents attend the IEP meeting (including detailed records of visits to the home, parents' place of employment, and telephone calls with narratives of the parents' responses). Figure 8.1 shows a typical notification letter along with a response form.

AGENDA FOR IEP MEETINGS

The following is a synopsis of the topics to be discussed at the IEP meeting. The decisions made on these items will be written into the IEP document.

1. To determine if your child is eligible to receive special education (review of assessment) by consensus of the multidisciplinary team.
2. To discuss the child's present levels of educational performance, which may include identification of a handicapping condition.
3. Individualized Education Program Planning, including:
   a. Development of annual goals, including short-term instructional objectives.
   b. Determination of the specific special education and related services to be provided to help meet those goals and the extent to which your child will participate in regular educational programs.
   c. When these services will begin and duration of these services.
4. Determination of placement.
5. Determination of the types of evaluation techniques (appropriate objective criteria) to be employed on an annual basis to review and measure whether the short-term instructional objectives are being achieved.

Figure 8.1
Notification Letter

HOMETOWN PUBLIC SCHOOLS
Address

Date

Dear: (Name of Parents and/or Legal Guardian)

Please be advised that a Planning and Placement Team (PPT) meeting will be convened on behalf of your child _____. The meeting is scheduled as follows for this date/time/location:

Day, Date, Time, Place
    The purpose of this meeting is to:

      ____   Review preplacement evaluation results and determine eligibility for special education placement

      ____   Develop, review and/or revise the Individualized Education Plan

      ____   Other, (Please specify)

      ____   Develop, review and/or revise transition services for students 15 or over

    The following individuals have been invited to attend (important individuals providing services to the child): Principal, Special Education Teacher, Nurse, Psychologist, Physical Therapist, Speech Therapist, Caseworker Board of Education Services for the Blind.

    This notice should reach you at least 5 days prior to the PPT date. Please make every effort to attend this meeting. You may bring anyone of your choosing to this meeting. The meeting can be rescheduled at a mutually agreed upon time and place. Our records indicate that you were given a copy of "Procedure Safeguards for Parents of Children in Special Education." (If it is an initial PPT meeting a copy will be attached). If you would like another copy or further explanation of your due rights please contact our office at (phone number).

                                                      Supervisor of Special Education

----

TEAR OFF AND RETURN THIS PORTION OF THE LETTER
IN THE ENCLOSED SELF-ADDRESSED ENVELOPE

    I will be able to attend the Planning and Placement Team meeting scheduled for this time and date Day, Date, Time, Place.

Student's Name   *School*   *Parent's Signature*

    I *will not* be able to attend the Planning and Placement Team meeting scheduled for this time and date. Day, Date, Time, Place.
    If you wish to meet on a more convenient date, please call my office at (Phone No.) between 8:00 A.M.–4:00 P.M., Monday–Friday, to arrange for another meeting date.

Student's Name   *School*   *Parent's Signature*

Source: Adapted from Danbury Public Schools, Department of Special Education.

This agenda is very lengthy, and all items might not be covered in one sitting. You as parents can request an adjournment at any time during the proceedings if you feel strongly that you need time to absorb information that has been presented. Or you may want to discuss some items privately with your spouse, or want to confer with other professionals. These are all legitimate reasons for adjourning a Planning and Placement Team (PPT) meeting for a few days. (In some states the meeting is called an IEP meeting.) Your local educational agency may find this inconvenient, but you do have this right within reason.

And, most important, placement may not be determined (decided with certainty) until all other issues are discussed and an IEP document is written. However, the law does stipulate that a temporary placement may be made with an interim IEP document written for the purpose of determining the proper placement for the child. In the interim IEP, a time limit on this placement should be specified so as to complete an evaluation of placement options. Parents must agree to this step.

NOW DOWN TO THE NITTY-GRITTY: A PARENT'S FIRST EXPOSURE TO THE IEP MEETING

What to Expect at the Initial IEP Meeting

To prepare you for your first formal meeting, let's go over some simple details of the meeting. First, you will be seated around a large conference room table with many people that you may not know. Then, the chair of the meeting, usually the district representative for special education or the principal, will introduce the attendees. Minutes of the meeting will be taken. The use of tape recorders at IEP meetings is not specified in the statutes. Therefore, parents or the agency may have the option to use one. If the public agency does use a tape recorder, the conversations recorded are considered educational records and must be treated like any other document in the educational file of your child. It is also likely that you will receive a copy of due process information or procedural safeguards for parents, describing your rights during this process. At the conclusion of the meetings, a copy of the IEP documents is to be in your possession.

It is a good idea to ask for a blank copy of the IEP document in advance; this will give you an idea of what information is recorded. Figure 8.2 is a copy of a typical IEP document. The actual form will vary slightly from district to district, but the information contained on the form must be complete. A discussion of the individual sections of the IEP document follows.

Figure 8.2
IEP Document

DANBURY PUBLIC SCHOOLS DANBURY, CONNECTICUT 06810-6211   PPT 5.1

PLANNING AND PLACEMENT TEAM MEETING AND INDIVIDUALIZED EDUCATION PROGRAM

Date: _____

1. IDENTIFICATION INFORMATION:

Student _____   Last IDE _____ Next IDE _____

Birthdate _____ Age _____   S.S.# _____ Race _____ Sex M F

Telephone _____   Student's Dom. Lang. _____

Address _____   Parent's Dom. Lang. _____

City _____ Zip _____   School _____ Grade _____

Parent/Guardian _____   Home School _____

Surrogate _____   Address _____

2. TYPE OF PPT: ____ Initial ____ Review ____ Triennial   3. DUE PROCESS EXPLAINED BY:

____ Diagnostic Placement ____ Central   _____

4. PPT MEMBERSHIP:

_____ Administrator   _____ Pupil Service

_____ Sp. Ed. Teacher   _____ Sp. Ed. Supr.

_____ Classroom Teacher   _____ Parent/Guardian

_____ Recorder   _____ Student

5. STUDENT EDUCATIONALLY DISABLED: ____ YES ____ NO   6. EDUCATIONAL DISABILITY:

_____

7. SPECIAL EDUCATION INSTRUCTIONAL SERVICES:

A. Primary Service

Area	Goal No.	Direct Hrs/Wk	Staff Responsible	Start Date	End Date	Next Rev.Date

B. Related Services

Area	Goal No.	Direct Hrs/Wk	Staff Responsible	Start Date	End Date	Next Rev.Date

C. Triennial Evaluation Design

Area	Assessment	Staff Responsible

D. OTHER RECOMMENDATIONS:

Copies: White/Cumulative Record Folder, Yellow/Parent, Pink/Supervisor of Special Education

127

Eligibility

In some jurisdictions, eligibility is determined at the IEP meeting. In other locations this is done at a separate meeting. If eligibility for special education programming is on the agenda, the results of the assessment will be discussed (see Chapter 5). At this point parents can bring to the table for discussion the results of any testing that has been done at their request (e.g., by outside consultants). A discussion by all members of the team regarding your child's needs will ensue. They will discuss what your child can do and what he needs help in. At this point, you have the opportunity to express your opinions on the types of activities your child will need to increase his ability to succeed in school, and what extra assistance is needed. Let the other team members sit up and take notice to your ideas and suggestions. If there is a consensus that a child is eligible, a discussion on his present levels of educational functioning (e.g., oral expression, reading, listening comprehension, fine motor) will take place.

Present Levels of Educational Performance

This part of the meeting is crucial in the process. At the outset it is important for you to know what is meant by "present levels of educational performance." What is included in this section should "accurately describe the effect of the child's handicap on the child's performance in any area of education that is affected, including: (1) academic areas (reading, math, communication, etc), and (2) nonacademic areas (daily life activities, mobility, etc.)" (NICHCY, 1981, p. 11). You are setting the stage for what extra help is needed to foster the educational progress of your child. Also note that the identification of a handicapping condition cannot be used as a sole basis for determining this performance.

Writing Goals and Objectives: Building Blocks for Future Educational Achievement

The evaluation team and the special education teacher will make suggestions on the areas that need to be worked on. Typically, several goals will be written in each development area: cognitive, social/emotional, motor skills, adaptive behavior/self-help, communication skills. There is no set number of goals and objectives on an IEP. The number is determined at the discretion of the team. Most of the goals will be based on the results of the assessment. But as a parent you may want to include a goal that you feel your child needs to attain. Communicating your opinions is very important in this step. It lays the groundwork for future meetings. Figure 8.3 shows goals and objectives for Adam.

Figure 8.3
Sample Goals and Objectives On an IEP

Student's Name: *Adam Cantor*
Annual Goal: To increase vocational/academic skills
(Written by Special Education Teacher)

Short Term Objective	Materials &/Or Methods	Evaluation Procedure	Target Date	Review of Each Objective
Be able to sort common household objects i.e. cups, bowls, plates, spoons, forks and knives.	Concrete objects Daily routine 3 objects	One time daily during 2 week period	6/95	__ Exceeded on __ __ Met on __ __ Did not meet criteria Comments
Adam will choose activity during free play time given 2/3 choices	Picture or object Class routine (Mayer Johnson Pictures)	1 time daily during 2 week period	6/95	__ Exceeded on __ __ Met on __ __ Did not meet criteria Comments
Sequence daily routine activities using pictures/symbols	Daily routine 5 activities (Mayer Johnson Pictures)	Sequence all 5 activities daily during 2 week period	6/95	__ Exceeded on __ __ Met on __ __ Did not meet criteria Comments

Note: Sample of new goal. A number of short term objectives may be written for each goal.

Figure 8.3 (continued)

Annual Goal: Improve independence throughout ADL skills demonstrating improved bilateral upper extremity muscle strength and range of motion (Goal written by Occupational Therapist)

Short Term Objective	Materials &/Or Methods	Evaluation Procedure	Target Date	Review of Each Objective
Adam will open a variety of fasteners (snaps, large buttons, zippers)	Adult facilitation Hand Over Hand Assistance Verbal cues Buttons & zippers— pull up & down	1 time per day over 5 consecutive days	6/95	__ Exceeded on __ __ Met on __ __ Did not meet criteria Comments
Adam will continue to engage in functional acts with active use of both upper extremities. (encouraging right to aim/point)	Verbal cues Therapeutic acts/exercise ADL Classroom acts	O.T./teacher observations 4/5 attempts	6/95	__ Exceeded on __ __ Met on __ __ Did not meet criteria Comments

Annual Goal: To improve functional communication skills
(Written by Speech Therapist)

Short Term Objective	Materials &/Or Methods	Evaluation Procedure	Target Date	Review of Each Objective
Select 1 item of 2/3 which does not belong to a given group or category.	Pictures/Symbols Teacher made/selected computer programs	50% in 10 trials	6/95	__ Exceeded on __ __ Met on __ __ Did not meet criteria __ Comments
Select/point to picture/objects found in a house which depicts its name or function	Same as above and daily routine	50% in 10 trials	6/95	__ Exceeded on __ __ Met on __ __ Did not meet criteria Comments

Figure 8.3 (continued)

Select/point to picture/objects found in school which depicts its name or function	Same as above and daily routine	6/95	__ Exceeded on __ __ Met on __ __ Did not meet criteria __ Comments

Indicate "STOP" by pointing to symbol or by holding up hand to communicate desire for an activity to cease	Teacher
	  facilitation
	Fading
	  to verbal prompt
	Daily routine
	Classroom
	  activities
		2 X day
		2 of 5 days
		
		6/95
			__ Exceeded on __
			
			__ Met on __
			
			__ Did not meet criteria
			
			Comments

Annual Goal: Improve use of his right hand to interact with objects.
(Goal written by musical therapist who sees Adam 50 minutes per week.
Funded through Board of Education Services for the Blind)

Short Term Objective	Materials &/Or Methods	Evaluation Procedure	Target Date	Review of Each Objective
Adam will actively participate in the music by using his right hand in fine/and or gross motor skills to interact with the musical instruments.	Strum the guitar Hold instruments	Level to progressively exceed the current baseline of 20 second duration and needing verbal prompts 19% of the time, physical prompts 31%, and refusing participation 50% of the time.	6/94	__ Exceeded on __ X Met on __ __ Did not meet criteria __ Comments Of note is the level of self-directed participation (21%) this year which was not present at all last year; with no prompting whatsoever, he is now using his right hand in an activity.

(Sample of goal—being reviewed. All goals can be developed that interrelate to one another. Note carryover of skills in goals and short term objectives written by members of the staff.)

Figure 8.3 (continued)

Annual Goal: Engage in Communication.
(Goal written by musical therapist)

Short Term Objective	Materials &/Or Methods	Evaluation Procedure	Target Date	Review of Each Objective
Actively participate in the music by communicating via nonverbal methods.	Introducing signs during first song of each session through physical prompting.	Observation of gestural language, pointing to a level that progressively exceeds the current baseline.	6/94	___ Exceeded on ___ _X_ Met on ___ ___ Did not meet criteria Comments Adam's sign vocabulary as known to this therapist consists of the following words: mom, dad, Julie, David, music, music lady, eat, drink, piano, guitar, yes, no, stop, finish, go, home, play, want, love. He typically needs physical prompting to sign the latter four. Adam further communicates during the music sessions by choosing from two offered instruments by pointing to the preferred one. Of note is Adam's increasingly appropriate use of signing "stop". At least once per session he exercises this control. Recommend continuing to address this goal, further increasing his signed vocabulary and applying his current vocab in appropriate situation.

How Are the Goals Achieved?

During your initial series of meetings the types of supports needed to reach the goals listed on your child's IEP will be determined. For example, a speech therapist may be identified as a resource. Your child may need one hour daily of direct instruction provided by a speech therapist for a year. Usually the duration of services correlates with the implementation of the IEP document to the date of review which is usually one year hence. However, this can be changed if the IEP team reconvenes at the request of the school system or the parent. Also under discussion is the level of service your child needs. For instance, does your child need services for part of the day with a specialist other than his regular education teacher; or does his teacher need extra help planning specific curriculum adjustments to individualize the program to meet his needs?

School districts are now responsible for supplying assistive technology devices, or services, or both, to children eligible for special education programming. These devices are defined as any item, piece of equipment, or product system that is used to increase, maintain, or improve the functional capabilities of individuals with disabilities. Assistive technology services are any services that directly help an individual with a disability to select, acquire, or use an assistive technology device (e.g., training and technical assistance to the users and their families as well as professionals, employers, or others working with children with disabilities; purchasing or leasing the device; designing, customizing, adapting, and repairing the device).

According to the IDEA:

> When the IEP of a student is being developed, reviewed or revised, the school district must assess, if appropriate, the student's need for an assistive technology device or service, determine those devices or services that will facilitate the student's special education (particularly those that will facilitate his or her education in the regular educational environment), list them in the IEP, and then provide them to the student. (NICHCY, 1993, pp. 6–7)

Placement Considerations

Numerous issues need to be discussed with regard to placement. Placement for a child with a disability is defined as "how the services the student needs can be provided in the way that preserves, to the maximum extent appropriate for the student, the student's ability to attend school and be educated with his or her non disabled peers" (Margolis, 1992, p. 1). Views on the types of educational environment best suited for children with disabilities will be up for debate. The IEP document must include a statement about "the extent to which the child will be able to participate in regular educational programs" (NICHCY, 1981, p. 14). Placement alternatives must be discussed based on the criteria set earlier. Parents should be given a list of possible sites. You do not have to agree immediately to the site proposed by the other members. It is reasonable to request an opportunity to visit any site so that you can visualize how your child would function in a given setting. Or you can request a trial placement. Once the team comes to a consensus on placement, it is noted on the IEP document. With this decision in place, arrangements will be made for your child to attend the program identified. Transportation issues must be resolved at this juncture, and the implementation of the placement is almost immediate (except when the program is not in operation at the time of the decision, such as during the summer or a school vacation).

How to Monitor Your Child's Progress

Goals and objectives are written into the IEP document not only as a starting point in the teaching process, but also as a way to monitor your child's progress. Next to the list of goals and objectives is a description of the mechanisms used to measure their attainment. This gives the team a point of reference to help measure whether the program is fitting the needs of the child. Discuss the types of evaluations that will be included in your child's IEP. For example, how will the teacher know if your child has achieved an objective? At the IEP meeting, a written statement will describe how each goal and objective will be measured. It may be a specific test or an observation made under certain conditions. Is this a realistic and proven testing tool? Have them explain to you the criteria for mastery. This section is important because it will allow you to judge whether the elements of the program are designed to meet your child's needs.

PREPARING FOR THE MEETING

This can be a stressful time for your family. The thought of facing a group of strangers at a formal meeting does foster anxiety. And even more stress-producing is the fact that you realize that decisions will be made at this roundtable that will have a major impact on your child's life as well as your own. Some parents may feel threatened by the sheer numbers of people present. They may feel, "it's us against them." This is not the case. Most special education professionals want parental input on decisions, and do not want to be your adversary. Be advised that community-based advocacy organizations will, if you request, provide a parent advocate to assist you at these meetings.

Decide on Your Participatory Style

You need to prepare for the meeting psychologically and emotionally. We know this is very difficult, but you need to put to rest feelings of inadequacy and intimidation, and become composed, confident, and optimistic. Recognize that the members of the team are working together in the best interests of your child. Even though there may be a high price tag on special education, early intervention is popular, a growing trend, and the law. Educators see the value of identifying youngsters in need earlier so that they can correct problems or more successfully guide their learning experiences. Most of the time, educators value the opinions of parents, especially if you have information that will help them devise a program that will address more appropriately the needs of your child. Thus, it would be foolish not to speak up. And if and when you do speak up, provide the team with constructive information. The team members are always interested in knowing how your child acts, reacts, and demonstrates skills in various situations at home. If they ask, then you have a golden opportunity to tell them what you want them to know (e.g., needs that you want to be addressed) in order to set up the program that you feel is most suited for your child. For we know that if a program is going to be successful, carryover at home and in the community must occur. Parents have to feel comfortable with the plan that is devised.

You need to decide what approach you will take with the team. Are you going to put all issues and concerns out in the open at the beginning of the meeting, or will you just react to what the other team members say? It is very important that you listen carefully to the points made by the team. Don't feel embarrassed to ask questions. If unfamiliar jargon is used, interrupt politely and ask for an explanation. You do not have to raise your voice to get your points across. Always ask them to discuss alternatives. We suggest that the best approach to take as a parent is to listen to the points that the group is offering, and make suggestions on how you see your child. Discuss your child's strengths and needs openly and frankly, and the advantages and disadvantages of each proposal. Do not be afraid to suggest alternatives or provide information on successful programs or services in different areas of your district or state.

Get to Know the Members of the Team

Try to alleviate as much stress as possible before the meeting takes place. If you can, call the special education supervisor or principal ahead of time, and ask to be introduced to the members of the team. Even if it's a brief phone call, you have broken the ice. This may relieve some of the tension at the beginning of the meeting.

Come Prepared to Participate Actively in the Meeting

Bring records with you. Record keeping and organizing all the reports you have collected over the years describing your child may not be one of your favorite activities. There are usually piles of paper on your kitchen counter or in a desk drawer. Having accessible records is important, therefore it is wise to set up a filing system that enables you to retrieve a specific report at a moment's notice. The simplest method is to keep your materials in a loose-leaf notebook. You may decide to purchase a filing cabinet or accordion folder. Bring these records with you so that you can participate in the conversation and discuss the information with the other members of the team.

Read critical reports over again leisurely. You cannot always remember every detail in a report. Before the meeting, preferably several days before, read over the reports or other documentation in your possession. It is a good idea to highlight (using colorful markers) important points in the report, including important recommendations. Do not expect to receive advance copies of the latest reports to be used at the PPT meeting from teachers or therapists. More than likely these reports are either being typed (most of the time they are handwritten), reviewed, or completed relatively close to the date of the meeting. We suggest that you call at least ten days prior to the meeting and request that you be sent a copy at least a few days before the meeting. Also, request IEP progress evaluations done by teachers before the meeting.

Be able to describe your child's strengths and needs. After you have reviewed your records, go through your diary or log of activities (described in Chapter 2) and draw a picture of your child's strengths and weaknesses. You may want to write down an example of how each strength and weakness is demonstrated, what your child will do, and what you would like to see improved (see Figure 8.4). This chart should include your child's functional levels in areas such as academic abilities, language skills, social interaction, and communication skills. Be able to talk about specific incidents in these areas. This will make your child seem more real. Also, discuss your child's best learning style. This is based on (1) how your child reacts to his environment; (2) his emotional response to specific situations; (3) how he relates to himself and others; and (4) how his physical limitations may interfere with his learning (see Figure 8.5).

List goals you would like to see incorporated into the IEP document. As you think about your child's strengths and needs, try to answer the

Figure 8.4
Descriptive Summary of a Child's Strengths and Weaknesses

Learning	Present Levels Can Do	Needs to Learn	Strengths
Gross Motor (Large Muscle)			
Fine Motor (Small muscle)			
Perceptual Skills Visual Auditor Motor			
Receptive Language (Understanding)			
Expressive Language (Speaking, Gestures, Sign)			
Social/Emotional (Self-Concept, relationships, peer interaction group vs. alone)			
Cognitive (Thinking skills)			
Adaptive (Learn from the environment, learn from experience)			

Figure 8.5
Diagnosing Learning Style

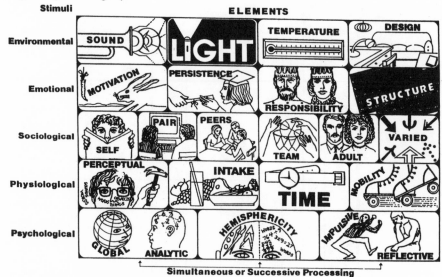

Source: Designed by Dr. Rita Dunn and Dr. Kenneth Dunn. Reprinted with permission of Dr. Rita Dunn, 1995.

following questions regarding the goals you would like to see incorporated in your child's IEP.

1. Is your child likely to use the skill in his/her immediate environment?

2. Is it functional, and a useful skill?

3. Is your child able to use the skill often?

4. Has your child demonstrated an interest in learning this skill?

5. Is success in teaching this skill likely?

6. Is the skill a prerequisite for learning more complex skills?

7. Is your child likely to be more independent as a result of learning this skill?

8. Does the skill allow your child to qualify for improved or additional services in a less restrictive environment?

9. Is it important to modify this behavior because it is dangerous to self or others? (*Directive Teacher*, Summer/Fall 1981, p. 37)

Write out a few goals. They don't have to be comprehensive. You might want to just write down areas you would like to see worked on.

Get the scoop on what's happening in your district regarding special education. Try to get the lowdown on the programs being offered, the personalities in the program, and the sensitive issues in the school district. There are a variety of ways to obtain this information. Tap the resources of the school system first. Obtain the official public relations pamphlets on special education from your district. Know what is available in your district. Many large school districts fund a parent resource center, where you can talk to other parents and parent educators whose job it is to advocate for parents. Information is available on your legal rights during the IEP process. Obtain a copy before the meeting, and read it.

Next, read your local newspaper. Articles describing issues on the front burner, including special education programs, appear often. Stories may be written about model programs, high-profile programs, and innovative techniques used in the district. The style section or local section may have run human interest stories on children and adults with disabilities in the past year. This will give you background on what's happening in your community.

Identify the players and participants in the program. Ask for the names of the teachers being considered. Talk to them, or to other parents who may be familiar with their teaching style and temperament. Think about whether these personality characteristics would be compatible with your child's learning style. Identification of the teacher is required as part of the placement procedure (sometimes teachers relocate or are reassigned, but for the most part the school district will have a good idea as to possible staffing). This should not be the sole determining factor of your placement decision, but must be considered. Another important person to talk to is the school principal. Her leadership style and beliefs about special education may influence your decision.

Visit possible placement sites. One of your primary objectives is to seek out a positive environment for learning. Visit the site(s) that are under consideration. What vibes do you get when you enter the front door? How are you treated? Observe the children in the building. Are they happy? The appearance of the building may give you clues. It does not have to be new, but it should reflect the pride and team spirit of its occupants. You may want to visit classrooms. This may occur during the IEP meeting process.

Note classroom attributes and deficiencies. Note the physical environment, including accessibility, location of the classroom, and instructional areas. Observe the methods and materials used to teach. Are there many manipulatives in the classroom that will be beneficial in your child's learning? Does the teacher stress academics over functional skills that may be of little use to your child? What types of socialization techniques are used? How do these children interact with regular education students?

Know Your Rights Under the Law

We have discussed the purpose of the IEP as well as procedures for parent involvement in the process, including what information must be relayed to parents in the notification process. We have noted who should participate in the IEP process and the items that need to be identified in an IEP program. Next we will consider the results of the IEP process. Namely, do parents have to sign the document? What if they disagree with parts of the program? What recourse do they have? We also discuss how to document your objections.

Parental consent. There are very specific times in the IEP process when your written consent is required before the school district can proceed. Written parental consent is needed before (1) an initial evaluation is conducted; (2) placement in a special education program for the first time; (3) placement in a nonpublic setting; and (4) outplacement. In the evaluation phase, we discussed how school systems may initiate due process procedures if you do not agree to an evaluation. This includes obtaining a court order based on state guidelines or following the due process procedures outlined in IDEA. An option for parents is to withhold consent through silence. Parents have a right to appeal due process hearing results even if they were not the party to initiate the process.

Many parents believe that they should wait until summer or the beginning of the school year to request that their child be considered for special education services. This is not necessary. Youngsters enter special education all year round. Thus, your PPT/IEP meeting does not have to be scheduled in September.

Documenting your concerns. There are no restrictions on how long an IEP/PPT meeting must take. If you are unhappy with some of the suggestions or would like additional services put on the IEP document, you can withhold consent until you obtain all the information you need. If a second meeting is requested, bring along a friend or advocate who can back you up and support your opinions. A member of the PPT will have the responsibility of taking minutes of the meeting. Make sure your opinions and suggestions are part of the record. You may want to read the minutes before you leave the meeting. Usually, the chair of the meeting will summarize the major areas of discussion, including type of placement and related services, and future actions to be taken by members of the team (e.g., collecting information on a piece of equipment; possible community-based activities). If a signature is requested, you will want to go over the paperwork carefully.

If you have some concerns you may sign the IEP document but include clearly written dates for reconvening the team to review your child's schooling (e.g., no later than October 31; or within 60 days). You may want to meet on a more informal basis with your child's teacher or with the related services specialist, to discuss your concerns and the child's progress, before you reconvene the entire team.

Other options. If this does not suit your needs, you can request mediation (if your state provides this option) or a due process hearing (see Chapter 10). Another option is to file a complaint with your state department of education, alleging that the state or agency violated a requirement of the IDEA. There is a sixty-day time limit for the state to resolve the complaint (see Chapter 10 for more information).

If the school district refuses your request for placement based on the results of testing, you may request an independent evaluation. The results of the independent evaluation must be considered by the school district when making any decisions about the educational program of your child. This action on your part may persuade the school district to provide special education services to your child.

POINTS TO REMEMBER

There will be occasions at PPT/IEP meetings where parties will disagree. The most important point for you to remember is to keep the dialogue going. When you offer a suggestion, be prepared to back up your request with relevant data. List your concerns succinctly, with conviction. Try to be flexible, and listen to what the other members of the team are saying. Put yourself in their position, and try to envision the obstacles they may face in providing a program that you may feel is necessary. You may be able to give them suggestions on how they might resolve the situation, since you know your child best. And if you are unhappy, let them know why. Call the chair, or talk to your child's teacher about your concerns. Provide them with feedback on your reactions to the meeting. For example, you may describe the most uncomfortable aspect of the meeting (e.g., The team does not listen to what I say. I believe they decided before the meeting what the placement or goals would be).

We have included two questionnaires to rate the IEP process. Use Figure 8.6 to rate your level of satisfaction with the IEP meeting, and Figure 8.7 to rate your level of satisfaction with your child's IEP. After completing these questionnaires, look them over, analyze your answers, and decide which procedures you would like changed or modified to have a better understanding of, and a more productive role in, the IEP process.

Figure 8.6
IEP Meeting Questionnaire

PPT/IEP MEETING	Strongly Agree	Agree		Disagree	Strongly Disagree
I believe that my rights were clearly explained to me at the beginning of the meeting.	5	4	3	2	1
All the people attending the PPT meeting were properly introduced to me.	5	4	3	2	1
I felt that all the school professionals at the meeting were needed to help plan for my child.	5	4	3	2	1
I wished some other school official attended the meeting.	5	4	3	2	1
I believe I was properly advised about my child's special needs.	5	4	3	2	1
I received enough information about my child's abilities, needs, and program.	5	4	3	2	1
I received legible copies of all reports IEPs, etc. that I would like to have for my records.	5	4	3	2	1
I felt like my questions were answered.	5	4	3	2	1
I believe my opinions were listened to.	5	4	3	2	1
I felt I was treated as a partner in the planning for my child's education.	5	4	3	2	1

	5	4	3	2	1
I believe we reviewed to my satisfaction various educational options to meet my child's needs.	5	4	3	2	1
I believe we had enough time at the meeting to plan my child's program.	5	4	3	2	1
I know who to contact in the school system if I would like another meeting.	5	4	3	2	1
If I would have liked to meet with school personnel prior to the PPT meeting to talk about my child, I knew whom to call.	5	4	3	2	1

Source: Special Education Parent Advisory Council. 1991. *Parent Survey.* Danbury, CT: Danbury Public Schools.

Figure 8.7
IEP Questionnaire

IEPs	Strongly Agree	Agree		Disagree	Strongly Disagree
I believe I helped in developing my child's IEP.	5	4	3	2	1
There was the correct number of IEP goals and objectives to address my child's needs.	5	4	3	2	1
The IEP goals and objectives were clear and meaningful.	5	4	3	2	1
I understand how the goals and objectives will be evaluated.	5	4	3	2	1
I believe the goals and objectives were clearly explained to me.	5	4	3	2	1
I know who in the school to call or visit if I have a question about my child's IEP.	5	4	3	2	1
I believe the IEP clearly described who in the school was going to be responsible for delivering my child's teaching program and related services.	5	4	3	2	1
I believe the IEP goals and objectives are realistic.	5	4	3	2	1
I understand what methods will be utilized to accomplish my child's IEP goals and objectives.	5	4	3	2	1

Source: Special Education Parent Advisory Council. 1991. *Parent Survey.* Danbury, CT Danbury Public Schools.

Working Through the Chain of Command in a Typical School System

A TYPICAL SCHOOL SYSTEM'S ORGANIZATIONAL STRUCTURE

To advocate effectively for your child, you will need to understand your school system's organization. This chapter is intended to give you some basic information about a typical school system, and more important, information on how to find out who is who within your own particular school district. Typically, a school district is organized as follows. A chief school administrator (called a superintendent of schools or a district principal) is the one individual to whom all other employees (teachers, supervisors, psychologists, etc.) in the system report. This chief school administrator is appointed by the district board of education (your elected officials). Reporting to the chief school administrator are deputy superintendents or assistant district principals for each of the major divisions (e.g., elementary schools, secondary or high schools, and pupil personnel services). Special education services are usually administered as part of pupil personnel services. Figure 9.1 is an organization chart for the Montgomery County Public Schools (MCPS), a rather large suburban school system in the Washington, D.C. area. Note that special education falls within the Office of the Associate Superintendent for Special and Alternative Education.

The MCPS Department of Special Education and Related Services has supervisors responsible for each area of service (e.g., speech and language, auditory, physical disabilities). These supervisors will work with the Central Placement Unit and Diagnostic and Professional Support Team personnel to bring together the services within the district (or outside of the district) to best meet the needs of an individual student. As

Figure 9.1
Organization Chart of a Typical Large Suburban Public School District

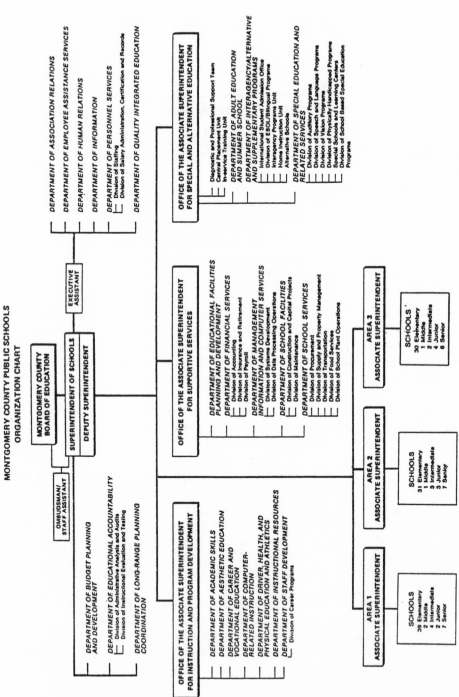

MONTGOMERY COUNTY PUBLIC SCHOOLS
ORGANIZATION CHART

MONTGOMERY COUNTY BOARD OF EDUCATION

SUPERINTENDENT OF SCHOOLS
DEPUTY SUPERINTENDENT

OMBUDSMAN/STAFF ASSISTANT

EXECUTIVE ASSISTANT

DEPARTMENT OF ASSOCIATION RELATIONS
DEPARTMENT OF EMPLOYEE ASSISTANCE SERVICES
DEPARTMENT OF HUMAN RELATIONS
DEPARTMENT OF INFORMATION
DEPARTMENT OF PERSONNEL SERVICES
  Division of Staffing
  Division of Salary Administration, Certification and Records
DEPARTMENT OF QUALITY INTEGRATED EDUCATION

OFFICE OF THE ASSOCIATE SUPERINTENDENT FOR SPECIAL AND ALTERNATIVE EDUCATION
  Diagnostic and Professional Support Team
  Central Placement Unit
  In-service Training Unit
DEPARTMENT OF ADULT EDUCATION AND SUMMER SCHOOL
DEPARTMENT OF INTERAGENCY/ALTERNATIVE AND SUPPLEMENTARY PROGRAMS
  International Student Admission Office
  Division of ESOL/Bilingual Programs
  Interagency Programs Unit
  Home Instruction Unit
  Alternative Schools
DEPARTMENT OF SPECIAL EDUCATION AND RELATED SERVICES
  Division of Auditory Programs
  Division of Speech and Language Programs
  Division of Vision Programs
  Division of Physically Handicapped Programs
  Special Schools and Learning Centers
  Division of School Based Special Education Programs

OFFICE OF THE ASSOCIATE SUPERINTENDENT FOR SUPPORTIVE SERVICES
DEPARTMENT OF EDUCATIONAL FACILITIES PLANNING AND DEVELOPMENT
DEPARTMENT OF FINANCIAL SERVICES
  Division of Accounting
  Division of Insurance and Retirement
  Division of Payroll
DEPARTMENT OF MANAGEMENT INFORMATION AND COMPUTER SERVICES
  Division of Systems Development
  Division of Data Processing Operations
DEPARTMENT OF SCHOOL FACILITIES
  Division of Construction and Capital Projects
  Division of Maintenance
DEPARTMENT OF SCHOOL SERVICES
  Division of Procurement
  Division of Supply and Property Management
  Division of Transportation
  Division of Food Services
  Division of School Plant Operations

OFFICE OF THE ASSOCIATE SUPERINTENDENT FOR INSTRUCTION AND PROGRAM DEVELOPMENT
DEPARTMENT OF ACADEMIC SKILLS
DEPARTMENT OF AESTHETIC EDUCATION
DEPARTMENT OF CAREER AND VOCATIONAL EDUCATION
DEPARTMENT OF COMPUTER-RELATED INSTRUCTION
DEPARTMENT OF DRIVER, HEALTH, AND PHYSICAL EDUCATION AND ATHLETICS
DEPARTMENT OF INSTRUCTIONAL RESOURCES
DEPARTMENT OF STAFF DEVELOPMENT
  Division of Career Programs

DEPARTMENT OF BUDGET PLANNING AND DEVELOPMENT
DEPARTMENT OF EDUCATIONAL ACCOUNTABILITY
  Division of Administrative Analysis and Audits
  Division of Instructional Evaluation and Testing
DEPARTMENT OF LONG-RANGE PLANNING COORDINATION

AREA 1 ASSOCIATE SUPERINTENDENT
SCHOOLS
  39 Elementary
  2 Middle
  4 Intermediate
  2 Junior
  7 Senior

AREA 2 ASSOCIATE SUPERINTENDENT
SCHOOLS
  31 Elementary
  1 Middle
  3 Intermediate
  3 Junior
  7 Senior

AREA 3 ASSOCIATE SUPERINTENDENT
SCHOOLS
  30 Elementary
  1 Middle
  2 Intermediate
  4 Junior
  6 Senior

a parent, you should become familiar with the people within such departments and units in your district; this will make it easier to get the information and services you need.

Depending on the size of the school district and the school-age population of the community it serves, the division handling special education will include supervisors with specific responsibilities for either age categories of special needs children, or specific kinds of special needs (e.g., emotional disabilities, physical disabilities, visually impaired). In some small districts, one supervisor will be responsible for all facets of special education administration. Smaller school systems (e.g., Danbury Public Schools, Connecticut) center the administrative services initially at the child's local school. The principal becomes the central point of contact for the acquisition of services. As Figure 9.2 shows, the Danbury Public Schools have one assistant superintendent responsible for administering special education programs throughout the district on all grade levels, with a director of pupil personnel services reporting to the assistant superintendent responsible for supervision of psychologists, therapists and counselors, nurses, and related services personnel. Special education supervisors report to the assistant superintendent. They are assigned to different grade levels (elementary, middle school, and high school). Each supervisor works with the principal to secure delivery of the special services. Also note that a supervisor may have more than one job; serving, for example, as an assistant principal of a building. During the five years we have lived in Danbury, the administrative organizational chart has changed twice. Due to fiscal and other factors, the assistant superintendent for special education and pupil personnel services was downgraded to a director's position. Eventually, the assistant superintendent for elementary education took on the extra responsibility of administering the special education programs for the district. Similar changes can occur in any district. It is important for parents to know who is in charge, both on paper and in reality.

Negotiating the School System Bureaucracy

It is often to your benefit to speak with other parents receiving services within a particular school system to educate yourself on how the system tends to operate. Groups such as Parent to Parent, can put you into contact with appropriate parents to glean this information. Sometimes, if you feel somewhat intimidated by large bureaucracies, the services of a parent advocate can be your best approach in dealing with the school district. Advocacy organizations can be located by calling your local Parent Training and Information Center.

Figure 9.2
Organization Chart of a Typical Small City Public School District

DANBURY PUBLIC SCHOOLS
ORGANIZATION CHART

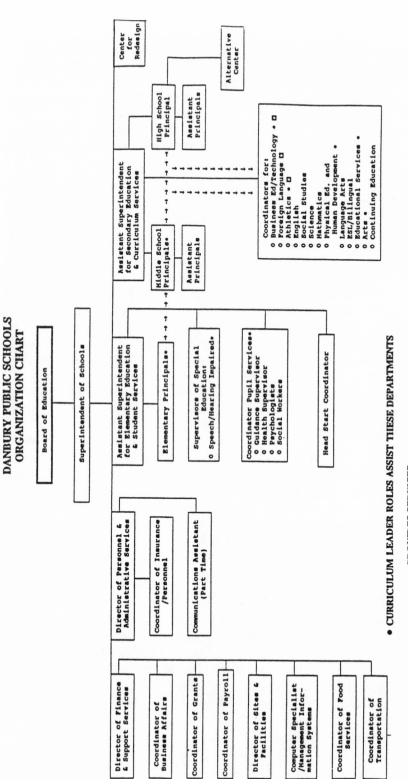

● CURRICULUM LEADER ROLES ASSIST THESE DEPARTMENTS

→ → → → → → PROVIDES SERVICES

☐ EVALUATED BY HIGH SCHOOL PRINCIPAL

THE SCHOOL'S ROLES AND RESPONSIBILITIES

At the school building level, your first point of contact will be the teachers—both the primary classroom teacher and other school-based professionals who will become the daily contacts for your child.

Role of the Teacher

The classroom teacher is a central focal point for your daily communication. But in addition to this role, the teacher must be an effective manager of all the other personnel that provide services to your child. The teacher must be aggressive in approaching this role, for he or she is the one who spends the most time with your child and is the link between your child and other professionals. The teacher will set the tone for facilitating cooperation among staff, establishing a clear communication system that will enable everyone to know what others are doing, and will receive information from others about progress or difficulties encountered.

Some teachers may be hesitant to bring up a matter that may evoke an emotional response in a parent. A teacher's comfort zone on when to approach parents varies according to his or her experience, education, and past communication with you in particular and with all parents in general. Thus, you have to let your child's teacher know when you want to be alerted to a potential problem.

Working with others. Teaching can be most effective when it is approached holistically. What is worked on in a therapy session should be transferable to your child's daily classroom activities. The teacher must build upon the therapist's work. For instance, if a speech therapist devises a communication sign for a nonverbal child, then the classroom teacher must use that sign during daily activities as reinforcement. In self-contained classrooms, the teacher is involved directly or indirectly in all facets of the child's program, from daily instruction to the delivery of therapies. A good working relationship between the teacher and therapists will promote team teaching and team building. Each member of the team will contribute expertise, thus building a stronger and more effective program for your child.

Fostering effective communication to nourish a positive relationship. A means of daily communication now becomes necessary. In our case, since Adam does not communicate verbally, we have developed a system whereby we write daily messages in a special notebook which travels with Adam. His teachers write messages back to us in the same manner. Adam's behavior can be adversely affected when he is not feeling well or has participated in numerous activities in one day. We always try to alert his teacher to this fact so that she can be aware of his mood

Figure 9.3
Today's Notes of Interest in Room Four

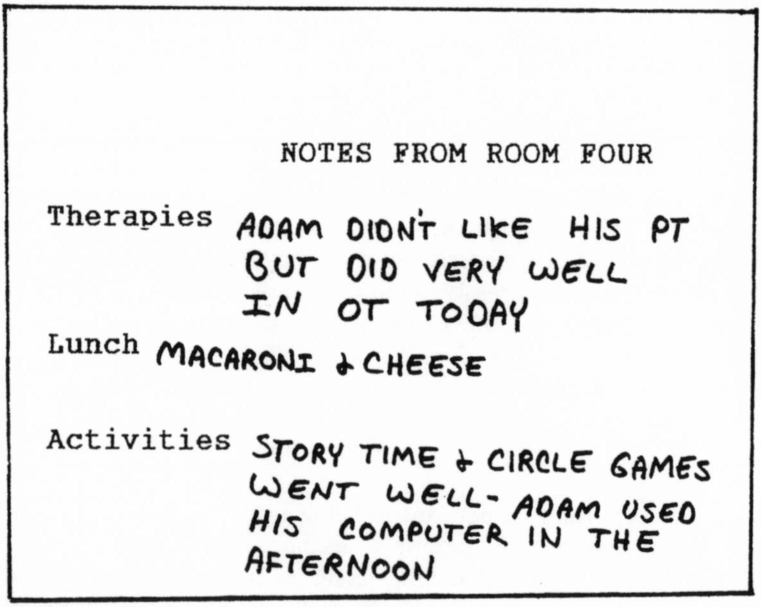

```
                    NOTES  FROM  ROOM  FOUR

    Therapies  ADAM DIDN'T LIKE  HIS  PT
               BUT  DID  VERY  WELL
               IN  OT  TODAY
    Lunch  MACARONI & CHEESE


    Activities  STORY TIME & CIRCLE GAMES
                WENT WELL- ADAM USED
                HIS  COMPUTER IN  THE
                AFTERNOON
```

and his willingness to participate in strenuous activities. A conference was even held to decide on strategies to employ during the school day if this occurred. Through written communication with our child's teacher, we identified areas of concern that needed to be discussed in greater detail in person. Thus the notebook served as a means of communication, improving the instruction delivered to our child. The notebook also serves a secondary purpose, as a permanent record of the services he receives on a specific day or week.

When Adam was younger, his teacher would send home a weekly newsletter (usually one page) describing the activities for the week. In another school, "Today's Notes of Interest in Room Four" (Figure 9.3) was sent home daily describing his activities, including therapies, with space for a short description of his responses and behavior. A standard form was used so that the teacher and other professionals could budget their time appropriately. However, when looking over these forms recently, we noticed that school personnel did not date them. Make sure that they do include dates, so that you have a log of what was going on, and when. This may be invaluable as you look back over the past year's instruction. It is a useful tool when you get ready for the IEP annual review. Expect the school to have copies in its files. It is a way to document instructional time spent in the classroom.

It is a good idea to let the teacher know how your child is doing at home (e.g., Adam is singing his favorite school songs at home; we went to the library, and Adam borrowed the same book that was read out loud to the class). This sends a powerful message. It tells the teacher that (1) your child is able to generalize what he has learned in school, (2) you are providing opportunities at home that reinforce the teacher's efforts in school, and (3) everyone is excited about learning.

Here are additional suggestions for establishing a productive rapport with your classroom teacher:

1. Develop workable procedures to visit the classroom during the school day. It is usually best to let the teacher know ahead of time that you want to visit. Some classrooms are equipped with observation rooms with a one-way mirror. In this way you are not a guest in the classroom, which might evoke behavior different from the norm. If your child knows you are there, he may try to impress you or gain your attention. This is okay at times, but other times you want to monitor your child's activities. You want to be able to observe during a typical day. If you want to talk to your child's teacher or specialist briefly, you might drive your child to school and talk to the teacher before the official day begins, or pick your child up at the end of the day.

Learn your child's daily schedule. This is usually posted either on the blackboard or on a bulletin board. Pick an appropriate time when the children's attention does not need to be directed solely at the teacher. You may decide to bring in a treat during snack time that is related to a holiday or a theme emphasized in the classroom, such as the fall harvest, changes in seasons, or Thanksgiving. You may bring in a family treasure to describe during circle time, or explain what your job is (e.g., nurse, firefighter) during a unit on community helpers. Your child is proud to see you come to see him in his class, and his teacher will appreciate the time you have taken to contribute to the class.

When in your child's class, always compliment the teacher on either an activity you thought was appropriate or creative, or on the festive appearance of the classroom. Say something that will let the teacher know that you appreciate her or his efforts. If your child learns a new skill, commend the teacher for his or her efforts. If you see improvement, why not share the good news with your teacher's supervisor? Or if an innovative curriculum is used in the class, why not publicize it in the local newspaper or through the school's PTO newsletter? This brings positive feedback to the teacher and to the kids in the class.

2. Volunteer to provide classroom assistance for routine days as well as outings. It is very important that you and your child's teacher get to know each other. When you are in the classroom as a volunteer, you become acquainted in an informal and nonpressured way. You can find out how the other person "ticks," and you learn each other's priorities and personality traits (e.g., whether you or the teacher is humorous,

gregarious, reserved, or shy). It will give you time to explore whether you agree or disagree on general issues, such as inclusion. Each of you will learn why you feel the way you do. Maybe this will be the time you begin to understand the obstacles your child's teacher faces every day. You might even change your opinion on certain issues based on these experiences. It will also give you time to express your ideas.

Sometimes volunteering in your child's class may be too disruptive. On occasion, children will focus their attention completely on the parent. If this happens, it is wise to volunteer in some other capacity, perhaps in the library; thus you are in the building, but not always on the heels of your child's class. You can still get an overall impression of what is going on. Children have often come up to me and asked if I am Adam's mom. They can't wait to tell me about their job in Adam's class. You can get a general sense of how things are going without disrupting your child's schooling. Most of all, you don't want your child's teacher to get the impression that you are a pest, or questioning every move.

Another way to foster a good working relationship with your child's teacher is to be in charge of hospitality. In this way you are not only helping the teacher but also getting to know the other parents in your child's class.

3. Establish a process to dialogue when differences of opinion arise, short of taking formal action. During your child's schooling there will be times when you will disagree with an aspect of the curriculum, such as how the subject matter is taught. Or you may disagree with the teacher's assessment of your child's progress. No matter what differences of opinion you may have, it is important to dialogue with the teacher in a constructive manner. The following suggestions are offered to help you through a tough situation.

In any sort of conflict resolution, you want to discuss the situation with the person most closely linked to the problem. In this case, you have invested a lot of time in a partnership with your child's teacher. Ideally, the partnership has been built on honesty, confidentiality, a spirit of cooperation, an interest in achieving the same goal—allowing your child to develop into an independent, happy individual—and an ability to communicate each other's ideas in a nonthreatening atmosphere. Thus, you are hoping that a difference of opinion can be resolved without intimidation, hostility, and an "us versus them" mentality. With this in mind, your first step is to inform the teacher of the problem and set up a meeting. You may write a short note to the teacher saying that you have concerns regarding a given subject and would like to discuss it. Or you may write a long explanation of the problem with backup documentation, which you feel is accurate and fair. This depends on your comfort level and how you feel your child's teacher will react to your concerns.

Set up a mutually convenient time, when both of you are not under pressure to be somewhere else in a half hour. Before you meet with the teacher, be sure you have your facts straight. If you have observed your child at home doing a certain task that was not seen as part of his activity during school, bring documentation with you. You may also wish to videotape your child at home.

Review your child's IEP before meeting with the teacher. It is unwise to talk about it with other teachers before you have discussed it with your child's teacher. During the meeting, give the teacher time to respond to your questions, as well as an opportunity to check on possible answers if the information needed is not at hand. It is a good idea to start off the meeting by saying, "I would like some clarification as to why . . ."

Teachers will always ask parents, "How does your child act at home when this situation occurs?" or "Have you seen your child_____?" You may want to discuss your concerns generally and then make a list of what you will do at home (e.g., collect data or keep a daily log). In this way you are working constructively with the teacher to find a way to solve the problem. This will enable you and the teacher to compare notes when you meet again. Take notes at the meeting and when you get home, so that you have a permanent record of the meeting. Before the end of each meeting you need to summarize what has been said and what each of you will do, and set up a time when you can meet again. Don't let it be open-ended. In this way you know your efforts will be productive. Take charge of the meeting by planning a course of action that is reasonable to all parties. As the process continues, you may want to inform the supervisor of the steps you have taken to work cooperatively. The supervisor may have knowledge of how other teachers worked out similar problems. Let her or him get involved on a positive note. Supervisors are there to provide support to both the teacher and the parent.

It is important that you take responsibility for finding some possible solutions to the problem. However, it is not your job to come up with a solution alone. You may suggest that your child's teacher approach other special education teachers or resources within the school system who might have information to proactively work out a solution that is acceptable to everyone.

Don't forget that you should ask your child how she feels about the situation. Get her feedback, and also watch how she behaves. Do you see signs that something is not right? Is she cooperative, or agitated, or unhappy? Has there been a dramatic change in her personality or behavior? It is important to communicate with your child's teacher, but you also must communicate with your child.

4. Develop language in the IEP that serves as a mechanism for deter-

mining successes in your child's cognitive and physical growth and development. The partnership that has developed between child, teacher, and parent will get stronger over time if positive steps have been taken. How do we know if a child has made positive gains in schooling over time? You may think it is through the results of individualized tests, but it's not—it is through the IEP. Therefore, the way the IEP is written is crucial in determining whether or not your child has made progress in his schooling. This includes the types of short-term objectives recorded on the IEP document, but even more important is how these objectives are presented. When the annual review takes place, the team leader will read the IEP verbatim to the entire group. The criteria used to measure how successful your child has been in achieving these goals are crucial. Success is measured by how well goals written at the previous meeting were achieved according to the criteria established on the document.

Everyone wants to see progress because it makes them feel good, and it also validates the existing program. It also gives a sense of security to teachers and other staff. Parents need to know that in order for a child to continue to receive a certain level of special education services, there must be measurable evidence of progress. Levels of service may be taken away if, in the opinion of the special education administration, these efforts have been futile. Therefore, you want to ensure that the IEP is written so that the goals included in the document are attainable. And if not, you need to investigate extensively whether the language used in measuring the criteria was inappropriate. Remember that even if you feel subjectively that your child has met the goals, this will not count for much on the formal IEP document.

All partners need to have their self-esteem enhanced to enable them to proceed to the next task. If we have experienced success, we will take risks to reach a higher goal. Thus, the IEP needs to be written in clear, measurable terms.

Roles of Related Services and Support Staff

Related services (e.g., speech therapy, physical therapy, psychological services, transportation) are provided because the IEP team has decided that they are needed to help your child meet the goals set in the IEP. After the initial IEP document is approved by parents, those who provide the services will be actively engaged in your child's schooling. At the IEP meeting, the levels of service your child will receive will be determined. For instance, a speech therapist may consult with your child's teacher only once a month, or may provide one-on-one instructional time with your youngster. However, regardless of the quantity of time or level of service provided, certain basic roles and responsibilities should be shared by all.

As mentioned above, clear and open communication among all team members needs to be in place. Related service personnel must be able to work together with the classroom teacher. A mutually agreeable approach must be taken. Is physical therapy conducted during circle time, or can the therapist follow the class to the gym and provide services there? A report must be written annually and attached to the annual review. These service providers are also responsible for developing ways to communicate with you throughout the year, either by written quarterly reports, monthly meetings, or telephone calls. We have found that team members are overworked and loaded with paperwork. Most therapists serve multiple buildings in a school system and are always on the run, which makes it increasingly difficult to talk to them on a regular basis. On many occasions we have received messages from physical therapists and occupational therapists through Adam's classroom teacher alerting us to a medical problem that needs attention. For example, if Adam has a red mark on his foot, the physical therapist may suggest that his braces need to be adjusted. On occasion we have spoken to therapists on the phone, or have seen each other in the classroom if we were able to be in the classroom during their scheduled time. This is an area where we would like to see improvement. Ideally, it is best to schedule an appointment in advance at a mutually convenient time. It is much easier to set up a conference with a related specialist housed in the same building.

These professionals are required to participate in determining when and where the services are to be delivered. This is usually not written into the IEP, except for the length of the session and how often it will be given. Who decides when it will be offered during the day? Related services personnel may travel to more than one school, resulting in a rigid time schedule. Do they then decide time and place? Here is where the classroom teacher steps in, discusses options, and helps everyone come to an agreement. But what if you as a parent feel that therapy given at the end of the day will not be beneficial, or that therapy time is in direct conflict with an academic subject time slot? We suggest that you set up a conference and talk to all parties concerned. Sometimes calling a meeting will motivate those concerned to find a solution. Questions may arise as to where the instruction is to be given. To alleviate this potential problem, you may stipulate this on your IEP (e.g., whether it will be in the classroom or in the resource room). In this way, the service is promptly initiated.

Role of the Principal

The principal should optimally be involved in the day-to-day supervision of classroom activities. In our experience, this has been inconsistent. In Danbury, special education services are delivered in the local school building. The principal is busy supervising the entire school program, which includes one or two special education classrooms on the average. The principal probably does not have a background in special education. At our son's preschool (a segregated center-based program serving only youngsters with multiple disabilities) the principal was totally involved in the program and made the final decision on every policy and procedure in the school. Hence, the level of direct supervision will reflect what the principal is comfortable doing. When we learn what the strengths of the individual principal are, we act accordingly. If the principal is not comfortable with close supervision of the special education classroom, then as parents we stay even closer to the day-to-day activities of our child's teacher. Where direct intervention is indicated, we make it our business to speak with the principal and express our opinions and needs.

DISTRICT LEVEL PERSONNEL

Role of the Special Education Supervisor

Generally speaking, at the district level, the special education supervisor should be monitoring the activities in the school building, including those in the classrooms, on a regular basis. This person gives teachers the additional resources and support necessary to guarantee that children learn successfully. However, we have found that the special education supervisor spends most of his/her work time doing paperwork connected with the IEP process, not giving hands-on assistance to teachers. If you feel that lack of supervision time is limiting your child's success, you need to meet with the special education supervisor to determine what adjustments are required. It becomes too easy for parents to take on the extra burden of supporting the teacher in the supervisor's absence. For instance, we felt that our child could learn more effectively if he had access to a computer. Not only did we have to suggest that an evaluation be done to determine if the computer would be appropriate, but we also did most of the legwork researching what hardware and software were appropriate. Once we initiated this course, the supervisor thought it was a good idea. However, if we had waited for suggestions from the supervisor and/or teacher, and not taken the initiative, Adam might not have had the computer to this day. We feel that this is an unacceptable situation, and you should feel the same way if you encounter similar experiences in your child's schooling.

OTHER CENTRAL ADMINISTRATION ISSUES

Every school district in the country has a public document specifying its educational mission and goals. In addition to this document, a plan is developed that explains how the specific instructional programs' goals will be achieved. Within this document, special education goals should be listed. Every year, a report is filed with the state department of education that describes how these goals have been met. A listing of activities, achievements, programs, and budget expenditures is included. It is important that parents read these documents and hold the school district accountable for reaching the goals it sets. Every year the general public is invited to comment on these documents. You can make suggestions on how goals can be modified to more accurately reflect the needs of special education students.

"They Thought You'd Never Ask": Put It in Writing

All school districts have as one of their goals increasing parental involvement in the educational process, either by moving toward school-based management, or fostering parent focus groups, PTOs, or mentoring programs. Take them up on their suggestions. Use every opportunity to monitor what the school administration is doing to reach its stated goals. If you want your ideas known about a district policy, write a letter to the superintendent. Take the case of a couple in Illinois who wanted to express their expectations on the placement of their daughter in a neighborhood school. They wrote a letter to their school superintendent requesting information on the district's School Improvement Plan. They wanted to know if any information or presentations were made to the school board on inclusion. They asked for specific dates, times, and materials used. They also asked how many in-service programs were offered to teachers and school administration. And they even asked about plans for future in-service training. Asking the right questions forces the administration to review what they have done to provide children with an appropriate education in the least restrictive environment. By being very specific, you prompt the district or board of education to take a look at their policies. You may even want to read your letter and their response out loud during a district function.

Often school districts are resistant to change because it usually costs money. We can always find reasons not to try something new. But in order to ready our children for society we need to be open-minded, willing to try new things and to take chances. Sometimes these risks can be minimized if we can show that innovative programs have been tried in other states with great success. As parents we need to relay this to the administration.

MONITOR SPECIAL EDUCATION FUNDS

Local educational agencies (LEAs) obtain funding for special education through the state department of education. When the school system identifies a child as in need of special educational services, the school district notifies the state of their need for assistance in providing a free and appropriate public education for the child. Thus, at budget time, specific budget lines are built for special education services (e.g., instructional lines, therapist lines, equipment lines). Dollar figures are then allocated to these lines based on projected needs per student to receive such services. Monies are then requested from the state to offset these projected needs. Why do we tell you this? Because your child needs specific services, and perhaps attends a class with six or fewer students in it, do not think that this places an undue burden on your local school system. In our son's case, we have received funding for a full-time instructional aide for his class, in addition to computer equipment and training for the classroom teacher in the use of the equipment; all this benefits the whole class. This funding for staff and equipment comes to our school system for our child. Our town budget does not suffer because of our child's needs.

How to Monitor Funding

When the school district receives funding from other sources it is held accountable for delivering appropriate services to its children. Know how your school system's budget is constructed. Learn to ask appropriate questions of the school officials charged with delivery of services. Also, make your questions and feelings known to the board of education members. Sometimes these folks do not understand how funding is obtained from external sources such as the state and federal government. Your questions will prompt the board members to ask appropriate questions.

How to Read a Budget

Figure 9.4 shows a portion of the Danbury Public Schools budget for special education services. Various line items are included for instructional staff and support staff. If a school system is unable to deliver a service for which line items appear in the budget, ask why.

Figure 9.4
Special Education Budget
Special Education/Pupil Services

Special Education	F.T.E.	Cost
Coordinators	3.5	$ 255,173
PPT Coordinator	.5	37,192
Teachers	77.4	3,957,444
Speech Pathologist	8.7	458,768
Physical/Occupational Therapist	1.8	70,088
Paraprofessionals	39.5	461,219
Clerical	2.71	72,975
Interpreter/Tutors	5.5	142,077
Extended Year—Salaries		61,850
Vocational Training—Salaries		50,085
Benefits		1,300,597
Legal Fees		12,000
Tutors—Special Ed		99,000
Homebound Instruction		62,000
Transportation		940,772
Professional Services (Visual, Psychological, Medical, Physical/Occupational Therapy)		81,587
Children's Insurance		750
Printing & Binding		2,500
Tuition		978,000
Special Class Supplies		28,790
Instructional Supplies		3,205
Textbooks		8,610
Clinical Testing		9,161
Education of Handicapped—Local		
	139.61	$ 9,254,678

Figure 9.4 (continued)

Pupil Services	F.T.E.	Cost
Coordinator	.9	$ 67,701
Coordinator of Guidance	.5	37,191
Guidance Counselors	16.0	959,018
Psychologists	10.0	536,723
Social Workers	9.7	464,865
Crisis Intervention	2.0	115,731
Clerical	2.0	64,914
Nurses	19.0	567,908
19.0 Public		
4.0 N/A Non-Public (Funded)		
.5 N/A Public (Funded)		
Substitute Nurses		10,000
Benefits		559,887
DSABC		10,000
Professional Services (Medical Advisor)		8,313
Rentals—Guidance		1,715
Transportation—Other (Guidance & Career Ed)		1,175
Postage		1,615
Printing & Binding (Guidance)		2,000
Guidance Supplies		6,544
Health Supplies		10,815
Achievement Tests		18,440
	60.1	$ 3,444,555
GRAND TOTAL—Special Education/Pupil Services		$12,699,233

Role of the Board of Education

Parents of children with special needs often overlook the role elected school board members play in the education of their children. These people are accountable for policy decisions and often administrative decisions made by the school district's professionals. Your board of education is a publicly elected policy body, and is *not part of the school administration*. The school administration works for the board of education. Your board is accountable to you! We advise you to become familiar with your local school board members. In fact, inasmuch as you will benefit directly from good policy decisions on special education services, get involved early in who gets elected to the school board. Prior to election time, become familiar with each board member's voting record on these issues. Turn out during campaign time and focus your questions on issues that will help get the right people elected. And then attend board of education meetings and lobby for the kinds of services and policies that will positively affect your child. Among these are:

- inclusion of children with disabilities in the mainstream populations whenever and wherever possible;
- applications for extramural funding to supplement existing special education funding;
- maintenance of professional levels of service adequate for special needs populations in the district (this includes classroom supervision of special education which supports the instructional process).

Also, invite board members to visit your school during a function in which your child participates. Board members want to hear from parents and want to see the schools in action. Take them up on it. They need to see what goes on in the classrooms and in class buildings. After all, you are their constituents.

Parents' Roles

To enhance your effectiveness as partners on the IEP team, it is important for you to become effective listeners and develop excellent communications skills. When communicating with school personnel, parents need to project a sense of (1) self-confidence, (2) personal competence, and (3) determination (Appoloni, 1984).

Most parents do not realize that how you say something may be just as important, or even more important, than what you say. The words you use and the nonverbal messages you send—through eye contact, posture, facial expressions, timing, and voice tone—all contribute to transmitting the intended message effectively. The listener decides whether or not you are serious about pursuing your ideas and opinions based on the messages he or she receives. These impressions will eventually play a role in the decision-making process.

As a partner on the IEP team, you advocate for what you think is in the best interest of your child. To attain your goals, you need to:

- build and maintain good relationships with those who are working directly with your child;
- communicate a sense of teamwork;
- be positive (e.g., smile and be friendly; leave any feelings of resentment or defensiveness at home);
- know agency personnel, school board members, the school psychologist, legislators;
- know your rights before you request services; and
- be prepared to describe essential aspects about your child in clear terms.

In other words, you need to be assertive when the occasion arises. Being assertive is no easy task, but it can be very effective in obtaining the appropriate education your child deserves.

Points of Contact for Parents When Concerns and Issues Arise

At this point, you should have a general idea who to approach when a problem or concern arises. Always start with the teacher, especially if it affects your child directly. If you are not satisfied with the outcome of your efforts, move on to the principal. He/she is responsible for the day-to-day activities in the classroom, including teacher supervision. If issues arise regarding transportation, health, and safety in the school building, contact the principal. If your concerns relate to the delivery of services, the special education supervisor is the one to contact. You may reconvene the IEP team at any time to discuss issues. Write a letter to the person in central administration responsible for special education requesting a meeting. Always use certified mail. This leaves a paper trail for future reference. Explain the reasons for your request. If issues are not resolved within a reasonable amount of time, you can invoke your right to due process. Several steps need to be taken before formal due process is initiated (see Chapter 10).

Let's look at one example of how a problem is identified and how a parent can take an active role in resolving it.

Scenario: Your child goes to the resource room two hours a day. When he comes back to the regular class, he feels lost, disorganized, and unhappy. The regular teacher feels that she cannot spend enough individual instructional time with your child for him to function satisfactorily in the class.

To resolve this issue you may arrange a meeting with the parties involved. This can be accomplished by phone or through the daily communication book.

Step 1. Talk to each teacher separately and then discuss the issue together at a mutually convenient time. You may decide that there needs to be more planning time when both teachers can get together to communicate and distribute information on what is going on in each situation. Parents can describe the effect that this is having on their child at home. The principal may be called to discuss a change in scheduling that would make it easier for a child to move from one class to the next.

Step 1 is an informal meeting. We suggest that after the meeting you write a summary that includes the purposes of the meeting, key concerns raised, the changes that have been proposed, and what actions will be taken. Request that this letter be included in your child's file. Also, include a date for a follow-up meeting with a proposed agenda. Send the letter to the principal and to other meeting participants, as well as to the special education administrator. Figure 9.5 is a sample of what you might want to include in the summary.

Take notes during the meeting. "Notetaking signifies to others that you are an active participant in what is occurring. When you are taking notes people around you are more likely to feel accountable. They become more productive and responsible and pay more attention to you" (Apollini, 1984, p. 3). Figure 9.6 gives suggestions on note-taking.

If this meeting does not resolve the issue on the table, you may call for an IEP meeting to discuss it in further detail (Step 2). Figure 9.7 is a sample letter requesting a meeting to review the IEP.

Step 2. During the PPT you may request that an aide be assigned to help your child on a part-time basis in the regular class. The team may be more receptive to this idea after you have tried to work the problem out at the teacher level. You may need to include goals for your child to better deal with transitioning from one class to another. Possibly the school psychologist needs to be consulted. These changes are instituted. A follow-up meeting is scheduled in six months to review changes.

Note that as the six months draw to a close, you will have collected information on your child's progress in school (e.g., conversations with your child, teacher, and therapists; observations both in school and at

Figure 9.5
Sample Letter Summarizing What Was Accomplished at a Meeting

Today's Date (include month, day, year)

Your Full Return Address

Name of Principal
Full Address

Dear (Name of Principal),

     I am writing this letter to inform you of the meeting I/We attended with (name of teacher and/or specialists) to discuss my/our son/daughter (name of child) program. The specific purpose of the meeting was to...(list purposes in a simple sentence). During our discussion, key concerns were raised by (participants). These were: (list).

     Under consideration were the following suggestions: (list). At the end of the meeting, the group decided to (list). We agreed to meet again on (date, time, and place) to discuss the effectiveness of these changes on our child's program.

     I (we) want to thank your staff for meeting with me(us) to discuss our concerns.

Sincerely yours,

Your Full Name

cc: Teacher/Participants
    Special Education Administratior

home). We suggest that before the PPT meeting you write a letter to either the principal or the special education administrator summarizing your concerns. If you decide that a change of placement is needed, include this fact in your letter (see Figure 9.8). PPT meetings can take many hours. By setting an agenda ahead of time the participants will be better prepared to discuss the issues.

Step 3a. A PPT meeting is held six months later to review the adjustments in the program. A discussion will center around the progress your child has been making in school. Your child is making good progress, and the team decides to continue with the current program, monitor the situation, and meet again in three months.

Step 3b. A PPT meeting is held six months after changes have been in effect. As you review the program, you feel that your child has not made any measurable gains. You request a change in the program. You feel that your child should stay in his regular class and that more time should be spent on developing a parallel program. The goals

Figure 9.6
Note-Taking Tips

1. Date, time, place, attendees with titles. State purpose of the meeting.

2. Group information into categories.
  a. information about assessment
  b. information about curriculum
  c. information about placement

3. Use an outline format.
4. Write key words and abbreviations.
5. Leave space in left hand margin for comments and questions made by participants.
6. Use a highlighter to underline important terms and phrases.
7. Write questions and list responses made by each participant.
8. Review notes and summarize them verbally to other participants.

Source: Apollini, T. (1984).

need to be changed to reflect what he can possibly achieve. The school suggests placing your child in a self-contained classroom for the full day. You object.

Before proceeding to Step 4, parents must analyze the situation carefully. Were all the members of the team present at the meetings held at Steps 2 and 3? Would the outcome be different if these absentees attended the meeting? Was the request for a change in the IEP in the realm of possibility? Were many issues on the table at one meeting, preventing a serious discussion on the most important issue? Did you refuse any compromise offered by the team (NICHCY, 1984)?

Step 4. Write a letter to the special education administrator requesting an administrative review. The special education administrator will review the case by reading the cumulative file and interviewing the teachers and the principal.

A written response is received:
4a. A recommendation is made to hire a consultant to observe your child and make suggestions on an alternative placement. You agree to this proposal. The consultant will interview parents to obtain their opinions and observations.

4b. The review confirms the team's decision that your child's most appropriate placement is in the self-contained classroom.

Figure 9.7
Sample Letter Requesting a Meeting to Review the Individualized Education Program

Today's Date (include month, day, year)

Your Full Return Address

Name of Principal
Full Address

Dear (name of Principal),

      I am writing to request an IEP review meeting. I would like to discuss making some possible changes in (child's name, grade level and teacher) IEP as I feel that .....

      I would also like to have (name of specialists) attend. I think his/her ideas about the changes we may make will be valuable.

      I (or my husband/wife and I) can arrange to meet with you on (days) between (give a range of time, such as between 8:00–10:00). Please let me know what time would be best for you.

      I look forward to hearing from you soon. My daytime telephone number is (000) 000-0000. Thank you for your time.

Sincerely yours,

Your full name

Source: Ferguson and Ripley (1991).

Step 5. You disagree with the findings and seek help and direction from an advocacy organization or from other parents.

(Note: Steps 4 and 5 are discussed in detail in Chapter 10.)

At this point you are not sure what course you should take. There may be more than one appropriate program for your child. The school district may not agree with your choice. They would rather have your child in a placement that is less threatening to others in the school building (both teachers and parents of other children). If you are the first parent to request an innovative placement, you may meet with more resistance. At this point, you will probably need to call on advocates to help you get ready to present your arguments to whatever forum you decide is most appropriate (mediation, due process hearing).

Before you file a formal request for a due process hearing, discuss the situation with others who have had experience in due process matters. A variety of resources are available, including advocacy organizations, officials of the state department of education, parent training information centers, and other parents. Try to find parents through your PTO, or through parent to parent organizations.

Figure 9.8
Sample Letter Requesting a Change in Placement

Today's Date (include month, day, year)

Your Full Return Address

Name of Principal
Full Address

Dear (name of Principal),

I am writing to request a meeting to discuss a change in class placement for (full name of your child). He/she is currently in (grade/school/name of teacher). I feel he/she would do better in (name of alternative placement).

I am most concerned about... (Keep this paragraph brief and mention your child's needs, not problems with people).

I would also like to have (name of teacher(s) and/or any specialists you would like) attend.

I (or my husband/wife and I) can arrange to meet with you on (days) between (give a range of time). Please let me know what time would be best for you.

I look forward to hearing from you soon. My daytime telephone number is (000) 000-0000. Thank you for your time.

Sincerely yours,

Your full name

Source: Ferguson and Ripley (1991).

HOW TO MOBILIZE PARENTS OF SPECIAL NEEDS CHILDREN TO ADVOCATE FOR OUR CHILDREN

You cannot do all of these lobbying activities alone. You need to mobilize other parents with like concerns. Take it from us, this is not an easy job. Too many special needs parents are embarrassed, frightened, or intimidated, or don't think their child's disability is serious enough to warrant involvement in a parent group. Working parents may not feel they have the time for involvement in a group. They tend not to want to rock the boat when it comes to advocating for their children. And many certainly will not confront a board of education at a public meeting to speak to issues facing their children. Hence, you need to organize these parents to construct a united front for such purposes.

Some methods proven to be reasonably successful include:

- Special grants for special projects (e.g., parent empowerment grants from the Connecticut State Department of Education, whereby parents are given seed money to help them organize programs or special events to help their children successfully transition from school to work). Activities have included swimming lessons for children; adult education classes; children participating in town parades (Memorial Day parades) by making their own floats and marching.
- Outings or activities sponsored by community groups such as Special Olympics and family coalition organizations. Many organizations will sponsor recreational activities, including Little League or Challenger Leagues for baseball and T-ball; Rotary or Lions Clubs may sponsor field trips to sporting events.
- Parent-sponsored school programs (e.g., parenting classes with topics of interest to parents with special needs, i.e., children transportation, after-school activities, respite care; recreational opportunities; fun activities including carnivals, bingo night, pizza night, international festivals, concerts).

Organize special needs parents as contacts at their children's schools for incoming special needs families. Another avenue to get parents together is to invite a well-known speaker who is dynamic and charismatic, and who has a story to tell that other parents can relate to. You probably can locate such a person in your area, either through a national organization that has local chapters throughout the country, such as ARC or C.H.A.D.D. [Children and Adults with Attention Deficit Disorder]. You may spread the word of an annual meeting of a national organization that is coming to your town. These meetings are announced well in advance. Even your local university or hospital may sponsor a workshop or seminar where parents can be part of the audience. We have also known parents to be inspiring to a group of parents who have just learned that their child has a disability. These are ways to start a parent network.

POINTS TO REMEMBER

Parents have many opportunities to participate in formulating and monitoring their child's schooling. Figure 9.9 is designed to help you assess your satisfaction with the implementation of your child's program. If, after completing the questionnaire, you discover that you are in disagreement with many of the items, it may be necessary for you to begin to question the effectiveness of your child's program. Prioritize the items that are most disturbing to you and communicate your concerns to the appropriate staff member.

Figure 9.9
Program Implementation Questionnaire

PROGRAM IMPLEMENTATION	Strongly Agree	Agree	Disagree	Strongly Disagree
I believe that my child has access to all appropriate school programs and activities.	5	4	3	2	1
I believe there is good cooperation between regular and special education so that my child is/will be successfully integrated into regular education opportunities.	5	4	3	2	1
I feel school staff is positive about special education.	5	4	3	2	1
I know who is responsible for each part of my child's program.	5	4	3	2	1
I believe the school provides me with enough information about my child's progress.	5	4	3	2	1
I know how my child's program is being evaluated.	5	4	3	2	1
I am satisfied with my child's program.	5	4	3	2	1
I feel my child's program is being implemented.	5	4	3	2	1
If I want to change my child's program I know who in the school to call.	5	4	3	2	1
I believe my child is appropriately placed.	5	4	3	2	1

Source: Special Education Parent Advisory Council. 1991. *Parent Survey*. Danbury Public Schools.

There are many professionals who in one way or another have an impact on your child's schooling. It is important for you to take the initiative and schedule an appointment to meet not only with your child's teacher, but also with the superintendent of schools. This contact should occur on a routine basis. We suggest that you extend your communications network by attending systemwide functions where you can chat with those in decision-making roles. This may seem like an unfair request, but it is well worth the few hours of inconvenience (e.g., finding a babysitter) in order to establish your child's existence in a positive light. Active involvement in your child's schooling demonstrates to the educational community at the local and central level that you support their efforts and are willing to participate on a cooperative basis. We need to stress to all those who will listen that as parents of special needs children we have dreams for our kids, just like any other parent, and we will do all we can to make those dreams come true.

10

Due Process

Sometimes, despite your best efforts to work with a school system, things do not go as you believe they should. You and your child should be receiving certain services, interventions, or programs, and you are not. Or the school system prescribes certain programs and then cannot deliver. Well, you are now in a position to begin due process.

In accordance with the Individuals with Disabilities Education Act (IDEA), if as parents you believe that your child's substantive rights to a free and appropriate public education (FAPE) have been violated, you may request an impartial due process hearing. To get a general picture of the time frame and series of events in the hearing process, see Figure 10.1, which outlines a typical due process procedure.

Due process is the appropriate course of action when the school system's representatives and you as parents cannot agree on (1) the specific handicapping condition or degree to which your child is affected; (2) the need for an evaluation; or (3) your child's placement in a special service or program. As parents, you must be informed of your rights, including the due process procedures, when a disagreement regarding identification, evaluation, or placement occurs that cannot be resolved.

Due process hearings may begin at the local level or go directly to the state department of education. This is determined by state statute. In Maryland, the first level of due process hearings is held at the local level. The hearing officer, as an impartial third party, cannot have any personal or professional ties with the local educational agency. He/she is paid by the local school district, however.

Figure 10.1
Due Process Guidelines

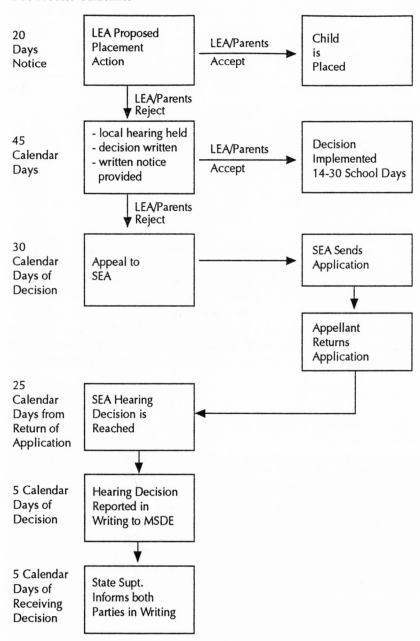

Source: *Project TEAM: Training in Educational Advocacy and Monitoring Manual.* N.D.
Rockville, MD: Association for Retarded Citizens, Montgomery County.

IF YOU DISAGREE WITH THE DECISION MADE BY THE HEARING OFFICER

If you disagree with the hearing officer's decision at the local level, you have the right to file an appeal with your state department of education. The state department of education will review the entire hearing process to make sure that your legal rights were protected, and the appropriate information was considered. Further information may be requested by the state, and a hearing may be conducted. You still have the same rights that were in effect during the local due process hearing.

If the initial due process hearing is held at the state department of education, you cannot file an administrative appeal. The next step would be to file a lawsuit either in state or federal court. The following flowchart illustrates the continuum. Note that the initial step can vary depending on the laws in your state.

| local district | → | state education | → | state court | federal district |
| level | | department | | or | court |

Section 300.508 of the IDEA describes your rights during due process. They include the following:

1. The right to examine all school records concerning your child.
2. The right to obtain an independent evaluation.
3. The right to an interpreter or translator.
4. The right to determine whether the hearing will be closed or open to the public. (Only parents have this right.)
5. The right to advice of counsel and representation by counsel at the hearing.
6. The right to bring your child to the hearing. (Only parents have this right.)
7. The right to keep your child in his/her current educational placement until all due process hearing appeals have been completed.
8. The right to written notification about the hearing in the primary language or mode of communication of the parent.
9. The right to present evidence and testimony, and to compel school personnel to serve as witnesses at the hearing.
10. The right to prohibit the introduction of any evidence which has not been disclosed to parents at least five days prior to the hearing.
11. The right to cross-examine and challenge all testimony presented during the hearing.

12. The right to receive a verbatim transcript of the hearing, at reasonable cost.

13. The right to appeal the decision of the hearing officer or hearing panel.

14. The right to receive from the school system reasonable attorney's fees as part of your costs when the hearing officer or judge rules in your favor.

At a due process hearing, a hearing officer will decide whether or not your child has in fact received a free and appropriate public education in the least restrictive environment. The appointed hearing officer will weigh the evidence and determine if the program is appropriate, whether resources on hand are sufficient, or if in fact the school system is out of bounds with respect to programming. The hearing officer may order the school system to provide any service that he/she feels is appropriate for your child. School districts must give your child access to these services even if they do not presently exist in the system.

RESOLVING A PROBLEM

Before you begin to invoke your right to due process there are intermediary steps you may take to try to resolve the conflict. You may request an administrative review, a conciliatory conference, or mediation (depending on your state and local laws).

Alternative 1: Administrative Review or Prehearing

The first alternative is to draft a letter to the superintendent of schools specifically stating your dissatisfaction with the actions of the school system with respect to your child. Herein, you must be very specific about which aspects of the findings and placement you disagree with.

- Has the school system not fully or accurately recognized your child's handicapping condition?
- Are you asking for an external evaluation?
- Is your child placed in an inappropriate class setting—not the least restrictive in your opinion?
- Do you believe that there is a program more appropriate for your child that the school system is unaware of, or unwilling to provide?

The school system will now initiate its administrative review procedure. It is under no obligation to discuss with you the procedures it follows during this process. The administration is obligated only to notify you of its decision.

Some school systems will immediately convene a meeting of all involved parties and try to resolve the problem amicably. Other school systems will exhaust the allowable time in their own investigation. In any case, the school administration might come back to you and ask for additional information. On occasion, they may ask you to supply them with names of independent evaluators, doctors, and others in the professional community who you feel are qualified to be called in as consultants. They may even request from you a list of acceptable alternative programs for your child. Administrative reviews can include a review of your child's educational records, interviews with those on the IEP team, and the content of the discussions held during an informal meeting.

We want to share with you our experiences in this process. As our son Adam needs extensive intervention, including a consistent behavior management plan, we felt that he was entitled to receive an extended school year (ESY—12 month) program and wanted the school district to consider this request. Adam was placed outside the county school system in a nonpublic preschool. In order for Adam to participate in an extended program, the local school district, as underwriter of the program, needed to be consulted, and their approval was required to proceed.

A major part of this review included a meeting with the Admission, Review and Dismissal Committee (ARD), which included members of the diagnostic and professional support team who reviewed Adam's eligibility for extended school year programming. The committee recommended a limited ESY program to the associate superintendent. This recommendation was based on relevant and compelling information presented to the team by school personnel. The school district required a substantial amount of time to develop a program. The planning took almost as long as the actual placement. As a result Adam lost valuable time that could have been spent in the program. Try to prevent the district from procrastinating. Do what you can to move the process along.

The specific ESY program was a continuation of some of Adam's IEP goals. A separate IEP was written for the ESY program. The goals were chosen based on the need to provide a behavior management plan. He was placed in a program (already in progress) that was scheduled to end two weeks later. Although we were interested in a twelve-month ESY program for Adam, this was denied. The school system was unwilling to take the necessary measures to identify appropriate funding to underwrite a twelve-month program for Adam. Thus the administrative review was a partial success but did not meet our full expectations.

If the decision of the administrative review is to support the initial determination by the placement or ARD committee, and you are still dissatisfied, then you may go on to a formal hearing by an impartial hearing officer. This is described in detail later in the chapter.

Alternative 2: Conciliatory Conference

In some states the conciliatory conference is an intermediate step before a due process hearing. The officer who hears the case has not been directly involved in the issues, but is paid by the school district. This may not suit you. The decisions made by this officer may or may not be binding. State and local laws dictate the roles of these officers. The advantage of proceeding with this alternative is to have another forum to discuss both sides of the issue and try to resolve the conflict.

Alternative 3: Mediation

Some states offer mediation, whereby a neutral mediator is employed. The mediator's job is to facilitate a resolution to the conflict by the two parties. In Connecticut there are two routes parents can take when proceeding through due process. The first is to go directly to a due process hearing (described above). Parents may decide to opt for "mediation in due process" as a first step. (This option may not be available in your state. Contact your state department of special education, due process unit, for information.) "Mediation is a flexible, informal way of resolving differences through understanding and/or compromise of the differing viewpoints" (State of Connecticut Department of Education, n.d., p. 1). Both the school district and the parent (or guardian) must agree to mediation and request it in writing. The State of Connecticut assigns a mediator at no cost to the parent or the school district. The mediation session takes place within thirty days of receipt of the written request. The state is often represented by the Due Process Unit of the Bureau of Special Education and Pupil Personnel Services, as in Connecticut. They will arrange a date acceptable to all parties, notify them of the time and place for mediation, and keep a record of the mediation agreement if one is reached. Attorneys representing either or both sides may attend the meeting. However, if one party elects to have an attorney present, it must notify the other party at least five days prior to the mediation. The mediator acts to facilitate an agreement between the parties. Thus, the solution to the problems must be developed by parents and the local school district.

Role of Each Participant in Mediation

Parents/guardian. The purpose of mediation is for all parties to approach the issue in good faith, with the intention of reaching an agreement. In order for mediation to work parents need to be partners with the school district. They need to consider all aspects of the school district's proposal. In addition, they must make every effort to understand the material presented. To ensure this, they must ask for clarification whenever any point under discussion is not understood. Parents must come prepared to present their viewpoint; they must be willing to disclose all relevant information and to spend the entire day at mediation. A parent or guardian may ask to meet separately with the mediator when necessary (e.g., to present sensitive material to the mediation officer). You have the right to bring an advisor or advocate.

School district representatives. In order for mediation to work, the school district must follow the same guidelines applicable to parents or guardians (see above). In addition, the teachers and staff who can disseminate information on the matter must be present, including a representative who has full authority to act for the school district. The mediation will take place in the local school district.

Mediator. As a representative of the state department of education, the mediator is a neutral party working to resolve differences in the identified issues. He/she will review records and documents as appropriate at the time of the negotiation. The mediator's job is to keep the discussion on target by helping to:

1. clarify the issues to be mediated;
2. make suggestions;
3. describe areas of agreement;
4. emphasize the present aspects of the case, limiting the discussion of the past to that which is necessary for understanding and planning; and
5. seek statements from each party as to their position or points of disagreement, requesting clarification as necessary. (State of Connecticut Department of Education n.d.)

Thus, he/she facilitates a constructive, open dialogue between parties. The mediator may meet separately with each party, with the discussion kept confidential.

Outcomes

In Connecticut, when an application for mediation has been received, the state department of education will immediately set a date for a due process hearing, to minimize delay if a mediation in due process does not produce an acceptable agreement between parties. If an agreement is reached, the hearing will be canceled.

The mediation session has three possible outcomes. The first is that no amicable resolution of the identified issues can be reached; in this case the mediator will end the session and notify the Due Process Unit. If an agreement is not reached, no notes or minutes are recorded or filed with the unit other than an attendance record. The second possible outcome is that the negotiator will recess the meeting and reconvene it at a later date. This happens when both sides agree that new information will be necessary to reach an agreement. The third outcome is that an agreement has been reached by both parties and signed. The mediator writes this agreement, which includes the names of programs, materials, schools, school personnel responsibilities, and parent responsibilities. A copy of this mediation agreement will be kept on file in the Due Process Unit. With mediation, a prompt solution to the disagreement may occur.

Procedures for Scheduling Due Process Hearings

If the above steps have not been satisfactory, a written request for a due process hearing may be sent either to your local school district or, in some cases, directly to the Due Process Unit of your state department of education. Some locales have preprinted forms available for your use. The Montgomery County (Maryland) Public Schools use a form to initiate this due process hearing (see Figure 10.2).

Written notification. Write a letter to the superintendent of schools stating your remaining dissatisfaction. It is important that you compose the letter very precisely, detailing your concerns and the specific actions that you are requesting (e.g., the kind of service or placement that you want for your child). Specifics are a must! If you are not comfortable writing such a detailed letter, then get help from a community-based advocacy group (to be discussed shortly). You will also want to send this letter by certified U.S. mail, with a return receipt indicating to whom and when the letter was delivered. This protects your rights to a due process hearing.

Timelines

The entire process, from receipt of written request to the rendering of a decision by the hearing officer, is completed within forty-five days after receipt of the written request for a due process hearing. This time requirement is stipulated by federal regulation (34 C.F.R. 300.512 [a]). Documentation by both parties (exhibits) must be sent to either the Due Process Unit (in the case of a due process hearing on the state level, as in Connecticut) or a designated person at the local level (in the case of a due process hearing on the local level) at least five days before the date of the hearing. Requests for a postponement of the initial hearing date or extension of time to file exhibits are enumerated in procedural guidelines. However, the hearing officer may postpone the hearing date so that an independent evaluation of the child can be obtained. He/she

Figure 10.2
Sample Form: Request for Due Process Hearing

STATE BOARD OF EDUCATION
P.O. Box 2219
Hartford, Connecticut 06115

Parental Request for Special Education Due Process Review

I (we) request the review of the (evaluation) (program) (placement) (other)

of _____, who is currently enrolled at

_____ school in the

_____ school district.

___ request for administrative review

___ request for mediation

_____
parent(s) signature

_____
parent address

_____   _____
date   parent's home and business telephone number

If mediation has been requested, the agreement of the local Board of Education
is required.

_____
agreement of local Board of Education
for mediation

One copy of this form shall be filed with the local Board of Education, and
one copy shall be mailed immediately by the local Board of Education to the
Due Process Unit, Bureau of Pupil Personnel and Special Educational Services,
State Department of Education, 25 Industrial Park Drive, Middletown, CT 06457
Upon receipt of this form, the Due Process Unit will schedule a hearing.
Should an administrative review or mediation resolve the disagreement, the
hearing will not be convened.

has the authority to request more information that will allow him/her to render a proper decision.

STEPS TO HELP PARENTS PREPARE FOR A DUE PROCESS HEARING

Where to Turn for Help

Under Section 300.506(c) of IDEA, school districts must provide information on free or low-cost services in your area that may assist you in your preparation. However, this information must be disclosed only upon parental request.

Protection and advocacy systems. Protection and advocacy systems (P&As) were established in response to the public's outcry concerning the treatment of persons with disabilities in state institutions. After testimony from many of their constituents, Congress enacted laws to address the needs of persons with disabilities. Four programs have been established to address their needs:

1. Protection and Advocacy for Persons with Developmental Disabilities (PADD) Program;

2. Protection and Advocacy for Individuals with Mental Illness (PAMI) Program;

3. Protection and Advocacy for Individual Rights (PAIR) Program (for persons with disabilities who are not eligible for the above programs); and

4. Client Assistance Program (CAP) (for persons with disabilities seeking vocational rehabilitation services under the 1984 Amendments to the Rehabilitation Act).

Copies of eligibility requirements for these programs can be obtained from your state P&A or at your local library. Figure 10.3 lists P&As. In fiscal year 1994, PADD programs devoted 34 percent of their caseload to obtaining a free appropriate public education under IDEA for children throughout the country. The results of some of these efforts are shown in Figure 10.4. Information and technical assistance to individuals, service providers, and other advocacy organizations are also available through your state P&A.

Advocacy groups. States and localities have many organizations specifically formed to help people with disabilities—or parents and friends of disabled people—gain and maintain the kinds of services they need or are legally entitled to. Advocacy groups may be affiliated with organizations such as ARC, special education or law departments of univer-

Figure 10.3
Protection and Advocacy Systems (P&As)

State	CAP	DD, MI, PAIR	State	CAP	DD, MI, PAIR
Alabama	Division of Rehabilitation Services and Children's Rehabilitation Services 2129 E. South Blvd Montgomery, AL 36111 205-281-8780	Alabama Disabilities Advocacy Program The University of Alabama P.O. Box 870395 Tuscaloosa, AL 35487-0395 205-348-4928, 205-348-9484 (TDD), 800-826-1675	Alaska	ASSIST 2900 Boniface Parkway, #100 Anchorage, AK 99504-3195	Advocacy Services of Alaska 615 E. 82nd Avenue, Suite 101 Anchorage, AK 99518 907-333-2211, 907-344-1022 Voice/TDD, 800-478-1234
Arizona	Arizona Center for Law in the Public Interest 3724 N. Third Street, Suite 300 Phoenix, AZ, 85012 602-274-6287 Voice/TDD	Arizona Center for Law in the Public Interest 3724 N. Third Street, Suite 300 Phoenix, AZ, 85012 602-274-6287 Voice/TDD	Arkansas	Advocacy Services, Inc. Evergreen Place, Suite 201 1100 North University Little Rock, AK 72207 501-324-9215 Voice/TDD 800-482-1174	Advocacy Services, Inc. Evergreen Place, Suite 201 1100 North University Little Rock, AK 72207 501-324-9215 Voice/TDD 800-482-1174
California	Client Assistance Program 830 K Street Mall, Room 220 Sacramento, CA 95814 916-322-5066	Protection & Advocacy, Inc. 100 Howe Avenue, Suite185N Sacramento, CA 95825 916-488-9950, 800-776-5746 818-546-1631 LA Voice/TDD	Colorado	The Legal Center 455 Sherman Street Suite 130 Denver, CO 80203 303-722-0300 Voice/TDD	The Legal Center 455 Sherman Street Suite 130 Denver, CO 80203 303-722-0300 Voice/TDD
Connecticut	Office of P&A for Handicapped and Developmentally Disabled Persons 60 Weston Street Hartford, CT 06120-1551 203-297-4300, 203-566-2102 TDD, 800-842-7303	Office of P&A for Handicapped and Developmentally Disabled Persons 60 Weston Street Hartford, CT 06120-1551 203-297-4300, 203-566-2102 TDD, 800-842-7303	Delaware	Client Assistance Program United Cerebral Palsy, Inc. 254 Camden-Wyoming Avenue Camden, DE 19934 302-698-9336, 800-640-9336	Disabilities Law Program 144 E. Market Street Georgetown, DE 19947 302-856-0038 Voice/TDD
District of Columbia	Client Assistance Program Rehabilitation Services Administration 605 G Street NW Washington, DC 20001 202-727-0977	Information Protection & Advocacy Center for Handicapped Individuals 4455 Connecticut Avenue, NW Washington, DC 20008 202-966-8081, 202-966-2500 TDD	Florida	Advocacy Center for Persons with Disabilities 2671 Executive Center, Circle W Webster Building, Suite 100 Tallahassee, FL 32301-5024 904-488-9071, 800-342-0823 800-346-4127 TDD	Advocacy Center for Persons with Disabilities 2671 Executive Center, Circle W Webster Building, Suite 100 Tallahassee, FL 32301-5024 904-488-9071, 800-342-0823 800-346-4127 TDD

CAP = Client Assistance Program; DD = Developmental Disabilities; MI = Mental Illness; PAIR = Protection and Advocacy for Individual Rights

Figure 10.3 (continued)

State	CAP	DD, MI, PAIR	State	CAP	DD, MI, PAIR
Georgia	Department of Human Resources Division of Rehabilitation Services 2 Peachtree St. NW, Room 23-307 Atlanta, GA 30303 404-657-3012	Georgia Advocacy Office, Inc. 1708 Peachtree St., NW, Suite 505 Atlanta, GA 30309 404-855-1234 Voice/TDD 800-282-4538	Hawaii	Protection & Advocacy Agency 1580 Makaloa Street, Suite 1060 Honolulu, HI 96814 808-949-2922 Voice/TDD	Protection & Advocacy Agency 1580 Makaloa Street, Suite 1060 Honolulu, HI 96814 808-949-2922 Voice/TDD
Idaho	Co-Ad, Inc. 4477 Emerald, Suite B-100 Boise, ID 83706 208-336-5353 Voice/TDD	Co-Ad, Inc. 4477 Emerald, Suite B-100 Boise, ID 83706 208-336-5353 Voice/TDD	Illinois	Illinois Client Assistance Program 100 N. First Street, 1st Floor Springfield, IL 62702 217-782-5374	Equip for Equality, Inc. 11 East Adams, Suite 1200 Chicago, IL 60603 312-341-0022 Voice/TDD
Indiana	Indiana Advocacy Services 850 North Meridian, Suite 2-C Indianapolis, IN 46204 317-232-1150 Voice/TDD 800-622-4845	Indiana Advocacy Services 850 North Meridian, Suite 2-C Indianapolis, IN 46204 317-232-1150 Voice/TDD 800-622-4845	Kansas	Client Assistance Program Biddle Building, 2nd Floor 2700 West 6th Street Topeka, KS 66502 913-296-1491 800-432-8276	Kansas Advocacy & Protective Service 2601 Anderson Avenue Manhattan, KS 66502 913-776-1541, 800-432-8276
Kentucky	Client Assistance Program Capitol Plaza Tower Frankfort, KY 40601 502-564-8035, 800633-6283	Office for Public Advocacy 100 Fair Oaks Lane, 3rd Floor Frankfort, KY 40601 502-564-2967, 800-372-2988 TDD	Louisiana	Advocacy Center for the Elderly and Disabled 210 O'Keefe, Suite 700 New Orleans, LA 70112 504-522-2337 Voice/TDD 800-662-7705	Advocacy Center for the Elderly and Disabled 210 O'Keefe, Suite 700 New Orleans, LA 70112 504-522-2337 Voice/TDD 800-662-7705
Maine	CARES, Inc. 4-C Winter Street Augusta, ME 04330 207-622-7055	Maine Advocacy Services 32 Winthrop P.O. Box 2007 Augusta, ME 04338 207-626-2774, 800-452-1948 TDD	Maryland	Client Assistance Program Maryland Rehabilitation Center Division of Rehabilitation Services 2301 Argonne Drive Baltimore, MD 21208 410-554-3221	Maryland Disability Law Center 2510 St. Paul Street Baltimore, MD 21218 800-233-7201, 410-235-4700 410-235-4227 Voice/TDD

State	CAP	DD, MI, PAIR
Massachusetts	MA Office on Disability, Client Assistance Program, One Ashburton Place, Room 303, Boston, MA 02108, 617-723-8455 Voice/TDD	Disability Law Center, 11 Beacon Street, Suite 925, Boston, MA 02108, 617-723-8455 Voice/TDD (DD, PAIR); Center for Public Representation, 22 Green Street, Northampton, MA 01060, 413-584-1644 Voice/TDD (MI)
Michigan	Client Assistance Program, Department of Rehabilitation Services, P.O. Box 30008, Lansing, MI 48909, 517-373-8193; Commission for the Blind, 201 North Washington Square, Box 30015, Lansing, MI 48909, 517-373-6425	Michigan P&A Service, 106 West Allegan, Suite 210, Lansing, MI 48933, 517-487-1755 Voice/TDD
Minnesota	Minnesota Disability Law Center, 4300 First Avenue North, Suite 300, Minneapolis, MN 55401-1780, 612-332-1441, 612-332-4668	Minnesota Disability Law Center, 4300 First Avenue North, Suite 300, Minneapolis, MN 55401-1780, 612-332-1441, 612-332-4668
Mississippi	Client Assistance Program, Easter Seal Society, 3226 N. State Street, Jackson, MS 39216, 601-981-8207 Voice/TDD	Mississippi P&A System for DD, Inc., 5330 Executive Place, Suite A, Jackson, MS 39206, 601-981-8207 Voice/TDD
Missouri	Missouri P&A Services, 925 S. Country Club Drive, Unit B-1, Jefferson City, MO 65109, 314-893-3333 Voice/TDD	Missouri P&A Services, 925 S. Country Club Drive, Unit B-1, Jefferson City, MO 65109, 314-893-3333 Voice/TDD
Montana	Montana Advocacy Program, 316 N. Park, Room 211, P.O. Box 1680, Helena, MT 59624, 406-444-3889 Voice/TDD, 800-245-4743	Montana Advocacy Program, 316 N. Park, Room 211, P.O. Box 1680, Helena, MT 59624, 406-444-3889 Voice/TDD, 800-245-4743
Nebraska	Client Assistance Program, Division of Rehabilitation Services, Nebraska Department of Education, 301 Centennial Mall South, Lincoln, NE 68509, 402-471-3656	Nebraska Advocacy Services, Inc., 522 Lincoln Center Building, 215 Centennial Mall South, Lincoln, NE 68508, 402-474-3183 Voice/TDD
Nevada	Client Assistance Program, 1755 East Plumb Lane #128, Reno, NV 89502, 702-688-1440, 800-633-9879	Office of Protection & Advocacy, Inc., 1135 Terminal Way, Suite 105, Reno, NV 89502, 702-688-1233, 800-992-5715, 702-622-0243 TDD
New Hampshire	Client Assistance Program, Governor's Commission for the Handicapped, 57 Regional Drive, Concord, NH 03301-9686	Disabilities Rights Center, P.O. Box 19, 18 Low Avenue, Concord, NH 03302-0019, 603-228-0432 Voice/TDD
New Jersey	Client Assistance Program, New Jersey Department of the Public Advocate, Hughes Justice Complex, CN 850, Trenton, NJ 08625, 609-292-9742 Voice/TDD, 800-792-8600	New Jersey Department of the Public Advocate, Division of Advocacy for the DD, Hughes Justice Complex, CN 850, Trenton, NJ 08625, 609-292-1750

Figure 10.3 (continued)

State	CAP	DD, MI, PAIR	State	CAP	DD, MI, PAIR
New Mexico	Protection & Advocacy System, Inc. 1720 Louisiana Blvd, N.E. Suite 204 Albuquerque, NM 87110 505-256-3100 Voice/TDD 800-432-4682	Protection & Advocacy System, Inc. 1720 Louisiana Blvd, N.E. Suite 204 Albuquerque, NM 87110 505-256-3100 Voice/TDD 800-432-4682	New York	New York Commission on Quality of Care for the Mentally Disabled 99 Washington Avenue, Suite 1002 Albany, NY 12210 518-473-7378, 800-624-4143 TDD	New York Commission on Quality of Care for the Mentally Disabled 99 Washington Avenue, Suite 1002 Albany, NY 12210 518-473-7378, 800-624-4143 TDD
North Carolina	Client Assistance Program North Carolina Division of Vocational Rehabilitation Services P.O. Box 26053 Raleigh, NC 27611 919-733-3364	Governor's Advocacy Council for Persons with Disabilities 1318 Dale Street, Suite 100 Raleigh, NC 27605 919-733-9250 Voice/TDD 800-821-6922	North Dakota	Client Assistance Program 400 East Broadway, Suite 303 Bismarck, ND 58501-4038 701-224-4625	The North Dakota Protection & Advocacy Project 400 E. Broadway, Suite 515 Bismarck, ND 58501 701-224-2972, 800-472-2670 800-366-688 TDD
Ohio	Client Assistance Program Governor's Office of Advocacy for People with Disabilities 30 East Broad Street, Room 1201 Columbus, OH 43266-0400 614-466-9956	Ohio Legal Rights Service 8 East Long Street, 6th Floor Columbus, OH 43215 614-466-7264 Voice/TDD 800-282-9181	Oklahoma	Client Assistance Program Oklahoma Office of Handicapped Concerns 4300 N. Lincoln Blvd STE 200 Oklahoma City, OK 73105 405-521-3756	Oklahoma Disability Law Center, Inc. 4150 South 100th East Avenue Suite 210, Cherokee Bldg Tulsa, OK 74146-3661 918-664-5883 Voice/TDD
Oregon	Oregon Disabilities Commission 1257 Ferry Street, SE Salem, OR 97310 503-378-3142	Oregon Advocacy Center 625 Board of Trade Building 310 Southwest 4th Avenue, Suite 625 Portland, OR 97204-2309 503-243-2081 Voice/TDD	Pennsylvania	Client Assistance Program (SEPLS) 1650 Arch Street, Suite 2310 Philadelphia, PA 19103 215-557-7112	Pennsylvania P&A, Inc. 116 Pine Street Harrisburg, PA 17101 717-236-8110 Voice/TDD 800-692-7443
Puerto Rico	Office of the Governor Ombudsman for the Disabled P.O.Box 4234 San Juan, PR 00902-4234 809-721-4299, 809-705-4014 TDD	Office of the Governor Ombudsman for the Disabled P.O.Box 4234 San Juan, PR 00902-4234 809-721-4299, 809-705-4014 TDD	Rhode Island	Rhode Island P&A System, Inc. 151 Broadway, 3rd Floor Providence, RI 02903 401-831-3150	Rhode Island P&A System, Inc. 151 Broadway, 3rd Floor Providence, RI 02903 401-831-3150

186

State	CAP	DD, MI, PAIR	State	CAP	DD, MI, PAIR
South Carolina	Office of the Governor Division of Ombudsman & Citizen Services, P.O. Box 11369, Columbia, SC 29211, 803-734-0457	South Carolina P&A System for the Handicapped, Inc., 3710 Landmark Drive, Suite 208, Columbia, SC 29204, 803-782-0639 Voice/TDD, 800-922-5225	South Dakota	South Dakota Advocacy Services, 221 South Central Avenue, Pierre, SD 57501, 605-224-8284 Voice/TDD, 800-658-4782	South Dakota Advocacy Services, 221 South Central Avenue, Pierre, SD 57501, 605-224-8284 Voice/TDD, 800-658-4782
Tennessee	Tennessee Protection & Advocacy, Inc., P.O. Box 121257, Nashville, TN 37212, 615-298-1080 Voice/TDD, 800-342-1660	Tennessee Protection & Advocacy, Inc., P.O. Box 121257, Nashville, TN 37212, 615-298-1080 Voice/TDD, 800-342-1660	Texas	Advocacy, Inc., 7800 Shoal Creek Blvd, Suite 171-E, Austin, TX 78757, 512-454-4816 Voice/TDD, 800-252-9108	Advocacy, Inc., 7800 Shoal Creek Blvd, Suite 171-E, Austin, TX 78757, 512-454-4816 Voice/TDD, 800-252-9108
Utah	Legal Center for People with Disabilities, 455 East South, Suite 201, Salt Lake City, UT 84111, 801-363-1347 Voice/TDD, 800-662-9080	Legal Center for People with Disabilities, 455 East South, Suite 201, Salt Lake City, UT 84111, 801-363-1347 Voice/TDD, 800-662-9080	Vermont	Client Assistance Program, Ladd Hall, 103 South Main Street, Waterbury, VT 05676, 802-241-2641, 800-622-4555	Vermont Protection & Advocacy, RR1 Box 1670, Starllsbono, VT 05487-9707, 802-453-2644
Virginia	Department for Rights of Virginians with Disabilities, James Monroe Building, 101 North 14th Street, 17th Floor, Richmond, VA 23219, 800-552-3962, 804-225-2042	Department for Rights of Virginians with Disabilities, James Monroe Building, 101 North 14th Street, 17th Floor, Richmond, VA 23219, 800-552-3962, 804-225-2042	Washington	Client Assistance Program, P.O. Box 22510, Seattle, WA 98122, 206-721-4049	Washington Protection & Advocacy System, 1401 E. Jefferson, Suite 506, Seattle, WA 98122, 206-324-1521 Voice/TDD
West Virginia	West Virginia Advocates, Inc., Litton Building, 4th Floor, 1207 Quarrier Street, Charleston, WV 25301, 304-346-0847 Voice/TDD, 800-950-5250	West Virginia Advocates, Inc., Litton Building, 4th Floor, 1207 Quarrier Street, Charleston, WV 25301, 304-346-0847 Voice/TDD, 800-950-5250	Wisconsin	Governor's Commission for People with Disabilities, 1 W. Wilson Street, Room 558, P.O. Box 7852, Madison, WI 53707-7852, 608-267-7422, 800-362-1290	Wisconsin Coalition for Advocacy, 16 N. Carroll Street, Suite 400, Madison, WI 53703, 608-267-0214, 608-267-0368 TDD
Wyoming	Wyoming Protection & Advocacy System, 2424 Pioneer Avenue, Suite 101, Cheyenne, WY 82001, 307-638-7668, 800-821-3091 Voice/TDD	Wyoming Protection & Advocacy System, 2424 Pioneer Avenue, Suite 101, Cheyenne, WY 82001, 307-638-7668, 800-821-3091 Voice/TDD	NAPAS	National Association of Protection and Advocacy Systems, Inc., 900 Second Street, NE, Washington, DC 20002, 202-408-9514, 202-408-9521 TDD	

Source: National Association of Protection and Advocacy Systems, Inc. (1993). *1993 Annual Report on State Program Activities.* Washington, D.C.: Author.

Figure 10.4
Sample Cases Represented by PADDs

LOCATION	SUBJECT
Alabama—Federal District Court	**Inclusion** Child with severe disabilities was ordered to be placed in a regular classroom. Court rejected school district's proposal to place child in segregated class with other children with multiple disabilities. The district failed to meet its burden to show that such a self-contained classroom would significantly enhance the student's education and that her IEP goals and objectives could not be implemented within the regular classroom with aids & services.
Indiana—Indiana Court of Appeals	**Special education services for children ages, 3–21** Affirmed a lower court decision. Ruled that the state department of education's regulations violated federal law by restricting special education services provided to students between the ages of 18–21.
Pennsylvania—Federal Court	**All children with disabilities receive the appropriate services.** Court order obtained requiring the state to ensure coordination of state services, including educational services for children with severe mental health needs.
New Jersey—Local School District	**Accessibility to Programs** District to provide accessible bathroom facilities and a larger resource room for a child with cerebral palsy; and a portable wheelchair lift to a pupil with spina bifida. Ensure that one of the schools in the district is fully accessible within the next year.
South Carolina—U.S. Supreme Court	**Reimbursement for Tuition Costs** A court may order reimbursement for tuition costs to parents who unilaterally withdraw their child from public school that provides an inappropriate education under IDEA and put the child in a private school that provides an education that substantially complies with the Act.

Source: National Association of Protection & Advocacy Systems, Inc. (1993). *1993 Annual Report on State Program Activities* p. 11–14. Washington, DC: Author.

Figure 10.5
Advocacy Organizations Providing Assistance to Parents—Education and the Law

Center for Law and Education	Larsen Hall 14 Appian Way Cambridge, MA 02138, 617-495-4666
Children's Defense Fund	25 E Street NW Washington, DC 20001, 202-628-8787
Disabilities Rights Education & Defense Fund	2212 Sixth Street Berkeley, CA 94710, 510-644-2555
Maryland Coalition for Integrated Education	7257 Parkway Drive Hanover, MD 21076
Mexican American Legal Defense & Education Fund	604 Mission Street San Francisco, CA 94105, 415-543-5598
National Association of the Deaf Legal Defense Fund	P.O. Box 2304 800 Florida Avenue, NE Washington, DC 20002, 202-651-5343
National Juvenile Law Center St. Louis University School of Law	3701 Lindell Blvd St. Louis, MO 63108, 314-652-5555
National Parent Network on Disabilities	1600 Prince Street Suite 115 Alexandria, VA 22314, 703-684-NPND
PACER Center	4826 Chicago Avenue South Minneapolis, MN 55417 612-827-2966 (800) 53P-ACER
WeCAHR (Western Connecticut Association for Human Rights)	11 Lake Avenue Extension Danbury, CT 06811

sities, or not-for-profit organizations started by parents (see Figure 10.5), or designated as Parent Training and Information Centers funded by the Division of Special Education Programs of the U.S. Department of Education (see Appendix F).

An advocate will review your case, the IEP as written, and other documentation attesting to your child's needs. The advocate will also review the proceedings to date and advise you as to the best course of action to be taken to receive services. An added bonus is that the people working for a local advocacy group will undoubtedly have knowledge of the internal workings and personalities of the local school system, which will help them devise a strategy to win the kinds of services and placement you seek. Politics always plays a part in these kinds of negotiations, and having a "friend in court" is a necessity.

Know Legal Precedents; If Necessary, Secure Legal Representation

Your advocate might or might not be an attorney. This depends on the kind of organization you have access to in your community. In our experience, hiring an attorney with a winning track record often made the school system reconsider our requests. Consider retaining a legal expert in special education law or the law of the disabled if your proposal demands a large capital outlay, if other children are requesting the same services, or if you are at a stand-off with the school system.

Legal organizations will assess your case based on the existing federal and state statutes, precedents within the state and federal court systems, and the IEP and related documentation specific to your child's situation. Many law schools will provide assistance. Legal service groups are available in many locales. Record keeping is essential on your part. You will need to pay close attention to how you organize your records and how you maintain a "correspondence trial" for all events surrounding your child's needs. We do not interface with the school system on formal or essential matters without written follow-up. And where matters relate to procedural issues such as IEP development, certified mail is essential.

Collect Evidence

Make sure that all of your records, both educational and medical, are organized for ease of reading and presentation. Correspondence should also be filed. Keep it in chronological order, separating it into categories. Request all documents from the school system that are currently not in your possession. Write for copies, citing the Freedom of Information Act as your authority for receiving copies of such materials. Where the materials or documents are records pertaining to your child, school policy usually dictates your rights to copies of such information (Buckley Amendment).

Solicit Expert Opinion

Often the opinions of psychologists, academics, medical professionals, and other individuals recognized as experts in a particular field can be useful in making your case. You have a right to have such persons testify on your child's behalf at these hearings. If these people were involved in evaluating your child for the purposes of placement, then the school system will definitely recognize them as appropriate to speak at a due process hearing.

Tape Record Meetings

It is not unusual, where actions have become somewhat antagonistic, for all meetings to be tape recorded, transcribed, or both. These recordings of the proceedings then become evidence for future actions or hearings.

WHAT OCCURS AT THE DUE PROCESS HEARING

Each party can present evidence, cross-examine witnesses, and require the attendance of any official, employee, or agent of the board of education who has information relevant to the issues being presented at the hearing. The hearing officer has the right to confirm, modify, or reject any diagnosis, evaluation, prescribed educational program, or exclusion or exemption from school privileges. He or she may also prescribe an alternative program.

The hearing officer will review previous documentation and may request an independent evaluation (to be paid for by the local board). An independent evaluator may be designated by the officer or agreed to by both parties. Parents may submit their own independent evaluation at their own expense. Attorneys may submit legal briefs if the hearing officer approves.

The written decision of the hearing officer will include "findings of fact" and "conclusions of law." If the hearing officer rules in favor of the parents, they may be reimbursed for legal fees.

What Parents Should Consider Before They Take That Big Step

Notice that the due process hearing goes into motion very quickly. It is important to be sufficiently prepared to state your case almost immediately after you request a hearing. We spoke with several persons involved in due process hearings; they made the following comments: Due process hearings today are more complex than they were ten years ago. Ten years ago, a due process hearing usually lasted one day, but today it can take ten to fourteen days. Many witnesses will be called during the hearing. It is an expensive process. When we asked who usually wins, we were told that parents win about approximately half of the cases.

Our experience in due process has also been mixed. As mentioned earlier, we were able to receive an extended school year (ESY) for Adam through an ARD meeting. The following year Adam was denied ESY on the local due process level. We proceeded to appeal the decision to the state board of education (hearing board), and our appeal was granted.

The Impact of Due Process on Families

Due process is not a very pleasant experience. You proceed with due process when you believe your child has not received a free and appropriate public education under the law, and you firmly believe that the school system *can* provide such an education for your child. When you begin a due process action, you are under enormous pressure to win the case! You feel this pressure not only at the time of the hearing but also continuously at home.

Time, however, is a critical factor. As noted above, the process moves quickly. Preparing your case will interfere with your daily activities, and as a result the time you spend with your child may be limited. You may have to make arrangements for child care and take time off from your job during the hearing. Tension in the family is heightened during this period. Your family is placed under a spotlight. The school administration will be watching your every move.

Prepare yourself and the family for the possible outcomes of the case. Have a contingency plan in mind. Change in placement may occur, and you will need to work with the school administration to implement the recommendations made by the hearing officer. Your child may not want to leave her present placement. Talk about what you are doing and the reasons for your actions. Answer all your child's questions as best you can. Remember, you must continue to keep your communications network operating during this crucial time.

If you so choose, the hearing can be open to the public. It is up to you to decide whether you want the media to be informed of your actions. It is important to publicize that your actions are based on an issue of ideology, not on a personal issue. Your actions should be based on what you believe is in the best interests of your child.

For us, winning an extended school year case was a moral victory, but we would have to go through the same procedure all over again for the next summer. It is important that you identify and access your support network (refer to Figure 4.2) during all phases of due process. You must think about and discuss with your family the options open to you if the decision is not what you expected.

Other Ways to Resolve Issues

In recent years we have accessed other means to secure services for our son Adam. Because he has multiple disabilities, Adam's IEP includes a comprehensive delivery of related services. On many occasions, both in his present district and in his first placement, Adam did not receive the related services stipulated on his IEP due to the district's inability to find therapists to deliver these services. The district's standard answer

Figure 10.6
Sample Letter of Complaint to State Department of Education

Your Name
Full Address

Date

Addressee (State Department of Education)

I would like to file a formal complaint with the Bureau of Special Education and Pupil Services regarding the lack of related services provided to (name of your child). According to his/her IEP, dated ----, (your child's name) is to (state service).

Enclosed is written documentation regarding (name of school system) inability to implement (your child's name) IEP during (appropriate dates).

If any other additional information is needed please call me at your convenience.

Sincerely,

Your Full Name

cc: (Superintendent of Schools)
(Administrator - Special Education)

was, "We have advertised and called the local hospitals, and we have had no luck recruiting therapists." School districts may not immediately notify you of this problem. We are very sensitive to it, and always inquire about staffing, especially during the extended school year. We have learned to relay our concern immediately to the appropriate administrative officer. This has been a problem for several years, and up until two years ago we worked out an arrangement whereby a consultant was hired to provide the services. However, these services were delivered in the consultant's office. After agreeing to this arrangement for several years, we decided enough was enough.

Filing a Complaint with the State Board of Education

We decided that a more direct approach to settle this problem was to file a complaint with the department of special education (see Figure 10.6).

Within a few days, the state department of education sent a letter of inquiry to the public school system. The state asked for a response in writing concerning issues we had raised, including the following:

1. Is the school system providing occupational and physical therapy services for Adam in the summer program as outlined in his IEP? If not, please explain the circumstances.

2. Are there other students in the summer program whose IEP requires occupational/and or physical therapy services? If so, are they receiving those services? If not, please explain the circumstances.

3. Please submit a copy of Adam's current IEP and the IEPs of other students in the summer program whose IEP requires occupational and/or physical therapy services. (Cappello, 1993)

This letter put the district on the alert. The system eventually found therapists to work with Adam at summer school. Sometimes you have to exert some pressure on your school district to make sure they are providing services that your child is entitled to receive. Remember that many times you have to be a detective, find out what's going on in your child's school, and take action.

Section 504 of the Rehabilitation Act of 1973 (The Civil Rights Act for Handicapped Persons)

Did you know that children who have impairments, but who do not require special education, are eligible to receive modifications to their regular education program, including certain services? These modifications or services include ramps for wheelchair access, interpreters for deaf persons, and braille materials and readers for students with visual disabilities. If these services are not available to your child, you can file a complaint with the Federal Office of Civil Rights (the civil rights and Section 504 enforcement agency for the U.S. Department of Education). Upon your written request, this complaint can be kept confidential. An investigation will be initiated. If the district is found in noncompliance with this statute, federal funds can be withheld.

POINTS TO REMEMBER

Parents may decide to pursue due process when no satisfactory resolution can be worked out between all parties. Before you jump in, consider all other options. In order to win your case, analyze the pros and cons for pursuing this course. Talk to people who have knowledge and experience in the courts regarding the issues you are raising. Call upon the resources described in this chapter to help you decide on your course of action. Before you make a decision, meet with other parents to discuss the issues. Maybe a letter to the editor of your local newspaper will be just as effective as a due process hearing. Also consider the time and financial resources that may be required. Once you embark on this course, a school system usually does not concede defeat easily. School systems usually have law firms on retainer who have been involved in many due process hearings. However, if the school system totally disregards your child's needs, or the school is not willing to consider alternatives, due process may be the proper course of action.

11

Where Are We Now? Where Do We Want to Be in Five Years?

As parents of a youngster with special needs, we often reflect on the past. However, we must also focus on the present and plan for the future. It is only human to evaluate the effectiveness of our actions. We do ask ourselves if, given a second chance, we would have done things differently with our child's schooling.

Parents do look at their child's overall abilities, social life, and acceptance in the community, and decide whether things are going as they think they should, or better than expected, or far below their expectations. Parents also analyze their child's academic progress. And as parents we must monitor the IEP services in terms of the child's changing needs. We must ascertain whether staff members are competent to work with our child. We need to monitor whether they are receiving adequate in-service training to keep abreast of high-tech instructional supports and whether they are encouraged to use an innovative curriculum. Often the test is whether our sons and daughters are happy and interested in school. We also need to ask whether the program is preparing our children sufficiently to enter society. The answers to these questions will help you assess the effectiveness of your child's program and help you decide whether it provides a foundation for continued academic success or acquisition of vocational skills needed to hold a job in the future.

Our son Adam has been in the same classroom for the past three years. We have worked side by side with the staff to devise and implement an individualized education program to meet Adam's needs. We have met frequently with the staff to request additional evaluations and assessments that we felt were needed to address issues affecting Adam's schooling. The acquisition of services for Adam was agreed upon with relative ease by the school district because it would be reimbursed for many of these services by the state of Connecticut (Board of Education, Services for the Blind). Since age five, Adam has been assigned an educational consultant who has the authority to approve services and equipment that allow him to benefit from his individualized education program. This has included the purchase of a computer, the services of a full-time tutor, music therapy (fifty minutes a week), and visits by mobility and visual specialists four times a year.

Adam's program is housed in a self-contained classroom in our neighborhood school. Some of Adam's classmates have moved, but the class census has basically stayed the same. Right now his three classmates are close in age, and are all nonverbal. We were not very happy that all the children were nonverbal, but we overlooked it because we believed that Adam was receiving individual attention and appropriate related services, including musical therapy, which he enjoys very much. There is a 4:3 ratio of children to adults in his class. For the first few years, we thought that this would enable Adam to excel. Many parents would be pleased with this arrangement, but we knew that something was missing in his program. The staff is loving and caring, but we needed to focus on identifying the barriers preventing Adam from achieving more success.

What Adam can really do is still a mystery. We do know that there is a lot locked up in his little body, and we desperately want to see him flourish. He is ten years old, and time is passing by quickly. We want to find out what he is capable of doing. But often he refuses to show us what he really can do. His aggressive behavior (e.g., pulling hair, scratching, and kicking) is holding him back. We sought to investigate why this behavior was continuing and what could we do to decrease it. To find out, we needed to address in depth the areas of (1) communication, (2) mobility, and (3) behavior. We have done this in the past, but we needed to take another look.

As a nonverbal child, Adam expresses himself through gesturing, pointing, and sign language. He has been using a "switch device" to choose: eat, drink, or stop. Three years ago we requested an augmentative communication evaluation. The evaluation was funded by the Board of Education, Services for the Blind. At that time Adam did not seem interested in using the device. He would attempt to throw it off the table. He also had difficulty activating the device. The team decided that Adam would not benefit from such a device and made other recommendations, including some intermediate steps that would prepare Adam for more predictable success with a communication device in the future. It was important for Adam to have the opportunity to make choices (such as choosing an activity during free play or deciding what he wanted for lunch). Adam needed to have some control over his environment. The team came up with a program using many pictures in his daily activities.

Accessing appropriate software programs for his computer enabled Adam to make choices as well. All these pieces of Adam's program were excellent, but still something was missing—motivation to move on. Last fall, we borrowed the communication device again, and finally Adam had some success. With his new device Adam is beginning to be able to express himself in more appropriate ways.

His receptive language is one of his strengths; however, his behavior has interfered with achievement. A behavior management plan has been part of his IEP for many years. It has been modified several times, with varying degrees of success. Adam is a child who can demonstrate a skill one day (e.g., crawl down the entire school hallway to deliver lunch money to the cafeteria) and then refuse to do it again for months at a time. When he was younger, Adam used more self-abusive behavior, such as biting himself and head banging, to escape from a demand made by his teacher, his physical therapist, or even his family. It was also a way to communicate his feelings. This behavior has decreased over the years, but has not been totally eliminated.

To stress mobility, a "walker" evaluation was conducted three years ago. Oddly enough, Adam would use the walker more as a crutch than as a support. He would lean back and refuse to walk with it. Finally the physical therapist decided to walk with Adam without any device. Adam is more cooperative and will walk with an individual for a longer period of time. He is able to maneuver his wheelchair more effectively when he is interested in his destination (e.g., wheeling himself along the driveway to the school bus).

Adam loves attention. When he receives verbal praise, he will do almost anything you want him to do. The tone of your voice can make a difference. He knows when you are angry or hurt, and he can get upset easily. Adam is a very social child. Even though he does not talk, he can get his feelings across through the use of gestures and physical action.

We have exhausted many options in his present classroom and feel that some dramatic change in Adam's program must be implemented. We authorized another psychological evaluation to analyze where Adam is and what we need to do to decrease his aggressive behavior. It was suggested that an already existing behavior plan be used with modifications; at the same time, his communication skills would be strengthened with the use of the augmentative communication device. However, the psychologist wanted us to travel to his office once a week along with Adam's teacher to receive training and to monitor the situation. The implementation of this plan appeared to us to be unworkable. In addition to the psychological evaluation, we decided to look at three alternative settings for placement.

The first alternative placement was in a self-contained classroom in a different school building (a ten-minute drive) with more verbal children.

Possibly a totally new environment with a new teacher and classmates would be effective in decreasing Adam's aggressive behavior. Our next option was to place Adam in a special education center outside the district where the staff was trained to work with children who had challenging behavior. The third possibility was to place Adam in a regular fourth grade classroom with appropriate supports—an option known as inclusion.

After visiting the out-of-district placement, we decided to eliminate this option from consideration. The director of the program was very accommodating and spoke honestly of the types of services the school could give Adam. The curriculum and type of class setting did not appear to be any different from Adam's current program. Adam would have to spend at least one hour on the bus each way. And finally, we knew that an out-of-district placement could create many problems in the future. In an out-of-district placement you are dealing with two distinct bureaucracies that may or may not have a strong relationship with each other. In this situation children and parents do not belong to any one group and are left in the middle. If problems arise, one organization may pass the buck to the other. Our past experience in an out-of-district placement was not a pleasant one. We would have chosen the out-of-district placement if we felt the program met Adam's needs. But as it turned out, this program did not meet our expectations.

We observed the self-contained classroom in the other in-district school building. We talked with the principal to get his views on special education and his perceptions of the strengths of the program. We talked to parents about the program. We put this placement on hold and decided to seek the recommendations of an advocacy organization. They suggested that we talk to a consultant who worked with school districts and parents on having children included in regular classrooms. We were open to any promising alternative.

At first, we were not very open to the idea of an inclusive education for our child. Adam's behavior was a big stumbling block. He has a tendency to grab kids' hair and knock glasses off, and his abilities are not known. How would he be able to function in a regular classroom when he cannot read or write? After talking to the consultant, many things fell into place. Adam had many of the supports that he would need to be placed in the regular classroom. He has a full-time aide who will follow him in any placement. In addition, he has his own computer with a touch window and unicorn board. Adam has good receptive language and has some sight word vocabulary. He can understand what is going on in his environment. He enjoys the same kinds of movies and TV programs that other fourth and fifth graders like. He has wheelchair mobility and can walk with assistance.

Thinking about placements, we tried to put ourselves in Adam's shoes.

Would we be happy to be in the same classroom for three years, repeating the same types of tasks over and over again? Would we be happy in a class with three other classmates who have limited abilities to communicate with each other? Does he have enough opportunities to establish relationships with peers? Adam does participate in a third grade music class. But is this really enough? Do the children in school know what Adam is really like?

We thought about the advantages of placing Adam in a regular classroom. He would be with his peers. Adam enjoyed going to summer day camp at the regional Y. There were many kids in camp all the time. We could tell that Adam was having a wonderful time. (He enjoys getting ready to go to school, but there was a level of excitement before and after camp that we never saw before.) Adam needs to learn to be self-sufficient. Maybe in this class he would be forced to learn how. There would be positive role models in the class. He might try harder to be accepted by the class. His self-esteem would be enhanced knowing that he was really part of a regular class.

Then we thought about the disadvantages of placing him in a regular class. How would the other children accept Adam? Would they tease him or complain to the teacher? Or would parents of other children complain to the principal that the teacher spends too much time working with Adam and not enough with the others in class? Would Adam's frustration increase because he would not be able to do all the things that the others could do? Would he act out even more to gain everyone's attention? Would the teacher be receptive to having Adam in the class?

After deliberating on these options, I wanted to go for it, but Jeff had some serious doubts. We agreed that we would take the first steps and request inclusion at the IEP meeting. We were surprised when the school system was willing to hire a consultant to help us implement an inclusion program.

Adam will remain in his self-contained class until all the pieces of inclusion are identified. The consultant has made her recommendations on how to proceed with inclusion. She has identified what steps need to be taken for inclusion to work. We all agree that Adam needs to become more proficient with the augmentative communication device. The principal has expressed some concerns about Adam's aggressive behavior in relationship to the safety of the children in the regular class. We understand his concerns. The consultant's recommendations include a "functional behavioral assessment" and development of a "behavior supports plan." We will work on this diligently so that an effective plan can be put into place.

We plan to meet again in the next few weeks to do a COACH (Creating Options and Accommodations for Children), an assessment and planning tool that (1) identifies and prioritizes a child's functional educational goals and objectives according to what the parents need and want the child to learn, and (2) enables the team to plan how those objectives can and will be met in typical settings at school, at home, and in the community (Giangreco, Cloninger, & Iverson, 1992). We also are planning to identify a fourth grade class. In the near future, we will work together to formulate a preliminary IEP that will be used in the inclusive setting. Before the actual change takes place the students as well as the teacher will attend a series of workshops to identify their concerns and to have the concept of inclusion explained to them in detail. Adam will have a chance to spend time with his new classmates at recess and at lunch. The teacher and staff will receive training to assist in the transition and initial program implementation. A student inclusion checklist will help determine what supports and systems changes need to be put into place to assure Adam's successful inclusion. During the transition period Adam can decide to return to his self-contained classroom but slowly build up his tolerance in the fourth grade class. The special education teacher will provide support to the regular classroom teacher. The consultant will work with us as well as the special education teacher and members of the IEP team to monitor and make changes in Adam's IEP as necessary.

We are embarking on a program that we hope will prove successful. We are willing to participate actively in making it successful. Adam has the support mechanisms in place to make it work. We have the commitment of the special education staff to make it work. We have an experienced consultant to help us set up and monitor the program. We know that Adam will need to live and work in his community. Thus he needs to be exposed to the real world now, not at age twenty-one.

WHAT DOES THE FUTURE HOLD?

We have talked about our fears and hopes in transitioning Adam into a new placement. All parents express anxiety and are apprehensive when their child moves into a new educational setting (e.g., birth to three program to preschool; preschool to elementary; middle to high school). Parents begin to think, What is ahead for my child? Will he be able to adjust? Is the new placement able to meet his needs? Parents should seek information on these new settings from other parents, teachers, and parent groups. They may become more vocal and express their concerns to the school administration or board of education. However, these actions lead to positive change. If we do not question the delivery of services and programs, who else will?

School systems make changes in special education programming when economic conditions force a consolidation of programs and/or staffing; when special education populations shift; when parents unite to pressure administration to make changes; and when they are directed to by hearing review boards or courts. Very rarely do school districts initiate change. Yes, the state and federal government are supposed to monitor special education, but how often do they voluntarily observe programs? Appropriate questions for administrators or the department of education in your state might be, How are special education programs monitored for compliance under IDEA and state statutes? Will they only audit programs when a complaint is filed by a parent or group of parents?

That is why it is important for parents to come together and have routine meetings with administrators. These meetings should focus on expressing parental concerns to those in decision-making roles. Specific questions should be developed based on these concerns. For example, the Montgomery County Special Needs Pre-School Parent Council invited an administrator of the school system to speak to them and answer questions about preschool programs. The group was working cooperatively with the department, and in its introductory remarks warmly welcomed the speaker to the meeting. This sets a tone of cooperation between parties. A major concern of the group was transitioning children from preschool to kindergarten. Specific questions included, Are kids being prepared for transitions? What do the teachers know about the programs children are transitioned to? How are other states/counties looking at prekindergarten options? Suggestions were given to the administrator for developing new programs (e.g., prekindergarten program for five-year-olds). These efforts are worthwhile because you are setting the stage for developing programs that will be in existence when children enter the schools in five years. Five years ago, our son Adam was able to attend our neighborhood school because parents who preceded us felt strongly that children with special needs should be educated with their friends and peers. Our actions should be based on what is best for our child; but we also have to consider the long-lasting effects on programming.

The transition to elementary school is not the only time parents will be confronted with this process. When children turn sixteen they must have a transition plan as part of their IEP as mandated by the IDEA. Many parents wait till their child is in high school before they begin to plan for this change. We suggest that planning begin at the elementary level. Goals should be written into your child's IEP that encourage independence and self-help, and vocational skills as appropriate. Community-based work experiences are becoming more popular in school systems. Children need to learn how to function in the real world.

Many parents rely on the professionals working with their child for advice. Remember that they are only one source of information. Solicit opinions by talking to various organizations such as inclusive education groups, Parent Training and Information Centers, the National Parent Network for Disabilities, and Parent to Parent.

INCLUSION

Since the mid-1970s parents have been seeking alternatives to the once popular segregated special education classroom. Most of these parents do not feel comfortable with the thought that their children might be isolated from their peers for the rest of their lives. The civil rights movement and the exposure of the conditions and mistreatment of residents in state institutions have given impetus to inclusion as a policy. P.L. 94-142, Section 504 of the Rehabilitation Act, IDEA, the Americans with Disabilities Act, and other laws were passed by Congress because of the grassroots efforts of individuals interested in promoting equal access to education, employment, and housing for those with disabilities. A majority of these individuals were parents just like you, interested in providing the most appropriate services to their children. Advocates for inclusion define it as

> maximum opportunity for students with disabilities to be included fully with their nondisabled peers in all aspects of school life, using whatever supports are necessary to facilitate social interactions, scholastic achievement, and full membership in the school community. Inclusion abandons the notion of a continuum of educational placements and is based on the presumption that we as educators have knowledge and the technology necessary to enable all children to receive an individualized and appropriate education in typical, age-appropriate classrooms. (Rammler, 1994)

Advocates for inclusion, including Rammler, believe that a child with disabilities will function best in a regular classroom with the appropriate supports. Most notably:

1. It is a realistic preparation for adult life.
2. It provides appropriate role models ("kids learn from kids").
3. It fosters opportunities to learn in natural contexts.
4. It allows children with disabilities to:
   a. have typical experiences
   b. experience greater challenge
   c. have equal opportunities
   d. make friends

They also believe that typical children also benefit from an inclusive education by being able to develop more accepting attitudes and respect for human diversity. The practice of inclusion has spread because many parents have seen a value in this approach. They believe that their child will learn best in this type of environment. In many instances parents in a school district got together and formed organizations to promote it in their school systems. These organizations then met on both the state and national levels to learn of each other's successes and strategies to implement inclusive education. A campaign was launched to promote inclusive education through newsletters, media coverage (e.g., the film *Educating Peter* on PBS), and fund-raising activities (e.g., receiving grants from the federal government, foundations, and private industry). Much has been written about inclusion by academics interested in this topic. Thus much attention has been placed on inclusive education due to the activities of parents seeking an alternative to the "segregated classroom/school." The Individual Education Program process allows parents the opportunity to request inclusion if they believe it is an appropriate setting for their child.

There are many forces out there that will have an effect on how our children will do. The attitudes of the school community as well as Mr. Average Citizen will play a part. The local economic conditions will influence your local school district's budget. In order to create the best educational climate for our children, both now and in the future, parents need to educate the community on who their children are, what they can contribute to the school, and what supports they need to be successful in school. We must also be involved on the state and federal level. In the 1990s, parents of special needs children are working to this end. The National Parent Network on Disabilities is one such organization. Parents have testified at congressional hearings on the reauthorization of funding. They have willingly given up their right to privacy and have come forward to express their views on education policy and practice. Parents have lobbied for "family support" legislation and have been successful in their efforts. On the local level, parents are active in their school's parent teacher organizations (PTOS). Others have set up a special education Parent Teacher Association (an affiliate of the National Parent Teacher Association) to lobby for appropriate and much needed programs in their school districts. Still others have run for seats on the board of education, the city council, or the state legislature. Parents sit on advisory committees to the school district or town committees on disabilities. There are many opportunities for parents to influence the way programs and services are offered to our children in the future.

IN CLOSING

Now that you have read our book, we hope that you will feel more comfortable in becoming an active partner in your child's schooling. At each step we included information to enable you to establish and maintain a strong and cooperative relationship with other members of your communications network. As an informed parent you will be able to ask the right questions at the right time to obtain the information you need to make appropriate decisions on your child's schooling. Your self-confidence has improved because you are knowledgeable about your legal rights as parents of a child with disabilities. It is also very important to make all members of the team feel part of the team effort. It is our responsibility as parents to praise them when they are doing well.

Most likely you will be working with these people for an extended period of time, and your child will interact with many of them on a daily basis. For this relationship to work you must be willing to meet and work with the team on a regular basis. Most important, you need to demonstrate your interest in your child's program not only by attending the PPT meeting, but by (1) being easily accessible for consultations, telephone calls, and interactions in the classroom; (2) supporting the activities in class by carryover at home; and (3) listening to the suggestions made by the professionals and communicating with them often.

Finally, don't be afraid to ask for help. Many resources are available to you. As we have shown, support is out there. There will be times when you will want to seek advice and guidance on some aspect of your child's schooling. Work with the team to identify strategies and resources, but also seek information from others who have no ties with the school district. Many times, the administration may not volunteer information that may help you to decide on a course of action. And the confidentiality issue may prevent you from finding parents that may have similar problems or concerns. We suggest that you become active in special education activities on the district level, so that you will have opportunities to meet parents and stay informed on districtwide issues. Most important, engage in family activities with your child.

Selected Genetic Related Disease Support Groups

Aarskog Syndrome

Aarskog Syndrome Support
Group
c/o Shannon Caranci
62 Robin Hill Ln
Levittown, PA 19055-1411
(215) 943-7131

Aicardi Syndrome

Aicardi Syndrome
Awareness and
Support Group
29 Delavan Ave
Toronto ON
Canada M5P 1T2
(416) 481-4095

Albinism &
Hypopigmentation

National Organization for
Albinism and
Hypopigmentation
1530 Locust St. Box 29
Philadelphia, PA 19102
(800) 473-2310

Anemia, Aplastic

Aplastic Anemia
Foundation of America
P.O. Box 22689
Baltimore, MD 21203
(800) 747-2820

Angelman Syndrome

Angelman Syndrome
Foundation
5959-77 SW 20th Avenue
Gainesville, FL 32607
(904) 332-3303

Arnold-Chiari Syndrome

c/o Maureen &
Kevin Walsh
67 Spring Street
Weymouth, MA 02188
(617) 337-2368

Arthrogryposis

National Support Group for
Arthrogryposis Multiplex
Congenital
P.O. Box 5192
Sonora, CA 95370
(209) 928-3688

Batten's Disease

Batten's Disease Support
and Research Association
2600 Parsons Avenue
Columbus, OH 43207
(800) 448-4570

Beckwith-Wiedemann
Syndrome

3206 Braeburn Circle
Ann Arbor, MI 48108
(800) 837-2976

Cardio-Facio-Cutaneous
Syndrome

CFC Support Network
157 Alder Avenue
McKee City, NJ 08232
(609) 646-5606

Chromosome 9 Disorders

Support Group for 9p
675 N Round Table Drive
Las Vegas, NV 89110
(702) 453-0788

Support Group for
Monosomy 9p
43304 Kipton Nickel Plate
Road
LaGrange, OH 44050
(216) 775-4255

Trisomy 9 International
Parent Support

Childrens Hospital of
Michigan
3901 Beaubien Blvd
Detroit, MI 48201-2196
(313) 745-4513

Chromosome 17p

Smith-Magenis Syndrome
11875 Fawn Ridge Ln
Reston, VA 22094
(703) 709-0568

Chromosome 18 & 13
Chromosome 18

Support Organization for
Trisomy 18, 13 and Related
Disorders
2982 S Union Street
Rochester, NY 14624

Chromosome Deletions

Chromosome Deletion
Outreach,
P.O. Box 532
Center Moriches, NY 11934

Chromosome Inversions

National Center on
Chromosome Inversions
1029 Johnson Street
Des Moines, IA 50135
(515) 287-6798

Cytochrome C Oxidase
Deficiency

Cytochrome C Oxidase
Deficiency Parental Research
and Support Foundation
1935 Park View Place
Aliquippa, PA 15001
(412) 375-6193

Down Syndrome

Association for Children with
Down Syndrome
2616 Martin Avenue
Bellmore, NY 11710
(516) 221-4700

International Foundation for
Genetic Research
400 Penn Center Blvd,
Suite 721
Pittsburgh, PA 15235
(412) 823-6380

National Down Syndrome
Congress
1605 Chantilly Drive
Suite 250
Atlanta, GA 30324
(800) 232-6372
(404) 633-1555

National Down Syndrome
Society
666 Broadway, Suite 810
New York, NY 10012
(800) 221-4602

Parental Assistance
Committee on Down
Syndrome
208 Lafayette Avenue
Peekskill, NY 10566
(914) 739-4085

Fragile X Syndrome

National Fragile X
Foundation
1441 York Street, Suite 215
Denver, CO 80206
(800) 688-8765
(303) 333-6155

Hemophilia

National Hemophilia
Foundation
110 Greene Street,
Room 303
New York, NY 10012
(212) 219-8180

Joubert Syndrome

Joubert Syndrome Parents-
In-Touch Network
12348 Summer Meadow
Road
Rock, MI 49880
(906) 359-4707

Sickle Cell Disease

American Sickle Cell
Anemia Association
10300 Carnegie Avenue
Cleveland, OH 44106
(216) 229-8600

National Association for
Sickle Cell Disease
3345 Wilshire Blvd,
Suite 1106
Los Angeles, CA 90010
(800) 421-8453
(213) 736-5455

Triad Sickle Cell Anemia
Foundation
1102 E. Market Street
Greensboro, NC
27420-0964
(919) 274-1507

Spina Bifida

Spinal Bifida Association of
America
4590 MacArthur Blvd
NW #250
Washington, DC
20007-4226
(800) 621-3141
(202) 944-3285

Tay-Sachs Disease

National Tay-Sachs and Allied
Diseases Association
2001 Beacon Street,
Suite 204
Brookline, MA 02146
(617) 277-4463

**Wolf-Hirschhorn
Syndrome (4p-)**

4p-Parent Contact Group
c/o Becky &
Tom Richardson
3200 Rivanna Court
Woodbridge, VA 22192

Wolf-Hirschhorn Syndrome
(4p-) Support Group and
Newsletter
Virginia Court
Amherst, OH 44002
(216) 282-1460

A Guide to Resources for Families

Disability	Name of Organization	Address	Phone Number
Attention Deficit Disorder	Children with Attention Deficit Disorders	499 NW 70th Avenue Suite 109 Plantation, FL 33317	(305) 587-3700
Autism	Autism Society of America	7910 Woodmont Avenue Suite 650 Bethesda, MD 20814	(800) 328-8476
Cerebral Palsy	United Cerebral Palsy Association	1522 K Street, NW Washington, DC 20005	(800) 872-5827 (202) 842-1266 Voice/TDD
Cystic Fibrosis	Cystic Fibrosis Foundation	6931 Arlington Road Bethesda, MD 20814	(800) FIGHT-CF
Fetal Alcohol Syndrome	National Organization on Fetal Alcohol Syndrome	1815 H Street NW Suite 710 Washington, DC 20006	(800) 666-6327
General Information	Association for the Care of Children's Health	7910 Woodmont Avenue Suite 300 Bethesda, MD 20814	(301) 654-6549
	The Association for Persons with Severe Handicaps (TASH)	29 W. Susquehanna Avenue Suite 210 Baltimore, MD 21204	(410) 828-8274
	Beach Center on Families and Disabilities	University of Kansas 3111 Haworth Hall Lawrence, KS 66045	(913) 864-7600

General Information (continued)	Human Services Research Institute (Family Support)	2336 Massachusetts Ave Cambridge, MA 02140	(617) 876-0426
	National Easter Seals Society	230 W. Monroe Chicago, IL 60606	(800) 221-6827 (312) 726-6200 (312) 726-4258 TDD
	National Information Clearinghouse on Infants with Disabilities and Life Threatening Conditions	University of South Carolina Benson Bldg 1st floor Columbia, SC 29208	(800) 922-9234 ext. 201
	National Rehabilitation Information Center (NARIC)	8455 Colesville Road Silver Spring, MD 20910	(800) 346-2742
	Pathways Awareness Foundation	123 N. Wacker Drive Chicago, IL 60606	(800) 955-2445
Genetics	Hereditary Disease Foundation	1427 7th Street Suite 2 Santa Monica, CA 90401	(310) 458-4183
Hearing Impaired	Alexander Graham Bell Association for the Deaf	3417 Volta Place, NW Washington, DC 20007	(202) 337-5220 Voice/TDD
	National Information Center on Deafness	Gallaudet University 800 Florida Avenue NE Washington, DC 20002	(202) 651-5051 Voice (202) 651-5052 TT

Learning Disabilities	Learning Disabilities Association of America	4156 Library Road Pittsburgh, PA 15234	(412) 341-1515
Mental Retardation	The ARC	500 E. Border Street Suite 300 Arlington, TX 76010	(817) 261-6003
Muscular Dystrophy	Muscular Dystrophy Association	3300 E. Sunrise Drive Tucson, AZ 85718	(602) 529-2000
Rare Disorders	National Organization for Rare Disorders	100 Rt 37 P.O. Box 8923 New Fairfield, CT 06812	(800) 999-6673 (203) 746-6518
Visually Impaired	American Council of the Blind	1155 15th Street, NW Washington, DC 20005	(800) 424-8666 (202) 467-5081
	American Foundation for the Blind	15 W. 16th Street New York, NY 10011	(800) 232-5463 (212) 620-2000
	National Association for Parents of the Visually Impaired	P.O. Box 317 Watertown, MA 02272	(800) 562-6265 (617) 972-7441

Appendix C

References for Parents of Preemies

Batshaw, M.L., and Perret, Y.M. 1992. *Children with disabilities: A medical primer.* 3rd ed. Baltimore: Paul H. Brookes.

Cohen, L. 1990. *Before their time: Fetuses and infants at risk.* Washington, DC: AAMR Monographs.

Jason, J., & Van Der Meer, A. 1989. *Parenting your premature baby.* New York: Henry Holt.

Lieberman, A., & Sheagren, T. 1984. *The preemie parents handbook.* New York: E.P. Dutton.

Marantz-Henig, R., with Fletcher, B. 1983. *Your premature baby: The complete guide to preemie care during that crucial first year.* New York: Rawson Associates.

O'Sullivan, S.B. 1985–1986. Infant-caregiver interaction and the social development of handicapped infants. *Physical and Occupational Therapy in Pediatrics,* 5(4): 1–12.

Rosenberg, S.A., Robinson, C.C., & Beckman, P.J. 1986. Measures of parent-infant interaction: An overview. *Topics in Early Childhood Special Education,* 6(2): 32–43.

Trute, B., & Hauch, C. 1988. Building on family strength: A study of families with positive adjustment to the birth of a developmentally disabled child. *Journal of Marital and Family Therapy,* 14(2): 185–93.

Children's Literature to Help Sisters and Brothers of Children with Special Needs Cope

PRESCHOOL AND PRIMARY LEVEL

Cairo, S. 1985. *Our brother has Down's syndrome.* Canada: Annick Press.

Two older sisters tell about their younger brother, who has Down syndrome. Large color photographs and a sensitive text describe their special brother and their family life. A clear explanation of Down syndrome is included. Nonfiction, Primary School Level.

Hirsch, K. 1977. *My sister.* Minneapolis: Carol Rhoda Book.

This story depicts a boy who has a sister with mental retardation. The boy's own play activities and friendships are contrasted with his sister's social abilities. Through various scenarios (e.g., vacation), the brother's emotions (resentment, embarrassment, anger, pride, and love) are explored. Fiction, Primary School Level.

Muldoon, K.M. 1989. *Princess Pooh.* Morton Grove, IL: Albert Whitman and Co.

This picture book shows how a young sibling learns to cope with her own feelings and reach a fond understanding of her ten-year-old sister, whose lifestyle involves a wheelchair. Fiction, Preschool–Primary Level.

Smith, L.B. 1977. *A special kind of sister.* New York: Holt, Rinehart and Winston.

The word "special" in this title emphasizes the qualities of the "normal" sibling while focusing on her feelings. Her brother, who has mental retardation, tends to fall ill frequently, which prompts her to contemplate feigning illness to gain more parental attention. Fiction, Primary School Level.

Sobol, H.L. 1977. *My brother Steven is retarded.* New York: Macmillan.

An eleven-year-old girl speaks directly to the reader in this book, illustrated with photographs about her oscillating feelings toward her older brother, who has mental retardation. The feelings range from anger to acute embarrassment to pleasure. Steven is portrayed as a person capable of accomplishment and an integral member of the family. His sister, Beth, worries about his future and the reactions of her friends, and reexamines her old fears that mental retardation might be catching. Biography, Primary School Level.

ELEMENTARY LEVEL

Bunnett-Stein, S. 1985. *About handicaps: An open family book for parents and children together*. New York: Walker and Co.

This book is a valuable resource for parents to utilize when explaining to their children that their brother or sister has a disability. It is written for both adults and youngsters. Nonfiction, Elementary School Level.

Emmert, M. 1989. *I'm the big sister now*. Morton Grove, IL: Albert Whitman and Co.

Michelle Emmert is the younger sister of Amy, who has cerebral palsy. Michelle explains what it is like living with someone who cannot sit up, use her hands, walk, talk, or read. Nonfiction, Elementary Level.

Jansen, L. 1984. *My sister is special*. N.P., Ohio: Standard Publishing Co.

Matthew has a sister who has Down syndrome. In this book Matthew shares his feelings about having a sister with disabilities. Fiction, Elementary School Level.

Thompson, M. 1992. *My brother Matthew*. N.P., MD: Woodbine House.

This tale is about how family life typically focuses on the needs of a child with a disability, and the effects that can have on the other kids in the family. Fiction, Elementary School Level.

PRIMARY TO MIDDLE SCHOOL LEVEL

Gold, P. 1975. *Please don't say hello*. New York: Human Services.

This story depicts a family with two boys, one of whom has autism, moving into a new neighborhood. Though the story is told from the brother's perspective, autism is explained through the mother's conversations with the neighborhood children. The stress of telling newfound friends about one's sibling and coping with their reactions is a major part of the story. Fiction, Primary–Middle School level.

Grollman, S.H. 1977. *More time to grow: Explaining mental retardation to children*. Boston: Beacon Press.

An illustrative story accompanies questions and activities for children, a guide for parents and teachers, and a list of recommended resources on mental retardation. Fiction and Nonfiction, Primary and Middle School Level.

MIDDLE–JUNIOR HIGH SCHOOL LEVEL

Byars, B. 1970. *The summer of the swans*. New York: Viking Press.

In this story about growing up, a young girl's miseries are shoved aside as she searches for her lost brother, who has mental retardation. Petty personal concerns are put into perspective in the light of her brother's predicament, and by the helping hand extended by Joe, a boy she "can't stand." Fiction, Middle–Junior High School Level.

Cleaver, V. 1973. *Me too.* New York: J.B. Lippincott.

This story explores the relationship between twin sisters, one of whom has mental retardation. Their father deserts the family, and Lydia becomes responsible for her sister, who must come home from boarding school. Lydia battles neighborhood ignorance and prejudice while attempting one summer to do what no one else has done—teach her sister. Lornie does not learn much from Lydia, but Lydia gains valuable insight into their relationship. Fiction, Middle–Junior High School Level.

Gehret, J. 1992. *I'm somebody too.* New York: Verbal Images Press.

This book is about the sister of a boy who has ADD. The themes explored in this book are an individual's desire to help, guilt, resentment, and being left out. Fiction, Middle School Level.

Meltan, D. 1976. *A boy called hopeless.* Independence, MO: Independence Press.

Fifteen-year-old Mary Jane describes her family's reactions when they find that her younger brother has a brain injury. They decide to participate in a rehabilitation program with him. Fiction, Middle–Junior High School Level.

Metzger, L. 1992. *Barry's sister.* New York: Atheneum, Macmillan.

This story is about a young girl named Ellen Gray and her brother Barry, who has cerebral palsy. The author explores Ellen's feelings about having a brother with a disability. Fiction, Middle–Junior High School Level.

Miner, J.C. 1982. *She's my sister: Having a retarded sister.* MN: Crestwood House.

Mary Lou's secret of having a sister who has mental retardation threatens to be revealed and ruin her social life when her sister moves back home. Fiction, Middle School Level.

Minneapolis Children's Medical Center, Exceptional Children with Communication and Interaction Disorders. 1989. *Having a brother like David.* MN: Minneapolis Children's Medical Center.

The story offers the perspective of Marty, whose brother, David, has autism. Marty shares experiences, thoughts, and worries as well as coping alternatives about life with David. Fiction, Middle School Level.

Roy, R. 1984. *Where's Buddy?* New York: Clarion Books.

Mike has a brother named Buddy. Buddy has diabetes and takes insulin to help stabilize his body. Buddy gets lost, and Mike frantically searches for him. Both brothers learn painful lessons in responsibility in this story. Fiction, Middle School Level.

Appendix E

Literature to Help Parents Cope with a Special Needs Child in the Family

Beavers, J., Hampson, R.B., Hulgus, Y.F., & Beavers, W.R. 1986. Coping in families with a retarded child. *Family Process*, 25 (3): 365–378.

Bristol, M.M. 1979. *Maternal coping with autistic children: Adequacy of interpersonal support and effect of child's characteristics*. Doctoral dissertation, University of North Carolina, Chapel Hill.

Burden, R., & Thomas, D. 1986. A further perspective on parental reaction to handicap. *Exceptional Child*, 33 (2): 140–145.

Cavanagh, J., & Ashman, A.F. 1985. Stress in families with handicapped children. *Australia and New Zealand Journal of Developmental Disabilities*, 11(3): 151–156.

Crnic, K.A., Friedrich, W.N., & Greenberg, M.T. 1983. Adaptation of families with mental retarded children: A model of stress, coping and family ecology. *American Journal of Mental Deficiency*, 88: 125–138.

Donovan, A.M. 1988. Family stress and ways of coping with adolescents who have handicaps. Maternal perceptions. *American Journal on Mental Retardation*, 92(6): 502–509.

Dyson, L. 1987. Parent stress, family functioning and social support in families of young handicapped children. Paper presented at the National Childhood Conference on Children with Special Needs, Denver, November 1–3, 1987.

Featherstone, H. 1980. *A difference in the family: Living with a disabled child*. New York: Basic Books.

Flynt, S.W., & Wood, T.A. 1989. Stress and coping of mothers of children with moderate mental retardation. Special Issue: Research on Families. *American Journal on Mental Retardation*, 94(3): 278–283.

Frey, K.S., Greenberg, M.T., & Fewell, R.R. 1989. Stress and coping among parents of handicapped children: A multidimensional approach. *American Journal on Mental Retardation*, 94(3): 240–249.

Gath, A. 1985. Parental reactions to loss and disappointment: The diagnosis of

Down's syndrome. *Developmental Medicine and Child Neurology*, 27(3): 392–400.

Goodman, C.R. 1988. *Helping families cope*. Paper presented at the International Conference of the Association for Children and Adults with Learning Disabilities, Las Vegas, February 24–27, 1988.

Harris, S.L. 1987. The family crisis: Diagnosis of a severely disabled child. *Marriage and Family Review*, 11(1–2): 107–118.

Hutliner, P. 1988. Stress: Is it an inevitable condition for families of children at risk? *Teaching Exceptional Children*, 20 (4): 36–39.

Johnson, S.J. 1985. A survey of stresses and resources for families with handicapped infants. *Dissertation Abstracts International*, 45(8-A): 2652.

Jones, C.W. 1987. Coping with the young handicapped child in the current family: An ecosystemic perspective. *Family Therapy Collections*, 23: 85–100.

Kazak, A.E. 1985. Family stresses and social support networks. An analysis of families with handicapped children. *Dissertation Abstracts International*, 45 (8B): 2692.

Mendler, A. 1990. *Smiling at yourself: Educating young children about stress and self esteem*. Santa Cruz, CA: Network Publishing.

Meyer, D., Vadasy, P., Fewell, R., & Schell, G. 1985. *A handbook for the Fathers Program: How to organize a program for fathers and their handicapped children*. Seattle: University of Washington Press.

Minnes, P.M. 1985. Coping strategies and family adjustment to stress associated with a handicapped child. *Dissertation Abstracts International*, 45(8-A): 2454.

————1988. Family resources and stress associated with having a mentally retarded child. *American Journal on Mental Retardation*, 93(2): 184–192.

Nasseef, R. 1989. How families cope successfully with a handicapped child: A qualitative study. Paper presented at the sixty-seventh Annual Convention of the Council for Exceptional Children San Francisco, April 3–7, 1989.

Perske, R., & Perske, M. 1973. *Hope for the families: New directions for parents of persons with retardation or other disabilities*. Nashville: Abingdon Press.

Simon, R. 1987. *After tears: Parents talk about raising a child with a disability*. Orlando: Harcourt Brace Jovanovich.

Singer, G.H.S., & Irvin, L.K. 1990. *Support for caregiving families: Enabling positive adaptation to disability*. Baltimore: Paul H. Brookes.

Wright, L.S., Matlock, K.S., & Matlock, D.T. 1985. Parents of handicapped children: Their self-ratings, life satisfaction and parental adequacy. *Exceptional Child*, 32(1): 37–40.

Parent Training and Information Centers

State	Organization	State	Organization
Alabama	Special Education Action Committee* P.O. Box 161274 Mobile, AL 36606 (205) 478-1208 (800) 222-7322	Alaska	Alaska PARENTS Resource Center 540 International Airport Rd Suite 250 Anchorage, AL 99518 (907) 563-2246 (800) 478-7678
Arizona	Pilot Parent Partnerships* 2150 East Highland Avenue, Suite 105 Phoenix, AZ 85016 (602) 468-3001 (800) 237-3007	Arkansas	Arkansas Disability Coalition Focus 10002 West Markham, 2917 King St Suite B7 Jonesboro, AR Little Rock, AK 72205 72401 (501) 221-1330 (501) 935-2750
California	Team of Advocates for Parents Helping Special Kids, Inc. (TASK) Parents 100 W. Cerritos Ave. 1801 Vincente Street Anaheim, CA 926805 San Francisco, CA (714) 533-TASK 94116 (415) 564-0722	Colorado	PEAK Parent Center, Inc. 6055 Lehman Dr, Suite 101 Colorado Springs, CO 80918 (719) 531-9400 (800) 284-0251
Connecticut	CT Parent Advocacy Center, Inc. 5 Church Lane, Suite #4 P.O. Box 579 East Lyme, CT 06333 (203) 739-3089 (800) 445-2722	Delaware	Parent Information Center of Delaware Inc. 700 Barksdale Road, Suite 6 Newark, DE 19711 (302) 366-0152
District of Columbia	COPE P.O. Box 90498 Washington, DC 20090-0498 (202) 526-6814	Florida	Family Network on Disability 5510 Gray Street, Suite 220 Tampa, Florida 33609 (813) 289-1122

Georgia	Parents Educating Parents Georgia ARC 1851 Ram Runway, Suite 104 College Park, GA 30337
Hawaii	AWARE/Learning Disabilities 200 North Vineyard Blvd. Suite 103 Honolulu, HI 96817 (808) 536-2280
Idaho	Idaho Parents Unlimited Parent Education Resource Center 4696 Overland Road Boise, ID 83705 (800) 242-4785 (208) 342-5884
Illinois	Designs for Change 6 N Michigan Avenue Chicago, IL (312) 857-9292 Family Resource Center on Disabilities 20 E Jackson Blvd Chicago, IL 60604 (800) 952-4199 (IL)
Indiana	Indiana Resource Center for Families with Special Needs 833 E Northside Blvd, Bldg 1 R South Bend, IN 46617 (800) 332-4433 (IN); (219) 234-7101
Iowa	Iowa Pilot Parents 33 N 12 Street PO Box 1151 Fort Dodge, IA 50501 (800) 952-4777 (515) 576-5870
Kansas	Families Together 1023 SW Gage Blvd Topeka, KS 66604 (913) 273-6343
Kentucky	Kentucky Special Parent Involvement Network 2210 Goldsmith Lane, Suite 118 Louisville, KY 40218 (502) 456-0893
Louisiana	Project Prompt 4323 Division Street, Ste 110 Metairie, LA 70002 (800) 766-7736 (504) 888-9111
Maine	Special Needs Parent Information Network PO Box 2067 Augusta, ME 04338-2067 (800) 870-7746 (207) 582-2504
Maryland	Parents Place of Maryland 7257 Parkway Drive, Ste 210 Hanover, MD 21076 (410) 712-0900
Massachusetts	Federation for Children with Special Needs 95 Berkeley Street, Ste 104 Boston, MA 02116 (800) 331-0688 (MA); (617) 482-2915

Michigan	Citizens Alliance to Uphold Special Education 313 S Washington Sq, Ste 040 Lansing, MI 48933 (800) 221-9105 (MI); (517) 485-4084	Parents Are Experts 23077 Greenfield Rd Southfield, MI 48075 (313) 557-5070	Minnesota	PACER Center 4826 Chicago Ave S Minneapolis, MN 55417 (800) 537-2237 (parents MN); (612) 827-2966
Missouri	Missouri Parents Act 1722 S. Glenstone, Ste125 Springfield, MO 64131 (800) 743-7634 (MO); (417) 882-7434

MPACT 8631 Delmar, Ste 300 St. Louis, MO 63124 (800) 995-3160 (314) 997-7622 | MPACT 1115 E. 65 Street Kansas City, MO 64131 (816) 333-6833 | Montana | Parents, Lets Unite for Kids EMC/Special Education Building 1500 N 30th Street Billings, MT 59101 (406) 657-2055 |
| Nebraska | Nebraska Parents Center 3610 Dodge Street, Ste 102 Omaha, NE 68131 (800) 284-8520 (NE); (402) 346-0525 | | Nevada | Nevada Parent Connection 3380 S Arville Blvd, Ste J Las Vegas, NV 89102 (800) 508-4464 (NV); (702) 252-0259 ext. 112 and 113 |
| New Hampshire | Parent Information Center 151 A Manchester Street PO Box 1422 Concord, NH 03302 (800) 232-0986 (NH); (603) 224-6299 | | New Jersey | Statewide Parent Advocacy Network 516 North Ave E Westfield, NJ 07090 (908) 654-7726 |

New Mexico	EPICS Project Parents Reaching Out 1127 University Blvd NE Albuquerque, NM 87102 (800) 524-5176 (NM); (505) 842-9045	EPICS SW Communication Resources PO Box 788 412 Camino Don Thomas Bernalillo, NM 87004 (800) 765-7320
North Carolina	Exceptional Children's Assistance Center PO Box 16 Davidson, NC 28655 (800) 962-6817 (NC); (704) 892-1321	Families First Coalition 300 Enola Road Morganton, NC 28655 (800) 822-3477 (NC); (704) 433-2662
Ohio	Child Advocacy Center 1821 Summit Road, Ste 303 Cincinnati, OH 45237 (800) 821-2400 (OH); (513) 821-2400	Ohio Coalition for the Education of Handicapped Children 933 High Street, Ste 106B Worthington, OH 43085 (614) 431-1307
New York	Advocates for Children of NY 24-16 Bridge Plaza S Long Island City, NY 11101 (718) 729-8866 Parent Network Center 452 Delaware Ave. Buffalo, NY 14202 (716) 885-1004	Resources for Children with Special Needs 200 Park Avenue S Ste 816 New York, NY 10003 (212) 677-4650
North Dakota	Pathfinder Parent Training and Information Center 1600 Second Avenue SW Minot, ND 58701 (800) 245-5840 (ND); (701) 852-9426	
Oklahoma	Parents Reaching Out in Oklahoma Project 1917 S. Harvard Avenue Oklahoma City, OK 73128 (800) 759-4142 (405) 681-9710	

Oregon	Oregon COPE Project 999 Locust Street, NE Salem, OR 97303 (503) 373-7477	
Pennsylvania	Mentor Parent Program Rt 257 PO Box 718 Seneca, PA 16346 (800) 447-1431 (PA); (814) 676-8615 Parent Education Network 333 E 7th Avenue York, PA 17404 (800) 522-5817 (PA); (717) 845-9722	Parents Union for Public Schools 311 S Juniper Street, Ste 602 Philadelphia, PA 19107 (215) 546-1166
Rhode Island	Rhode Island Parent Information Network Independence Square 500 Prospect Street Pawtucket, RI 02860 (800) 464-3399 (RI); (401) 727-4144	
South Carolina	PRO-PARENTS 2712 Middleburg Dr, Ste 102 Columbia, SC 29204 (800) 759-4776 (SC); (803) 779-3859	
South Dakota	South Dakota Parent Connection PO Box 84813 Sioux Falls, SD 57118 (800) 640-4553 (SD); (605) 335-8844	
Tennessee	Support and Training for Exceptional Parents 1805 Hayes Street, Ste 100 Nashville, TN 37203 (800) 280-7837; (615) 639-0125	

Texas	Parents Resource Network 277 N 18th, Ste 2 Beaumont, TX 77707 (800) 866-4726 (409) 838-2366 Special Kids PO Box 61628 Houston, TX 77208 (713) 643-9576 Project PODER 2300 W Commerce, Ste 205 San Antonio, TX 78207 (800) 682-9747 (210) 222-2637
Utah	Utah Parent Center 2290 E 4500 S, Ste 110 Salt Lake City, UT 84117 (800) 468-1160 (UT); (801) 272-9576
Vermont	Vermont Parent Information Center 1 Mill Street Burlington, VT 05401 (800) 639-7170 (VT); (802) 658-5315
Virginia	Parent Education Advocacy Training Center 228 S Pitt Street, Ste 300 Alexandria, VA 22314 (800) 869-6782 (703) 836-2953
Washington	PAVE/STOMP Specialized Training of Military Parents 12208 Pacific Hghwy, SW Tacoma, WA 98499 (206) 588-1741 Touchstones 6721 51st Avenue S Seattle, WA 98118 (206) 721-0867 Washington PAVE 6316 S 12th Street Tacoma, WA 98465 (800) 572-7368 (206) 545-2266
West Virginia	West Virginia Parent Training and Information Center 104 East Main Street Colonial Village, Ste 3-B Clarksburg, WV 26301 (800) 281-1436 (304) 624-1436
Wisconsin	Parent Education Project of Wisconsin 2192 S 60th Street West Allis, WI 53219 (800) 231-8382 (WI); (414) 328-5520
Wyoming	Wyoming PIC 5 N Lobban Buffalo, WY 82834 (800) 660-9742 (WY); (307) 684-2277

Glossary

Achondroplasia—A condition wherein the growth of bones is stifled, causing extreme shortness of arms and legs.

Alphabeta protein—A type of blood test that highlights Down syndrome and other birth defects.

Americans with Disabilities Act, P.L. 101–336 (ADA)—Federal legislation that prohibits discrimination based on disabilities in the areas of employment, public services, transportation, public accommodations, and telecommunications.

Annual review—A school meeting to discuss and review a child's Individualized Education Program.

Apgar score—Assessment of the condition of a newborn within one minute of birth and after five minutes of life.

Aphasia—The inability to comprehend spoken or written language or to express words in speech, writing, or gesture.

Apnea—Difficulty in breathing.

ARD meeting—Admission, review, and dismissal meeting that includes members of a school district as well as parents. Its purpose is to discuss and make recommendations as appropriate for providing a special education program to a child (may be called a PPT meeting in some locales).

Assessment—A process that determines the strengths and weaknesses of a child through the use of testing both formally, using standardized tests, and informally, through observation by both parents and professionals; and information gathered by questioning parents and collecting a medical history.

Assistive technology—Any item, piece of equipment, or product system that is used to increase, maintain, or improve the functional capabilities of individuals with disabilities.

At risk—A term used with children who have, or could have, problems with their development that may affect later learning.

Attention deficit disorder—A developmental disorder characterized by impulsivity (the tendency to act or speak quickly without thinking about the meaning or consequences), distractibility, and inattentiveness.

Attention deficit hyperactivity disorder—A developmental disorder characterized by impulsivity (the tendency to act or speak quickly without thinking about the meaning or consequences), distractibility, and inattentiveness, accompanied by excessive movement (overactivity).

Audiologist—A professional concerned with the measurement of hearing.

Auditory association—The ability to identify and accurately choose between sounds of different pitch, volume, and pattern.

Auditory discrimination—The ability to recognize differences between similar sounds and words, such as bet and bat.

Auditory memory—The ability to repeat a sequence of sounds; the ability to remember what has been heard.

Auditory perception—The ability to receive and understand sounds.

Auditory processing—The ability to discriminate, associate, sequence, and remember auditory (by hearing) stimuli.

Auditory reception—The ability to understand the spoken word.

Autism—One of the thirteen different categories of disabilities that IDEA lists under which children may be eligible for special education and related services. Major symptoms are delayed and abnormal language, an inability to relate to people, and repetitive behaviors usually resulting from abnormal brain development.

Birth defect—Any physical condition or malady resulting genetically or from gestational injury.

Bradycardia—Slowing of the heartbeat.

Brain damage—Structural injury or insult to the brain.

Brain shunt—A device implanted in the brain to allow fluid from the brain to be absorbed into other parts of the body.

Buckley Amendment—The Family Educational Rights and Privacy Act of 1974 (P.L. 93-380), written to preserve family rights of disclosure of educational records that are maintained by institutions receiving federal education funds (including your local school district).

Case manager—A person who acts as a central resource person for families to access needed services.

CAT Scan—An x-ray of the brain.

Center-based program—A self-contained educational program wherein all services are delivered within the school's confines.

Central auditory processing disorder—Inability to process and interpret auditory stimuli in the absence of a peripheral hearing loss.

Cerebral palsy—A term used to describe a condition of motor dysfunction (problems with movement) caused by a lack of oxygen to the brain, usually before, during, or shortly after birth.

Child Find—A state and local program that identifies individuals from birth to age twenty-one who may be in need of special education and related services. This program makes a special effort to identify children from birth to age six.

Cleft palate—An opening in the upper palate of the mouth.

Clinical nurse specialist—A member of a multidisciplinary team in a clinical setting who coordinates care among the various disciplines and ensures continuity of care. This professional may provide supportive counseling for the family, teach self-help skills, and address educational needs of the child and family when they are accessing clinical services.

Cognitive—A term that describes the process people use for remembering, reasoning, understanding, and using judgment.

Corrected age—The age that a premature baby would have been if born at forty weeks gestational age.

Cri du chat syndrome—A condition in which genetic material is lost on chromosome 5. It is often initially diagnosed by a distinctive cry at birth.

Cystic fibrosis—The number-one genetic killer of American children. This disorder affects the lungs, pancreas, and sweat glands.

Developmental delay—A term used to describe a young child who is slower than his peers in reaching specific milestones, but has the potential to catch up.

Developmental milestones—The average age when a child is able to complete certain tasks.

Developmental pediatrician—A pediatrician specializing in the areas of child mental and physical development.

Disability—The result of any physical or mental condition that affects or eliminates one's ability to develop, achieve, and/or function in an educational setting at a normal rate.

Down syndrome—The most common chromosomal disorder, caused by an extra chromosome contributed either by the egg or sperm cell.

Due process—The process designed to protect the rights of parents and their child with a disability and to provide a method for conflict resolution between parents and schools.

Dysgraphia—The inability to copy or write symbols or words.

Dyslexia—The inability to see or perceive letters and words as they really are.

Dyspraxia—The inability to perform nonhabitual or new coordinated movements.

Early intervention services—Services designed to stimulate the development of a disabled infant and to provide training and support for the family.

EEG (electroencephalogram)—This test measures the brain wave pattern through electrodes placed on the scalp.

Evaluation—Procedures used to determine whether a child has a disability and the nature and extent of the special education and related services the child needs.

Extended school year (ESY)—A kind of special education program provided to a child for more than 180 school days.

Fetal alcohol syndrome—A maternally inflicted condition wherein a baby is born with birth defects due to a mother's consumption of alcohol while pregnant. Such babies may have lowered intelligence, speech delays, poor fine motor coordination, or ADHD.

Fine motor skills—Those skills pertaining to the smaller muscles of the body, especially those in the hands, fingers, toes, and eyes, and those related to the production of speech. Fine motor coordination is based on gross motor ability.

Fragile X syndrome—The most common inherited form of mental retardation.

Free appropriate public education—Legal terminology in IDEA by which all children have the right to a public education without cost to families no matter how severely disabled they are.

Genetic counselor—A professional specializing in the translation of genetic concepts into understandable and practical information on birth defects and inherited diseases to assist families to make informed personal decisions on pregnancy and the care of a child with a defect.

Geneticist—A professional specializing in inherited or genetic disorders. A geneticist studies the chemical and physical nature of genes and chromosomes to determine how a disorder is inherited and the risks of recurrence.

Gross motor skills—Skills pertaining to the movements of larger refined muscles of the body for activities such as walking and balance.

Home-based program—A program in which designated professional(s) travel to a child's home to provide one-on-one service.

Hydrocephalus—A medical term referring to the accumulation of excess cerebrospinal fluid in the ventricles of the brain. Often referred to as water on the brain.

Hypertonia—A condition of too much muscle tone, or increased resistance to stretch.

Hypotonia—A condition of too little muscle tone, or no resistance to stretch; demonstrating floppiness when handled.

IDEA—The federal Individuals with Disabilities Education Act, (Public Law 102-119), which provides guarantees for a free appropriate public education to children with disabilities.

IEP—Individualized Education Program; a written statement of the educational program designed to meet a child's special needs by identifying goals for the child, and specific means for achieving these goals in a coordinated team effort.

IFSP—Individualized Family Service Plan; a written plan for infants and toddlers with special needs and their families to ensure that the children receive a well-planned and coordinated program for early intervention services.

Inclusion—The process of developing and implementing a special education program that will enable a child with a disability to be educated in the same classroom with nondisabled peers.

Jaundice—A condition that often occurs in newborns. It appears as a yellow discoloration of the skin and eyes and is caused by immaturity in the brain stem.

Kleinfelter syndrome—A genetic disorder in which an extra X chromosome is present in males.

LEA—local educational agency; the term used in many state and federal laws to identify the educational agency responsible for providing educational services to children. (In most cases, this is the local school system.)

Learning disability—An abnormal condition often affecting children of normal or above-average intelligence, characterized by difficulty in learning skills in areas such as reading and writing. It is usually related to slow development of perceptual motor skills.

LRE—least restrictive environment; a term in the section of the IDEA that requires children with disabilities to be educated with their nondisabled peers, to the maximum extent possible.

Marfan syndrome—A disorder of connective tissue.

Mediation—A process by which parents and the local education agency work together to develop a mutually agreed upon resolution to a conflict with the help of a neutral party who acts as a facilitator.

Microcephaly—The medical term for an abnormally small head.

Multidisciplinary team—A group of professionals with expertise in different areas who come together to share their knowledge with each other and to develop a plan of action to solve problems.

Muscle tone—The amount of tension present in a muscle when it is resting or when it is working; the resistance of muscles to stretch.

Neuro developmental exam—A comprehensive exam made up of a series of tasks designed to test coordination, memory, sequencing, fine motor skills, and the ability to follow directions.

NICU—neonatal intensive care unit; a hospital unit especially designed to provide state-of-the-art medical care to high-risk infants.

Occupational therapist—A professional specializing in providing treatment that helps encourage individual developmental or physical skills that will aid in daily living. Works on developing fine motor and self-help skills such as dressing and eating.

Ophthalmologist—A physician who treats eye disorders.

Orthopedist—A physician who evaluates movement and motor function in children and assesses the need for gait correction through the use of splints, braces, traction, and, when necessary, surgery. Recommends appropriate adaptive equipment for proper positioning and/or maximum independence.

Orthotist—A technical specialist who makes braces and splints.

Pediatric neurologist—A physician who usually confirms the diagnosis of cerebral palsy and other neurological conditions and is often responsible for the care of children with seizure disorders, learning disabilities, and mental retardation.

Perineonatologist—A physician who specializes in the care of the developing fetus.

Personal-social skills—Those skills designed to facilitate independent living in a developmentally challenged person.

Physiatrist—A physician specializing in physical medicine and rehabilitation.

Physical therapist—A professional specializing in the remediation of or compensation for mobility, muscle strength, and postural deficits.

Placement—The classroom, program, service, and/or therapy that is selected for a student with special needs.

PPT—Planning and Placement Team; a group of educational professionals, including a special education teacher, a representative of the special education administration, and other professionals as needed, who evaluate, discuss, and make recommendations as appropriate for providing a special education program to a child.

Program—In special education, a service, placement, and/or therapy designed to help a child with special needs.

Psychologist—A professional specializing in the mental processes affecting behavior.

Psychomotor—A term used with reference to the causing of voluntary movement.

Public agency—An agency, office, or organization that is supported by public funds and serves the community at large.

Related services—Professional services a child might need in order to benefit from an educational program (e.g., occupational therapy, transportation, speech).

Rett syndrome—A sex-linked neurological disorder found in females.

Screening—A process for gathering information to determine whether or not further evaluation is needed for possible delivery of special education services.

Seizure—An excessive periodic discharge of electrical activity in the brain.

Sensory integrative dysfunction—An irregularity or disorder in brain function that makes it difficult to integrate sensory input effectively.

Service coordinator—Someone who acts as a coordinator of an infant's or toddler's services, working in partnership with the family and providers of special programs.

Sickle cell anemia—An inherited blood disorder occurring among blacks and Hispanics of Caribbean ancestry.

Special education—Instruction designed to meet a child's special individual needs, often not limited to instruction in a classroom.

Special needs—A term to describe a child who has disabilities or who is at risk of developing disabilities, and who therefore requires special services or treatment in order to progress.

Speech therapist—A professional specializing in the identification and treatment of speech and language problems, including the ability to reproduce sounds, interpret spoken language, and convey meaning.

Spina bifida—A malformation, apparent at birth, characterized by a defect in the spinal column (open spine).

Standardized test—A test developed to measure an individual's skills, knowledge, or abilities based on a specific population's norm. This kind of test is validated for use with that specific population.

Syndrome—A collection of abnormalities that go together to form a recognizable pattern.

Tactile defensiveness—An oversensitivity to touch or movement usually exhibited by children with developmental disabilities, which may interfere with their ability to learn.

Tay Sachs disease—An inherited progressively degenerative disease caused by an enzyme deficiency that affects the nervous system. It is most commonly found among Jews of Eastern European ancestry.

Visual discrimination—The act of distinguishing differences in visual stimuli.

Visual evoked response test—A test commonly performed to verify that a child can see. This test, however, does not measure visual acuity.

Visual memory—The ability to recall items from visual stimulation. It includes immediate and delayed recall of numbers, words, sentences, and paragraphs.

Visual motor function—The ability to draw or copy forms or to perform constructive tasks.

Visual motor integration—The ability to translate what a person sees into a physical action.

Visual processing—Taking in, understanding, remembering, and using information received by visual stimuli.

References

American Medical Directory. 1993. Chicago: American Medical Association.

Anderson, W., Chitwood, S., & Hayden, D. 1990. *Negotiating the Special Education Maze: A Guide for Parents and Teachers.* Rockville, MD: Woodbine House.

Apollini, I. 1984. Self Advocacy: How to Be a Winner. *Information from the National Information Center for Handicapped Children and Youth.* Washington, DC: National Information Center for Handicapped Children and Youth (NICHCY).

Arcfacts: Public Law 99-457 Amendments to the Education of the Handicapped Act (factsheet). 1986, October. Arlington, TX: Association of Retarded Citizens (ARC).

Association for Retarded Citizens Montgomery County. (N.d.). *Project TEAM: Program Course.* Rockville, MD.

Beckman, P., & Boyes, G. 1993. *Deciphering the System: A Guide for Families of Young Children with Disabilities.* Cambridge, MA: Brookline Books.

Blaber, M.E., et al. N.d. *One Step at a Time: A Parent's Guide to Cerebral Palsy* (pamphlet). Newington, CT: Newington Children's Hospital.

Cappello, N. 1993. Letter to Danbury Public Schools. Middletown, CT: Bureau of Special Education and Pupil Services.

Center for Parenting Studies. N.d. *Organizing Support Programs for Parents of Premature Infants.* Boston: Wheelock College.

The Central Admission, Review and Dismissal Process: A Parent's Guide to the Central Placement Process (brochure). N.d. Rockville, MD: Montgomery County Public Schools.

Children's Defense Fund. 1989. *94-142 and 504: Numbers that Add Up to Educational Rights for Children with Disabilities. A Guide for Parents and Advocates.* 3rd ed. Washington, DC: Author.

Cluman, B. 1987. Fighting for Education Rights: Severely Disabled Children Can Benefit from Education. *Exceptional Parent,* 17(4): 48–56.

Dawkins, C.; Freedman, M.; Johnston, C.; & Walker, J. 1994. Perspectives on Early Intervention. *Exceptional Parent,* 24(2): 23–24.

Dorros, K., & Dorsey, P. 1988. The Pressures of Early Intervention. *Exceptional Parent,* 18(6): 72–77.

Ferguson, S., & Ripley, S. 1991. *A Parent's Guide: Special Education and Related Services: Communicating Through Letter Writing.* Washington, DC: National Information Center for Children and Youth with Disabilities.

Fine Motor/Adaptive Checklist. 1967. Rockville, MD: Montgomery County Public Schools.

Frankenburg, W.K., & Dodds, J.B. 1969; 1989; 1990. *Denver Developmental Screening Test II.* Denver: Denver Developmental Materials.

Georgia ARC. 1994. *Education Update,* 14(3): 6.

Giangreco, M.F., Cloninger, C.J., & Iverson, V.S. 1992. *C.O.A.C.H.: Creating Options and Accommodations for Children.* Baltimore: Paul H. Brookes Publishing Co.

Gliedman, J., & Roth, W., for the Carnegie Council on Children. 1980. *The Unexpected Minority: Handicapped Children in America.* New York: Harcourt Brace Jovanovich.

Glover, M.E., Preminger, J.L., & Sanford, A.R. 1978. *EARLY—LAP: The Early Learning Accomplishment Profile for Developmentally Young Children, Birth to Thirty-Six Months.* Winston-Salem, NC: Kaplan Press.

Heather's Story: The Long Road for a Family in Search of a Diagnosis. 1991. *Exceptional Parent,* 21(2): 92–94.

How to Teach Our Kids. *Newsweek* (Special Edition: *Education: A Consumer's Handbook*). 1990, Fall-Winter.

Individualized Education Programs. 1981. Washington, DC: National Information Center for Handicapped Children and Youth (NICHCY).

Iowa Governor's Planning Council for Developmental Disabilities. 1990. *Families who have children with disabilities and the Iowa Family Support Program: Evaluation findings.* Des Moines, IA: Author.

Irwin, L. 1991. Look at the Good Side. *Exceptional Parent,* 21(2): 100.

Jason, J., & Van Der Meer, A. 1989. *Parenting Your Premature Baby.* New York: Henry Holt.

Keith, S. 1984, October. *Preschool Education Program: Birth to Three* (newsletter). Rockville, MD: Montgomery County Public Schools.

———. 1985. *Classroom Topics, Birth to Three: A Newsletter for Parents of Infants and Toddlers in PEP* (newsletter). Rockville, MD: Montgomery County Public Schools.

Klein, S.D., & Schleifer, M.J. 1993. *It Isn't fair: Siblings of Children with Disabilities.* Westport, CT: Bergin & Garvey.

Lamm, D., & Fisch, D. 1984. Disabilities Explained. In Melton, D. *Promises to Keep: A Handbook for Parents of Learning Disabled, Brain Injured, and Other Exceptional Children.* New York, NY: Franklin Watts.

Levin, T. 1992. *Rainbow of Hope: A Guide for the Special Needs Child.* North Miami Beach, FL: Starlight Publishing.

Margolis, L. 1992. The Least Restrictive Environment and the Law. *MCIE Update,* 4(1): 1–2.

McGovern, R., ed. 1991. *Project Heal: Infant and Toddler Assessment and Intervention* (newsletter). Wethersfield, CT: Help, Education and Advocacy League of the Mental Health Association of Connecticut.

Melton, D. 1984. *Promises to Keep: A Handbook for Parents of Learning Disabled, Brain Injured, and Other Exceptional Children.* New York: Franklin Watts.

Messenger, K.P., & Gliedman, J. 1980. Medicine and Handicap: A Promise in Search of a National Commitment. In Gliedman, J., & Roth, W., for the Carnegie Council on Children. *The Unexpected Minority: Handicapped Children in America.* New York: Harcourt Brace Jovanovich.

Montgomery County Public Schools, Office of Special and Alternative Education. N.d. *Support System Worksheet.* Rockville, MD: In-Service Training Unit.

Moore, C. 1983. *An Update to: A Reader's Guide for Parents of Children with Mental, Physical, or Emotional Disabilities.* Baltimore: Maryland State Planning Council on Developmental Disabilities.

National Board for Professional Teaching Standards. 1987. Towards High and Rigorous Standards for the Teaching Profession. Excerpts cited in *American Educator* (1990), 14(2): 43.

National Information Center for Children and Youth with Disabilities. 1993. Questions and Answers about the IDEA. *News Digest*, 3(2).

National Information Center for Handicapped Children and Youth (NICHCY). 1985, October. Psychological Testing of Children with Disabilities. *News Digest*, U.S. Government Printing Office -0-483-237.

1993 Annual Report on State Program Activities. 1993. Washington, DC: National Association of Protection and Advocacy Systems.

Novick, B.Z., & Arnold, M.M. 1991. *Why Is My Child Having Trouble at School? A Parent's Guide to Learning Disabilities.* New York: Villard Books.

The Official ABMS Directory of Board Certified Medical Specialists. 1994. New Providence, NJ: Marquis, Who's Who.

Parent Information and Training Center. 1988. Special Education Step by Step. *Plaintalk for Parents of Students Receiving Special Education Services*, 1(1): 2.

Parent Support Networks: A Workbook for Creating Successful Community Support Groups. 1993. Augusta, ME: Maine Parent Federation.

A Parent's Guide to Understanding Sensory Integration. 1986. Torrance, CA: Sensory Integration International.

Points to Consider when Prioritizing Annual Goals. 1981. *Directive Teacher* (Summer/Fall).

Project TEAM, Training in Educational Advocacy and Monitoring Manual. N.d. Rockville, MD: Association for Retarded Citizens, Montgomery County.

Rammler, L. 1994. Why Inclusive Education? Presentation to the Danbury Public Schools, September.

Rimland, B. 1989. In Powers, M., ed. *Children with Autism: A Parents' Guide.* Rockville, MD: Woodbine House.

Ripley, S. 1993. *A Parent's Guide: Accessing Parent Groups.* Washington, DC: National Information Center for Handicapped Children and Youth (NICHCY).

Schleifer, M.J., & Klein, S.D., eds. 1989. Editorial Report. Final Regulations Early Intervention Programs for Infants and Toddlers with Handicaps. *Exceptional Parent*, 19(6): 46–48.

————, eds. 1990. Parents and Professionals (editorial). *Exceptional Parent*, 20(3): 48.

Sibling Information Network. 1993a. *Children's Literature for Sisters and Brothers of Children with Special Needs.* Middletown, CT: A.J. Pappanikou Center on Special Education and Rehabilitation.

————. 1993b. *Issues Relating to Developmental Disabilities: A Bibliography for Families.* Middletown, CT: A.J. Pappanikou Center on Special Education and Rehabilitation.

Simkin, P., & Edwards, M. 1979. *When Your Baby Has Jaundice* (pamphlet). Seattle: Pennypress.

Simon, R. 1987. *After the Tears: Parents Talk about Raising a Child with a Disability.* Orlando: Harcourt Brace Jovanovich.

Smith, S. 1978. *No Easy Answers: The Learning Disabled Child.* Washington, DC: National Institute of Mental Health, U.S. Department of Health, Education and Welfare.

Special Education Handbook: Information about Services for Students with Special Education Needs. 1991, March. Fairfax, VA: Fairfax County Public Schools, Department of Student Services and Special Education.

Speech, Language and Hearing Checklist. 1967. Rockville, MD: Montgomery County Public Schools.

State of Connecticut. Connecticut's Interagency Birth to Three Initiative. 1990. *Birth to Three Council Newsletter*, 1: 5.

State of Connecticut Department of Education. N.d. *Mediation in Due Process: A Guide for Participants.* Hartford: Bureau of Special Education and Pupil Personnel Services, Due Process Unit.

State of Maryland Department of Education, Division of Special Education. 1981. *Legal Rights: A Handbook for Parents.* Baltimore, MD: Author.

State of Maryland Department of Education. 1982. *Parent Helper: Handicapped Children Birth to Five, Communication.* Baltimore: Division of Special Education.

State of Maryland Department of Education, Maryland Infants and Toddlers Program Interagency Coordinating Council. 1989, March. *Fact Sheet: Public Law 99-457 H, Part H Infants and Toddlers Program.* Baltimore, MD: Author.

————. 1989, Fall. Family Centered Care. *Around the State Family Support Network*, 1(2).

Tommasone, L., & Tommasone, J. (1989). Adjusting to Your Child's Diagnosis. In Powers, M., ed. 1989. *Children with Autism: A Parents' Guide.* Rockville, MD: Woodbine House.

What Every Parent Should Know about Testing. 1992. Chicago and Princeton, NJ: National PTA and Educational Testing Service.

Where to Call for Help: A Nationwide Directory of United Way Information and Referral Services. 1992. Alexandria, VA: United Way of America.

Your Baby's First Year: A Guide to Infant Growth and Development. 1990. Evansville, IN: Mead Johnson and Co.

Index

About the Authors

RUTH F. CANTOR does volunteer work and is an advocate for inclusion of children with special needs into the reglular classroom and community setting.

JEFFREY A. CANTOR is Associate Professor, Adult Education and Corporate Training at the City University of New York, Lehman College. He is the author of several books including *Delivering Instruction to Adult Learners* and *Cooperative Education and Experiential Learning*.

Jeffrey and Ruth Cantor are parents of an 11-year-old son, Adam, who has been receiving appropriate special needs services and programs since birth. Both parents are actively involved in parent–teacher and parent-support organizations for special needs children.